(p. 41
43
48
48
v. impt)

GH00838730

p53

207!
208!

p. 190.
v impt

or
leerny

Jo Jackson King was born in 1968 into a family in which child development, parenting and education have been a passion for generations. Jo grew up reading books collected over those generations: Froebel, Montessori, John Holt, A. S. Neill's *Summerhill*. She then sat in libraries and read still more – along the way collecting a degree in literature and one in occupational therapy.

357
259

Jo next began working with families as an occupational therapist alongside her mother, Barbara, another occupational therapist. She discovered then that the most effective therapist for a child is an empowered and knowledgeable parent.

265!

But none of her work and research prepared her for how parenting feels from the inside. With the arrival of her first baby she finally got it: how desperately parents want to help their children and how complicated parenting is made by a parent's own emotions – and by conflicting information.

Jo lives on a pastoral property in Western Australia with her extended family – the subject of her bestselling first book, *The Station at Austin Downs*. She teaches her children on School of the Air, works as an occupational therapist, runs workshops for parents and professionals on child development and contributes as a speaker at professional conferences. Jo can also be heard on ABC radio.

all emotions are ok
all behaviours are not

5 ✓   10 ✓

p216

concentration
attention
self regulation
highly active children become
extroverts.

RAISING THE
BEST
POSSIBLE
CHILD

28-32

How to navigate parenting myths
and bring up confident, happy kids

JO JACKSON KING

ABC
Books

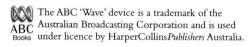 The ABC 'Wave' device is a trademark of the Australian Broadcasting Corporation and is used under licence by HarperCollins*Publishers* Australia.

First published in Australia in 2010
by HarperCollins*Publishers* Australia Pty Limited
ABN 36 009 913 517
harpercollins.com.au

Copyright © Jo Jackson King 2010

The right of Jo Jackson King to be identified as the author of this work
has been asserted by her in accordance with the *Copyright
Amendment (Moral Rights) Act 2000*.

This work is copyright. Apart from any use as permitted under the
Copyright Act 1968, no part may be reproduced, copied, scanned,
stored in a retrieval system, recorded, or transmitted, in any form
or by any means, without the prior written permission of the publisher.

HarperCollins*Publishers*
25 Ryde Road, Pymble, Sydney, NSW 2073, Australia
31 View Road, Glenfield, Auckland 0627, New Zealand
A 53, Sector 57, NOIDA, UP, India
77–85 Fulham Palace Road, London W6 8JB, United Kingdom
2 Bloor Street East, 20th floor, Toronto, Ontario M4W 1A8, Canada
10 East 53rd Street, New York NY 10022, USA

National Library of Australia Cataloguing-in-Publication data:

Jackson King, Jo.
    Raising the best possible child : how to navigate parenting myths and bring up
        confident, happy kids / Jo Jackson King
    ISBN: 978 0 7333 1630 2 (pbk.)
    Includes index.
    Bibliography.
    Parenting.
    Parent and infant.
    Child rearing.
    Australian Broadcasting Corporation.
649.1

Cover design by Jane Waterhouse, HarperCollins Design Studio
Cover image © Radius Images/Corbis
Typeset in Bembo Std 11.5/14pt by Letter Spaced
Printed and bound in Australia by Griffin Press
70gsm Classic used by HarperCollins*Publishers* is a natural, recyclable product made from wood
grown in sustainable forests. The manufacturing processes conform to the environmental
regulations in the country of origin, Finland.

5 4 3 2 1   10 11 12 13 14

With grateful thanks to my three sons:

Tim, who found references for me and dedicatedly read each draft through for errors of meaning at which he then laughed immoderately;

Sam, who generously let me write about him and also kept up a supply of comic relief for his serious mother;

and Rafael, who arrived just as I was embarking on the bulk of the research for this book and who happily snuggled and breastfed while I read and wrote in the very early hours of the morning.

Contents

About this book

I've always been a great reader of parenting books.

I remember reading one book that argued forcefully for 'positive parenting'. The central message was this: 'If you only pay attention to positive behaviours in your children, they alone will be reinforced, and the behaviours you don't like will steadily disappear.'

At the time I was in my early thirties with two little boys. I retold the message to my husband Martin and my mother — how exciting it would be to be able to drop the discipline and just focus on the good things!

'In my experience, if you ignore children who are behaving badly they will scale up their behaviour until you do notice,' advised my mother.

But I ignored her. Perhaps I had already internalised the message that I should only pay attention to what I wanted to see and hear?

We started our new parenting approach at breakfast the following day. Tim (four and a half years old) did not like to sit at the table to eat. In fact, he did not even really like to eat. He appeared at the doorway and slowly approached the breakfast table. Martin and I beamed at him approvingly. Tim reached the table only to promptly duck under it and drop to the floor beneath.

Instead of asking him to sit and eat, we steadfastly ignored him and talked of other things. One little hand shot up to the edge of the table, and then another. I thought for a moment that he had capitulated and was going to swing himself out and eat with us. But then the hands began a dialogue, with the right having a deep growly voice and the left squeaking plaintively. It was quite clearly the story of Dad telling Tim to eat, and Tim resisting.

I could see Martin was going to say something about this and so I reminded him in a whisper of the new rule. 'We only notice good behaviour.' He did not look particularly happy about it — but he nodded his agreement.

The dialogue presently stopped and I could hear scuffling sounds under the table. Luckily I am constructed so that I can talk ceaselessly and I was able to give an excellent impression of ignoring these intriguing noises. However Martin was not performing well in the supporting role, and my attention was eventually caught by the expression on his face. He is hard to read at the best of times, but at that precise moment his expression was so utterly impassive — so wooden — that he would not have been out of place in a shop window display.

I was to find out later that Tim had been biting his leg at the time.

But we finished our breakfast with me still in ignorance of this. Martin went to work and I continued on with my new parenting method.

One of the boys' habits I particularly disliked was 'play-wrestling'. Someone was always hurt. Later we instituted a rule that they could only wrestle with their father — which has stood the test of time — but on this particular day I adhered firmly to the rule of ignoring what I didn't want to see.

While I hung out washing I could hear the stealthy sounds of Tim and Sam beginning to wrestle. About here is where I would normally have broken it up. Roll, roll, and thump of them together on the floor. And then, over in the other direction — roll, roll, thump. And then a howl.

I picked up my basket and walked swiftly past the combatants, now well separated and attempting to hide tears.

They did not wrestle again.

I seized upon this first bit of evidence that my new parenting approach was working with a delightful feeling of inner certainty. This was the way forward! But shortly after I could hear the steady sound of objects being thrown. Out on the veranda my sons were throwing Lego pieces at each other. I feverishly raced back to consult the book. This, it said, was normal. Wait them out. And, soothed by the writer's utter certainty, I sat with a cup of tea and kept to my chair as each son simultaneously began crying. Right now, I told myself, they were learning that the consequence of throwing things is that someone gets hurt. I was forgetting that this had been experienced before and was showing no sign of leading to a change in behaviour.

It was time for morning tea — which we shared in perfect amity. There was no mention of the throwing by them and no mention of the toys everywhere by me. I ignored the widely spread Lego; as evidence of negative behaviour it was beneath my notice.

Later that day the boys were left to play together again on the veranda. And this time they played in contented silence. There was no play wrestling, no throwing. They were utterly engaged in whatever it was they were doing. I gratefully read some more of my parenting book. I marvelled that the author — a young male postgraduate student without children — had such a grasp on what worked with children and how extraordinarily easy his system was! Why was it not commonly used?

And with that thought I began to wonder just what it was that my children were doing on the veranda, so I decided to investigate.

They had taken four large bottles of poster paint and squeezed each out onto the vinyl floor. The colourful mass was then diluted with water and distributed widely. They had then invented a game of 'flicking'. You dipped your paintbrush into the paint and water and then 'flick': you saw just how much red, purple, blue and green paint you could throw up onto the white walls and ceiling.

When your mother leaves you to play for more than an hour, that is a great deal of paint.

It is very odd, some seven years later, to be the one who is writing a book on parenting. In my defence, it was not my idea to write this book.

I became friends with the editor on my first book and, being the mother of two young children, she quickly got into the way of 'picking my brain' about child development. Not only am I an occupational therapist, but my mother is also, which between us gives me some 50 plus years of clinical experience to ratchet through, looking for answers.

To add to this, I am, tragically, more than a little like a hound. If I am asked a question I 'take the scent' and am off on the hunt straightaway.

I remember not having an answer for my sister-in-law Minnie's question about one of her children who was briefly ill.

'We have Health Direct in WA, Minnie. You just call 1800 …' I said, giving her the number in full twice, and rather hopefully.

'Oh, I have that too. I just call …' and she rattled off a string of numbers.

'I wonder why it is different to the one we call?' I said.

'Let me just repeat that for you,' she said.

The number sounded somewhat familiar.

'It's yours,' she said eventually, as it was evident I wasn't going to make the connection.

And, sure enough, having spoken and read and nutted out the illness I was back to her in short order with a few ideas to deal with it. Once a question has been asked I'm programmed to return with a range of answers. 'Even,' my husband Martin has just added, 'when a person doesn't actually ask you to do it.

But my editor Jo Mackay did actually ask me. First of all she asked if there was a book with all the occupational therapy knowledge in for parents, and when I said, no, there wasn't, as Mum and I had often looked for such a book, she asked if I could write one. And then she came up with the name — the one on the cover. I pointed out to her that her original concept had not come close to the scope of this one. This book goes a long way beyond occupational therapy. This would need to draw from a much wider pool of knowledge. But she was not to be roped into a discussion of how difficult the project would be. She changed the subject and said how she had been longing for a book that was not about turning your child into Einstein or getting them to read at two or having them sleep through the night at three minutes old …

So off I went to find out just how to help a child become her 'best possible' self. I went back to university and I read thousands of articles and books and I talked and talked with my mother on our morning walks.

Into this book I have put everything I could find about how children learn to learn, think, move, talk, read, make friends, concentrate, empathise and, above all else, recover from setbacks and become transformed by adversity into the person they want to be. It is also the story of my own journey through the research, and how it profoundly changed the way I parent my children.

But this is not just my journey — and when you read 'I' it is not just my voice or Mum's voice you are hearing. We tend to interpret the saying 'it takes a whole village to raise a child' to mean that everyone needs to help a parent directly with their child. I think there is another interpretation that is just as valid. I believe it is equally about everyone contributing to a parent's 'thinking' about each individual child.

Martin and I are surrounded by people — parents, grandparents, teachers, family members, colleagues — who will happily talk with us about the issues we face in rearing our sons and the issues they face with their own children. Parenting is a richer experience when this is happening and easier, too. When you have someone who will say, 'Have you thought about …?' then your decisions are going to be smarter ones.

The same village that helps me raise my children has shared the journey of writing this book. I hope you can hear their loving voices asking, 'Have you thought about …?' as you read.

What does 'the best possible child' mean?

When a baby is born she could grow into a range of different people. One of these is a person who that child will be happiest being, which is what every parent wants for their child, and that is the 'best possible child' of this book.

Even as we get older this is still the case — ahead of us is always a range of different selves. We know that a decision will take us closer to one potential self, and further from another.

But just what capacities does a child need to become the person — happy, resilient and wise — she wants to be? And just what do we need to do to help our child be that person?

Should we focus on 'skills'?

I'm going to cover skills in detail in this book — talking, movement skills, reading, maths and writing skills and so on — because they are important, and, being an occupational therapist, this stuff is my bread and butter. But are they the deciding factor in life success? I know — and you probably do, too — skilled people who are still not making the success of life they could. So this, it seems to me, is the least likely answer to the question.

Should we focus on 'good behaviour'?

Again, you will find this covered in the book in great detail, but is good behaviour the 'make or break' factor? You can perform well in a role, such as worker or student, but not delight in it — and not, at the end of the day, be happy. So it seemed to me that a main focus on having an obedient child was not going to achieve our desired outcome.

Should parents try to create 'good motivation'?

This seemed to be far closer to the answer — and yet there are people who are highly motivated but who, in the end, are still not the person they want to be.

For me, none of these answers, alone or even together, were hitting the mark. And they weren't hitting the mark because I've seen that for some children education (to improve skills), discipline (to improve behaviour) and opportunity (to improve motivation) don't help. There was something that some children had and some children didn't. What was it and how could I shape my parenting to ensure my children had it?

This question is increasingly a focus in the child development literature.

Like parents, researchers have been disturbed by the fact that today's children are not performing as well as those in earlier generations. The change has been one that has happened during my lifetime — so in just the last forty years.

When I remember back to my classrooms in primary school and high school there was a very small percentage of children who were struggling. On graduating from university I expected that a classroom would have five to ten per cent of children who could benefit from occupational therapy. Ten years ago I had mentally 'upped' that number to between 10 and 15 per cent. And it has risen since.

The Australian Early Development Index, a best practice, whole population measure of child health, is now used to measure how well a community is supporting its children. And what does it show for Australia as a whole? It shows that about a quarter (23.4 per cent) of all children are deemed to be 'at risk' — socially, educationally and in terms of physical and mental health.[1] This is way, way too high.

So what have the researchers uncovered? What sort of parenting does put a child on track for her best possible self?

There are three main branches of early child development research. Each has come up with a very similar answer. Alas, each uses a different name for this concept and has a slightly different set of 'what is included', but the answers are hearteningly supportive of each other. And what they are all saying is this: What a child needs for success is to be able to manage stress, stay focused and navigate both her own and other people's emotions.

In everyday language, we would use terms like 'emotionally savvy' or 'wise' or 'self and people smart' to describe these abilities. In the literature they talk of 'effortful control' and 'emotional self-regulation' and 'executive function'. I'm going to use 'self-regulation' as I'm increasingly seeing the term appear in other writing for parents.

Each set of research is important in understanding how self-regulation develops and just why it is so valuable.

Attachment theory connects self-regulation to a particular type of relationship between parent and child, and believes that the main benefit of self-regulation skills further down the track is that they allow a child to create meaningful and enjoyable intimate relationships.

The *neuroscience* shows these skills grow as a result of the physical and emotional connection (brain to brain, heart to heart) between mother and child. Researchers would point to good health and good brain development as key results.

Another perspective comes in the *temperament research* literature, and to my astonishment this has been the most useful research of all. Previously I had held a grudge against the temperament theorists. I was astounded when my dear little Tim, my elder son, began behaving badly. His hand would inch ostentatiously towards an object he knew was forbidden — a power-board or toilet brush — while his eyes were defiantly fixed upon mine. I began to look for answers.

The first set of parenting information I encountered was based in the temperament literature. I dutifully filled in the checklist and was horrified to be told that he was 'anti-authoritarian' and at high risk of developing a conduct disorder. Sometimes what you read as a parent can be destructive and this certainly, though temporarily, was.

What I'd failed to realise is that behaviour, like everything else, follows a pattern of development. Tim had recently turned two. He had hit that stage of systematically defying me just to see what the consequences would be.

But this new temperament research was quite different from what I'd encountered years earlier. It dives right into questions such as 'Which sort of kids find it easiest to develop self-regulation skills?' 'Fearful or fearless?' 'Intense or laid back?' And the researchers also go on to ask, 'How should parents respond to different temperaments to create a child with good self-regulation skills?'

The temperament theorists have a different take on why self-regulation is important. Their research shows it leads straight to a child who develops a working set of socially appropriate internal rules. Without this set of rules children are more likely to grow up to abuse drugs, to be aggressive towards others and to generally behave in ways that deny them an easy life.[2]

And from there the research travels to exactly the destination I was looking for: a breakdown of the factors that lead directly to self-regulation.

So what are the qualities required for self-regulation?

Imagine you are learning to fly a small aircraft. First of all you are trying to learn how to monitor your plane for the slightest hint of something going wrong. This ability to be aware of subtle changes, to detect a new note in the engine, or an unexpected drop or increase in speed requires that your *perceptual sensitivity* is calibrated accurately to the outside world. The person who is not very sensitive will be at risk here, but so too is the oversensitive person. They will have difficulty screening out some signs to focus on the ones that really count.

Those perceptions help us know what to attend to, but we also need the separate ability to be able to *shift attention* to the right part of a task. We are not born able to do this, and, as adults, we only remember how difficult this is when we are immersed in new learning — for example, following the instruction 'look at the blinking light', you have to shift your attention to the blinking light on display. You must look just at this light and not any of the other fascinating gauges and lights, and then go back to your previous focus of attention.

The ability over time to keep directing your thinking between internal knowledge and the external situation while keeping in mind what you are trying to achieve is called *concentration*. You need that too.

You also need to be able to prevent habits, urges or emotions from interfering with your goals. This is called *impulse control*. If you hop back into your imaginary aircraft ... you discover that you don't just 'learn' how to fly, but that you also need to 'turn off' all the habits you have developed in driving a car. It is your feet that turn the plane to the left or to the right, rather than your hands. So as well as remembering to use your feet, you will have to suppress the habit of using your hands to do the job. Impulse control is the ability to stop yourself doing something.

Impulse control is fed by two other important skills: *empathy*, which is the ability to know how someone else is feeling, and something called *theory of mind*, which is the ability to predict what somebody else knows.

Both of these allow us to 'mind-read' other people to a sufficient degree to negotiate relationships — or a runway on which a number of small planes are landing.

Together these self-regulation tools — perceptual sensitivity, shifting attention, concentration, impulse control, empathy and theory of mind — create a human control system so flexible and powerful that with them in place your child will be able to become her 'best possible self', regardless of temperament.

Fortunately each one of these skills is something that you do shape with your parenting, and you shape them particularly by how you relate to your child. Just how that happens is the story of this book.

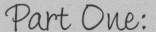

Part One:

The active ingredient

The active ingredient in child development is the quality of the relationships that children have with the important people in their lives. That's what it's all about.

Dr Jack Shonkoff, frequently described as the world's leading authority on child development.[1]

Chapter 1

Introducing attachment theory

He longed to become Real, to know what it felt like; and yet the idea of growing shabby and losing his eyes and whiskers was rather sad. He wished that he could become it without these uncomfortable things happening to him.

Margery Williams, *The Velveteen Rabbit*, 1922.[2]

This part of the book is about you rather than your child. For me, this information has been more powerful than anything else I've found in the research literature on parenting.

If it is the relationship our babies have with us that contributes most to their self-regulation skills and creates that 'best possible' self — and we know that it is — then what do we bring to that relationship? How do our lives, thoughts and emotions shape the relationship between us and our children?

These are the questions that attachment theory asks and seeks to answer.

The study of love

Researchers of attachment theory study all the different patterns that exist in intimate relationships and how those patterns, in turn, shape us. They study romantic relationships, parent–child relationships and other very close relationships and describe these powerful and intimate reciprocal relationships as 'attachments', or 'attachment relationships'. After studying millions of attachment relationships the researchers are able to see patterns into which these relationships fall.

They begin with looking at very little babies. All the things babies do — cry, smile, nestle, gaze — are designed to communicate to their parents their deep need to be kept as close as possible in order to feel safe and loved.

When a baby cries, that is an 'attachment behaviour'. When a parent has a pattern of responding to that cry, the baby knows that he is safe. But when a parent has a pattern of responding differently, such as not coming, or coming inconsistently, then the baby knows that his survival may be on the line. It is at this point that a baby knows he must either increase or change the signal to get help.

You can see that the way in which the parent responds to their baby will create the pattern that the child must match in order to ensure his survival.

If you are a new parent of a little baby you may hear the advice, 'That's no way to stop him crying, you're just rewarding him by picking him up'. And the advice sounds convincing, but not if you are using the attachment perspective and empathising with your baby.

What you can say is, 'Let's look at this from the baby's perspective. He can't meet his own needs and needs me to do things for him. Even if I don't pick him up, he is still going to be needing me. So to get my attention he's going to have to get more and more upset, and eventually I will pick him up.

'So if I don't pick him up I'm training him to get very upset immediately because nothing else works to get my attention. If he can't trust me to fulfil his needs, then he'll stick close to me because he won't trust me when I'm out of his sight. That means he'll explore less and won't develop so many skills. And my baby will turn into a whingeing, clingy preschooler.

'Or perhaps I could follow your advice and not pick him up at all when he cries. How would that turn out? Looking at it from my baby's perspective, he still needs me but obviously, his cries disturb me so much that I can't respond. To make me feel safe he'll have to pretend that he has no emotional needs. He'll learn to switch them off. And then he won't be able to recognise them in other people either. My baby will turn into a preschooler who won't have the empathic skills needed to make friends.

'But if I do pick him up, he learns that empathy is seeing how someone feels and valuing that in your actions. He'll know that I'm always going to be there to meet his needs and he will soon discover that it isn't necessary to get upset and cry to get his needs met. So, eventually, when he wants me, he'll just call out once and wait. Because he trusts me he'll turn into a happy little explorer because he knows Mum will be there watching and protecting. He will develop lots of the skills needed for independence. And my baby will grow into an independent, sociable and cheerful preschooler.'

(You will notice that I haven't suggested a snappy rejoinder. I am simply no good at these.)

Parents also often hear statements like 'there is no such thing as a naughty child' and 'just ignore undesirable behaviours'. Again, attachment theory provides a child's perspective on this kind of parenting practice — because the other great finding of attachment theory is that children need to feel safe, and that part of making them feel safe is having clear, enforced rules for behaviour. The great flaw in the parenting strategy of 'only noticing positive behaviours' — the one I describe in 'About this book' — is that it makes children feel less safe.

Attachment theory makes explicit something that we intuitively know: our children respond to our emotional patterns. Rather than offering 'strategies' for parenting, it offers us the chance to look at our emotions, how those emotions affect the way we respond to our children, and how that in turn shapes our children's characters.

This is contrary to what I was taught while studying at university. At that time researchers believed that the active, the *magic*, ingredient for child development was 'stimulation'.

'Is your baby getting enough stimulation?' was the question you were likely to be asked by the health professionals. But it was the wrong question.

We were doing all the right things with our babies by playing, touching, kissing, holding, singing to, talking to and cuddling them, but the most important thing in doing all this was *not* stimulation. It was the fact that this playful interaction built the knowledge that mother and child had of each other and strengthened the emotional connection — the *attachment* — between them.

Why 'attachment' is the real active ingredient

The most powerful forces in a child's development are his emotional states. These states are so powerful because emotion is the language the brain/body speaks to itself. The message is carried in chemicals — neurotransmitters, hormones — but the messages carried are emotional ones: fear, longing, discomfort, pain, sadness, despair, excitement, curiosity, exhilaration, confusion ... All of these different emotions drive or hinder brain/body growth throughout our lives. Will your child's main emotion be a feeling of love? Then it is oxytocin, the love and learning hormone that causes brain cells to grow and interconnect, that will prevail. Or will his main emotion be fear? Then it is cortisol and the catecholamines, the stress hormones that, in sufficient quantities, destroy neural connections, that will dominate.

And what creates these emotional states in a child? A child's emotional states are mostly (but not totally, because temperament is a factor) created by the quality of his relationship with you. It is the way you respond, the pattern of your response to him, that creates the feelings he has.

If a distressed baby is immediately comforted, he will spend less time in that distressed state. If he turns to share something with you, and you respond with delight straightaway, his happy feeling is going to be strengthened. The phrase in the literature on attachment theory and the interlinked neuroscience is, 'states become traits' — in other words, the feelings a baby has more of now are going to shape his character down the track. The skills of self-regulation start in infancy but there is no aspect of development untouched by this. Not even movement or thinking or language skills, even though they seem so far removed from the ambit of emotion.

You will perhaps be wondering why I haven't written 'love' here — why, in fact, love is not the magic ingredient. It would be a much nicer sentiment!

All parents love their babies and children. But it is how we respond to them that is the way our love is expressed, and there are ways of responding that are not going to help a child to that best possible self. No matter how much we love our children, it is *how that love is expressed* that counts.

To give a personal example, when my children have been distressed

I have always responded immediately. My babies and toddlers and even preschoolers have all been the sort who 'didn't need to cry', so rapidly do I respond. Except for this: once my children were five years old or older I no longer could bear it when they 'gave way to despair'. My behaviour when faced with a despairing child could not have been less supportive. While I was comfortable with them expressing every other negative emotion — extreme anger, great sorrow — I found it deeply bothersome and did about all I could to outlaw 'despairing crying'.

By trying to outlaw 'despair' I was still expressing my love and concern for them but not in a way that was going to help them. Working through just why I did this has been, as the Velveteen Rabbit suggests of becoming Real, uncomfortable and a bit sad. Nonetheless, it has been a very important part of 'becoming' a parent for me, and you might like to keep my 'out-of-character' behaviour in mind as you read through this part of the book. The other thing that I would like you to bear in mind is that a relationship can be repaired at any time, with changes in brain and body to match.

The importance of your own attachment relationships

There have been a number of studies where pregnant women were asked about their own childhoods. Interestingly, each study showed the same thing. Researchers have found that by listening to the story of a woman's childhood, her relationship with her parents and other attachment relationships, they can predict how securely her child will attach to her.[3, 4]

Many of my friends have freaked out when they read this. People immediately jump to the conclusion that I'm saying the research suggests that if they had a difficult childhood then they will struggle to parent. That's not it at all. Some of the very best parents I know had very unpleasant childhoods themselves, childhoods on which they have reflected and come to terms with and used to build a very different kind of childhood for their own children.

The key word is 'reflection': the ability to find meaning and use for past experiences, whether for good or bad. If we can tell the story of our own relationships and childhood in a way that hangs together and pulls meaning from all that has happened to us, then we are going to be able to parent well. This has been known for many years, but, until recently, no-one was able to explain why. In the last few years, however, researchers think they have worked it out.[5,6]

Being able to tell a coherent life story shows that you have moved on from your past. You are not trapped by circular thoughts of 'if only' and 'what if'. You haven't avoided thinking about the parts that hurt you, you've reflected on it all and come to terms with it and moved on. This lets you become a parent who is free to be in the here-and-now with your babies and children.[3,9,10]

But being able to 'live in the present' with your child is only one-half of the story. The other significant factor is that telling your life story, complete with ups and downs, shows that you are comfortable with a range of emotions.

The parent who has not turned away from experiencing life's pain is a parent who can cope with an unhappy child. This is important as a parent, and never more so than when you are dealing with a newborn. If we imagine an 'emotional compass', babies initially tend to have that needle in the sad end of the spectrum. They don't know how to get their needs met, they are helpless to meet those needs themselves, it's a strange new world out of the womb — and so they often feel sad and needy and fearful to begin with. But a baby who is lonely or frightened or sad is a baby you can relate to. You've had those emotions and you came out the other side, so you know that, with your help, your child will too.[9,10]

A parent who is mostly living in the present moment and mostly coping with the full spectrum of emotions in themselves and their children fits into an attachment pattern called 'free' or 'autonomous'.

At the generational crossroads

This is a fictional story that someone who has worked through their childhood issues might tell.

'My mother was very young. There was a lot she missed out on, having me. So it was a resentful relationship: she resented having me and I resented her having me when she hadn't really been ready. But I got over it as a teenager. I always had my head in a book, and I encountered someone just like her in one of those sprawling family sagas. You met the controlling grandmother and then her children and then their children in turn, and you could just see it all, travelling down the generations. That was what the book was about. So I was able to see the situation from the outside, and that actually helped a bit because I stopped asking for what she couldn't give and so she resented me less.

'But before that, I remember coming home with my first school award and she just wasn't interested. She just said, "Oh yes". And at this point the next-door neighbour came in and Mum immediately began to play the proud parent. It was something she did and it obviously made her feel better about her life, but it always made me feel worse. I wasn't worth the bother, but other people were. But she just wasn't ready for a child — she hadn't been herself first. The role of mother was something that she played on the outside for society, but often she would confide in me or friends she trusted that she still always dreamed about what she'd have done if she hadn't got pregnant so young.

'But after meeting her in that book I was able to think, "You poor sausage, you never got over it," and "Well, that won't be me, I'm going to get over it, I'm not going to stay stuck in the past." And there were other people who were interested in me and took the trouble to get to know me and I learned a lot from them.

'Mrs Simon, one of my high school teachers, was the main person. She was a very warm person, and back in those days teachers could give hugs, and although I was a very reserved girl she would always hug me. She was a big squashy lady, and she always smelt like oranges and wore bright friendly colours. She always joked about "keeping the books up to me", and spent time talking to me about them. I came to terms with my Mum with her help. If Mum was late picking me up she would take me home with her own children who were all younger, and I would sit in her untidy small kitchen and we'd have cheese on toast and warm chocolate and then play cards. And I deliberately set about learning to be a parent from her, even though I was only thirteen. And she knew that, because she really knew me. My eldest son is named Simon after her.

'Mum hasn't changed. She loves me, but she is too caught up in *her own life to be interested in mine. And I accept that because I'm not one of those people who keep trying to go back and change someone. I'm one of those people who seek out and celebrate the good relationships I can have instead.'*

This woman, with her strong emphasis on the value of attachment relationships, would have children who were securely attached to her. The message from the attachment literature is that having had a 'good childhood' or 'good parents' isn't a prerequisite. What is required is that you've worked it all through.

But not everyone is free to parent. Some people are emotionally preoccupied, still working through the wounds left by their own childhoods. Some people seem to have blanked out their memories of their own childhoods, refusing to look too closely at the painful emotions. In both cases, they are not responsive to some emotions in either themselves or other people and so they do not recognise those emotions in their child. Nor do they find it easy to cope with a child's quest to stay very close to a parent and to be treated tenderly.

When this is the case, it will lead to a child having more of the negative emotions — fear and sadness. This in turn impacts on body and brain development, and these children are the ones who most struggle with self-regulation skills and are least likely to grow into resilient, happy and wise adults.

In the next chapters the different attachment patterns are described. You will probably find something of yourself in a couple of them, because most of us dip in and out of them.[11, 13] Every mother can be too preoccupied with something to listen to a child to the degree they would wish, or not quite in a place to bring the same degree of warm comfort to a sad child as they would like. And there are patches of 'psychological sunshine' in the lives of parents who still have bleeding wounds left from their childhood, during which they are able to parent far more responsively.[5]

But what you should be looking for is an overall pattern into which your parenting fits. If you do feel very stressed a lot of the time, and during these times you find that you stay in one of the insecure or disorganised parenting patterns, then it is time to see what you can do to prevent an insecure and/or disorganised attachment pattern being passed down to your children and their children's children and so on, down the generations.[3, 4]

You might be wondering what the various terms mean: secure, insecure, organised, disorganised? What does a secure and organised attachment look like? How does it feel? How do you know if you have one with your baby, or if you haven't? Can an insecure attachment become secure? Can a secure attachment become insecure? Does your own attachment to your parents play a role? If you have a bad relationship with your parents, does that mean the attachment you experienced as a baby wasn't secure or organised? What things support secure, organised attachment and what things hinder it?

In thinking about this for myself I found three different sets of literature very helpful. First of all were the descriptions of the different attachment types: secure versus insecure, organised versus disorganised. I came to believe that learning to see the different attachment patterns was something all parents could benefit from. Then came the 'ghost-busting' approach, which is all about identifying exactly what in your children's behaviours causes you to stop being a 'warm and responsive' parent. Finally, I also came across the writings of Haim Ginott.

Although Ginott's work fits in the 'managing behaviour' part of child development literature, it also provides the nuts and bolts of creating a secure attachment in your children. So I have included his theory in this part of the book also, and the bonus is that in following his approach you will also spot any gaps in your own emotional compass. His work resonated most powerfully with me and guided me through managing myself when I found myself uncomfortable with my children's despair.

Chapter 2

Organised and disorganised attachment

'Now we'll all go to bed,' said Moominmamma.
'It's not good for children to hear frightening stories
at night.'

Tove Jansson, *Comet in Moominland*, 1946.[14]

Attachment theory tells us that for your child to be their 'best possible' self, the attachment between you and your child needs to be both secure *and* organised.

As we've seen, a 'secure attachment' occurs when you are comfortable with a full range of emotions in yourself — happiness, sadness, anger, fear — and accept all of those emotions in your child too. The term 'organised' — the focus of this chapter — is added to that if you can ensure your child feels safe — both physically and emotionally.

Making a child feel safe goes beyond the cocoon of mother and child: the world around your child and the kind of support you have also count greatly. One of the biggest costs of domestic violence, or drug and alcohol abuse, or intergenerational poverty or being held in detention centres is that they all alter the way in which parents express their love to their children. Children whose parents live desperate lives in desperate circumstances frequently show a particular set of behaviours. As toddlers these children begin to stumble in the presence of their parents, they freeze, they display fear as a parent moves towards them, they carry out strange, repeated rocking movements, or they wander about in a dazed fashion. That is the most extreme scenario, but children who simply have short periods where they have a blanked-out expression may be displaying elements of disorganisation.

What is the explanation given for this in the attachment literature? Feeling safe is an essential building block in childhood. So what makes a child feel safe? Mostly it is us, their parents. A child is hard-wired to respond to her parents as her safe haven, to return to them when danger threatens, to go to them for comfort, to stay near them much of the time to simply feel safe. But what if it is the parents who are the frighteners, the dangers, the people who hurt?

In such a situation the program for normal development has been utterly disrupted or 'disorganised', say the attachment researchers. The baby's world doesn't make sense at the most basic of levels. And a baby in such a world cannot find a way to adapt.[12, 15, 16]

A clinical puzzle

My view of the stereotyped movement patterns seen in children with disorganised attachment is slightly different. Many of these movements are the same ones you will see in newborns, the reflexive movements that all children are born with. As these children never feel safe they keep many of the movements that do have a survival function. It is in this way that the emotional state of the child directly impacts on all movement skills. This is not a generally held conclusion, mind you, but it is what my mother and I think. It was a conclusion we reached after months and months of trying to understand why we were seeing such an unusual clinical picture in the Aboriginal children with whom we worked.

I can remember the phone call from Mum that was to give me my first inkling of this clinical puzzle. I work mostly from home scoring and collating results, writing up programs for schools and parents and so on, and Mum was out in the communities, directly working with people. This is a well-established pattern we have, so I was very surprised when she asked me to come and help her with assessing kindergarten, pre-primary and Year One children.

'I think I'm going mad,' she began. This is something she says surprisingly often, but I've not yet found that she's really slipped over the edge. 'These results just cannot be right. I need you to come and do the same assessment on the same children.'

'Well, what are you finding?' I said, curious but not terrifically willing to get out of my comfort zone.

'I won't tell you just yet,' she said. 'Let's see if you find the same thing.'

This was all very intriguing so, sure enough, I was in the school the next day. Matching up our assessments at the end of the day, we had made exactly the same observations. Some of the children didn't have eyes that moved together, which is something babies have usually mastered by two months of age. There were other things wrong too, things that working closer to Perth we had only seen occasionally but which, in this case, were showing up as whole class patterns.

As well as our observations there were those of teachers, who reported that the children struggled far more than usual with transitions between activities, often resulting in them becoming aggressive or emotional. Acting out by one member of a class left the rest of the class very stressed and they had difficulty calming down again and learning. Learning was very difficult for these children even on good days and academically they were very behind. In adolescence, when schoolwork required abstract thinking skills, the children were simply lost.

There were also ongoing problems in terms of children appreciating that others had different feelings and perspectives on an event, which led to bullying. The children had very poor self-esteem and the teachers found it very difficult to build relationships with them — and you need a relationship with a child before you can educate that child.

As well as my personal journey through the research, solving this clinical puzzle has been the other great journey I've been on for the last four years. I would like to share this one with you too as, like so many researchers and clinicians before me, I have learned the most about human development from children who are very disadvantaged. The biggest strides in understanding the vital importance of attachment *were made because of the work done on children from orphanages who were later adopted into First World countries.*

Sometimes you only realise the value of something when it is missing. Just what happens to children's brains when they don't feel safe is a message we all need to heed.

The most recognisable group of children with disorganised attachment come from families that most people would quickly perceive as troubled. This is where a parent is not simply frightened, but is the frightener. It is when parents are frightening or dangerous to their children that the worst damage is done. Who can the child run to for protection when it is the protector who is hurting them? It is a crashing discordance, a betrayal and contradiction so great that the growing brain cannot encompass it, leading to all kinds of psychological damage.[15, 17]

But a frightening or harsh parent is not the *only* kind of parent who can create a child with a disorganised attachment. It was a real shock to me, finding this in the literature. In fact, I did not include much detail on disorganised attachment in the first draft of this book. I believed that it would be the rare reader of parenting books who had experienced or was creating such an attachment in their children. But at a recent workshop I was staggered to see research showing that in the mainstream population, 15 to 20 per cent of mother–child pairs were classed as disorganised.[18]

And when I chased up the exact breakdown of that figure — what percentage was disorganised insecure and what percentage was disorganised secure — I found that just over half of all disorganised attachments were 'disorganised secure'.[19] This means that parents who are mostly sensitive, responsive and warm are still not managing to make their children feel safe. What can be the explanation?

Other parenting that leads to a disorganised attachment
Fear is such a strong emotion. It says to our brains and bodies, 'Your survival is under threat. Drop everything else! Deal right now with what is before you!' If the brain experiencing fear is a developing

brain, then the message is, 'Your survival is under threat. Drop all non-essential brain and body development. Grow the size and speed of your flight and fright circuitry.'

Children can be made fearful by all kinds of things in our parenting, not just by harsh, neglectful or abusive parenting. They are made fearful by a parent who is frightened themselves. Fear in a parent is transmitted directly to a child when she sees the 'frozen mask' expression on a parent's face. Whether the parent is frightened because of an abusive relationship, a dangerous setting — such as a war zone or a natural disaster — or because they are remembering in a 'flashback trance' such a situation in the past, does not matter. That expression of fear is the same, and, for survival reasons, children are hard-wired to detect it: and then, immediately, to begin growing the right kind of brain to survive in those conditions.

Children are also made fearful by parents who withdraw from them. Deep inside, children know that they cannot make themselves safe and they need the protection of a parent. When parents withdraw they know they are not safe.

They are also made fearful by parents who behave very oddly. Drug and alcohol affected or mentally ill parents may not be violent towards their children, but disorientated or highly emotional behaviours are terrifying for children to witness in their parents. Again, the child knows that they cannot be kept safe by such a parent.

Parents who miss or who misread their children's emotional signals also frighten their children. The child thinks, 'I asked for a reassuring cuddle and she is poking me in the ribs and laughing. I can't possibly be safe in this situation.'

Babies and toddlers are made fearful when parents suddenly disappear from their lives. If a baby or toddler can't yet understand the explanation that because Mum and Dad are going away for a week or two she will be staying with Auntie and while she's there she will be able to hold a conversation with you over the phone, then she is too young to be left.[20]

Children are made fearful when a parent threatens violence, abandonment or suicide. Certainly, such threats tend to lead promptly to compliance in children — and parents will sometimes make them in a 'mock-threatening' manner — but, if the threats work, you know they are being taken seriously by children. Basically, if you frighten your child, then she is not going to develop as she should. The parent who controls their child by fear may have an obedient child but that child is not going to be able to become their 'best possible self'.

And, at the other extreme, very permissive parenting makes children fearful. Although this made sense, it was not something that had ever occurred to me. Frequently Martin used to tell me, 'Don't waver. Tell the children yes or no and then that's the end of it.' And in fact, much of the time he was the person who was firm and I simply went along with him. This worked just fine when he was around a great deal, but at the moment he is working away from our property five days a week.

Fortunately, I found this research around the time he started being away more. So rather than feeling 'mean', which was my feeling before, I now repeat to myself, 'Knowing limits helps children feel safe.'

Having observed Martin for many years, I have learned a few things about enforcing rules. Fewer words is better — saying more sounds like you feel a need to defend your decision, which in turn undermines the request and invites argument. Assume they are going to do exactly what you have asked, as that lends an unquestionable authority to your tone; and also know that what you are asking is completely reasonable. Every now and then you will need to defend a decision, so be prepared to back up your request by explaining your reasons to your child.

Chores, too, are very important here. Nothing conveys to children their sense of place more than knowing they are contributing and that they are needed. This is a big part of feeling safe.

The outcomes of disorganised attachment

So how does disorganised attachment show itself in addition to the odd behaviours discussed at the beginning of this chapter? The most well-known marker begins when the child is around three years old. Where the parent won't provide that feeling of safety, the child begins to control the environment and her parents to make that happen. This shows itself in two different ways.

The first of these is by becoming the caregiver for the parent. You will see the child working to help the parent keep their head straight: entertaining them, directing them and reassuring them. Often, unfortunately, other adults are so impressed by this behaviour in a child that they praise the child for it. 'What an amazing child she is! So mature and caring! You don't need to worry about a thing with her around!' In fact, this is a child who is not having a childhood. In the long term, despite how good those care competencies look, this child is on track for an unhappy adulthood.

Controlling behaviours: whingeing and temper tantrums

Just in these last two weeks I have realised that children very quickly give you direct feedback about how 'organised' they are feeling. The cold weather has come and Rafael has been strongly resisting being dressed in warm clothes. Well, I don't like wearing layers and layers of clothing either, so although I continued to argue for the clothes to go on, my face and voice were not entirely congruent with my message.

Within days he was 'whingeing', that mosquito-pitched tone which is like a spike into a parent's brain stem. From clothes the protest was extending to the eating of vegetables, and suddenly it struck me: Rafael was trying to control me. And although he doesn't have temper tantrums, I realised that some temper tantrums may also be an attempt to control a parent with a display of rage.

So if he was trying to control me, did that not mean there was a gap in my parenting? Having checked through the research I found that two and a half year olds have a stage of attempting to control Mum and Dad, but as Rafael is nearly four this didn't apply to him, so I realised that this is precisely what those behaviours meant.

It was my usual gap: not a strict-enough adherence to rules. There is always that little catch-up for a child between when you make a change to parenting and when it shows in their behaviour. However, within three days of my enforcement of 'warm dressing' (no going over to Grandad's for sausage and jam and toast otherwise) and all food being eaten, the whingeing had stopped. To further support this I took my own recommendations and began insisting that Rafael helped far more around the house. Now I just have to stick to it!

The second strategy is never approved by soci[e] who controls their parent negatively. Just yester[day] apparently in a good mood, suddenly walk up to [...] her with all his strength. These children bully, coerce a[nd] attack their parents in order to control them.

In both cases, knowing that parents can be controlled gives [a] child that essential feeling of safety that the parents have not provided in their parenting. The imperative of coping with fear and of simply surviving has been met, but at a profound cost.

Without a 'corrective attachment experience' — in other words, if they don't somehow find someone with whom they can have a secure, organised attachment — these children are placed on the path to difficulties with self-regulation skills, with all the consequences that has. Children with disorganised attachment are anxious and show difficulties with thinking, empathy and impulse control from a very early age. They grow into teenagers who struggle to control aggressive impulses and to empathise with others. School performance in the teenage years is suddenly much poorer as their thinking skills may be 'stuck' at a 12-year-old's level.

Finally, a disorganised attachment can also show itself as 'indiscriminate attachment'. This behaviour is one where a child attaches herself to a complete stranger within seconds of seeing her and is 'all over them', trying to elicit the kind of care a child normally only gets from a parent.

One of the things I find most extraordinary is that we don't question this behaviour when we see it in other cultures: we don't see it as aberrant and dangerous and a marker for pathology. When we see it in non-Indigenous Australian children we say, 'Oh, that's not right, that child is at risk, that child has no sense of "stranger danger"' and 'How odd it is they don't seem to know that some behaviour should only be directed to family members.' But when it is seen in Aboriginal children, for example, we often say, 'Oh, they are so lovely and friendly.' And while Aboriginal culture is a lot warmer than ours, this remains aberrant behaviour when physical affection is directed to a complete stranger.

Knowing about the disorganised and organised half of attachment classifications really helped me to 'sharpen up' the questions I asked myself on the way to a parenting decision. I now ask myself, 'Is that

an animal and seems unable to recognise the pain the animal feels (both emotional and physical) is on track to grow into an adult who is comfortable hurting other people in the same way.

When these children go on to parent themselves, unless they have been lucky enough to have developed a secure attachment with someone else, they too will not respond to emotional clues in their children, and so this pattern is transmitted to the next generation.

Dismissive parenting and avoidant attachment

This is a fictional story that a person beginning to come to terms with a childhood in which they had been dismissively parented might tell.

'My mother didn't ever — either she didn't notice or she didn't choose to — respond to how I felt. And she went away from me, I mean, she actually moved away from me if I cried or reached out to her. I always had food, I always had a bed, I went to school, the house was kept clean — but I never had love. I never saw love on her face. It was always still, frozen, barren of emotion.

'My sister was the favourite. I learned, though, how to be like Mother wished. If I was very happy she didn't mind me being around. If I didn't ask for love or cuddles or comfort, I could be near her. So I would just do sums, sitting near her feet. I would colour in, and if I didn't look at her, I didn't irritate her. So that was how I could still be close. But she always encouraged me to go off and do my own thing. I always got approval for that. A tiny bit of warmth. If I hurt myself, though, I would want so much to ask for a cuddle I would have to walk away. I'd go off by myself to get over it. Because her pushing me away when I needed to be held was worse than the injury. And if I cried, she was just hostile for days. It wasn't worth it.

'I remember breaking a finger at the beginning of the holidays once. I hid it, of course, and she didn't notice, but the teacher worked it out at school on the first day. And I asked her not to do anything about it, but she thought it was abuse, and so she did. Of course there was a lot

of trouble over it, and my mother was very angry with me, because people then said she was a neglectful parent.'

The mention of her mother's frozen expression is important. It's called the 'still face' in parenting literature and it has been shown to be as distressing to babies as a very frightening angry expression on Mum's face. That still expression is the embodiment of neglect, as the frightening expression is the embodiment of abuse. This is a fearful child, so this relationship would be classified as disorganised as well as insecure.

You can see that 'still face' in most adventure movies: the frozen expression that the hero shows in response to threat.[25] When you see it on the face of a mother looking at her child, you know that the mother is perceiving a threat. What kind of threat? Perhaps a threat to her child — she may see a child showing neediness as advertising their vulnerability and therefore unsafe in a predatory world. Or perhaps a threat to her own equilibrium, which may depend on her keeping emotionally distant from the rest of the world? Or is the mother simply depressed? Whatever the cause, the effect on the child is much the same. Instead of a smile leading to oxytocin release and brain growth, the 'still face' leads to the release of catecholamines and the loss of brain circuitry.[26]

The distressing thing is that when people say to vulnerable new mothers things such as, 'You will spoil that child if you keep picking her up', they are promoting a dismissive pattern of attachment. And that's tragic because these children then don't have such a rich experience of life, because life's richness comes from emotions and our relationships with other people. Dismissive parenting leads straight to isolation.

In other ways these children can look like strong performers. They do eventually acquire strong skills, as a result of their parent's keen interest in that aspect of development. They are often successful in work roles as a result. They are keenly motivated.

What these children tend to lack is one of the prerequisites for good impulse control, however. For someone to be able to stop themself doing or saying something that will damage a relationship with another person, they need first of all to be able to empathise with another person. They need to be able to imagine just how those words or that action or non-words or non-action will appear from the other person's perspective. And, because this child has very rarely experienced that empathy from his parent, he will mostly lack it himself.

This is a huge deficit. Success in life is, above all else, about our relationships.

So how do these children behave?

As babies, they seem only distantly connected to their parents. The frequent smiling and patting of Mum that you expect to see isn't there. In fact, the very strong body-to-body connection between mother and child is missing altogether. Physical contact is brief and the child is often seen to be avoiding it. They are usually a little distance away from their parents exploring, but their exploration and play is not characterised by the richly varied themes and absorption you see in the securely attached child.

Mum and I believe, and this is not something studied in the literature, that you see more repetition in the play of these children. It can look a bit like an autism spectrum disorder, but it owes more to the fact that these children aren't really playing but pretending to play while keeping a close watch on Mum. It sets the children up for the need for an unvarying pattern to play and a small repertoire of activities that can be enjoyed.

At school these children might be successful students but not the most successful, as they do not ask for help when they require it. Unsurprisingly, their social skills are markedly poor. Teachers notice, too, their difficulties in telling stories that make emotional sense and which can take into account multiple viewpoints. And for this same reason — appreciating that different people have different views of the same event — these children struggle with conflict resolution with their peers. So they fit very quickly into a pure bully or victim profile, or a bully/victim, with the roles alternating.

Although very few parents fall into the category of 'dismissive', a dismissive element is common in Australian parenting styles. Statements like 'It only counts if it is bleeding' or 'Build a bridge and get over it' or 'Tell it to someone who cares' or 'That's not worth crying over' or 'Come on, it's not that sad' are all dismissive. By saying such things our child hears that we believe his feelings are not strong enough to justify his behaviour.

In fact, we are asking them to 'feel less', which is not possible, so what they do is listen to their feelings less. Teaching children to disconnect from their emotions is not a good idea as it puts them on the pathway for mental illness later on. If you are feeling little prickles of annoyance with me at this stage — or have even thrown the book across the room (for me, this is a real sign that something has hit a nerve and I need to pay attention) — then you and I have something in common. My insistence that my sons shouldn't feel despair was dismissive.

The childhood that won't let go

On the other end of the attachment scale are the parents who, far from 'forgetting' their childhoods, cannot be in the present moment with their own children as their own childhood attachments are still their main focus. In the parenting literature these parents are called 'preoccupied'.

Where the dismissive parent teaches the child to avoid expressing and, in fact, consciously feeling negative emotions, the preoccupied parent does the reverse. By only inconsistently responding because she's spending all that time in her own past, this parent teaches her children to amplify all emotions in their efforts to get her to respond.

And often these parents need very strong signals to break through their preoccupation. Because of this, children exaggerate their neediness into whining and crying, even over quite small events, in order to keep their mother on the spot and paying attention. As a result these children do not learn to manage their mood, but they exaggerate emotions in order to keep Mum up to the mark, and on top of that they are most unlikely to leave her side to go and explore. The confidence to explore comes when a child knows that his parent is always watching over him, ready to help if it is required and to share the moment with him. The preoccupied parent is hardly to be relied upon and the child knows this, and remains glued to her side.[16] All in all, these are the very whiny, very angry, very clingy kids. They are called 'ambivalent' or 'resistant' in the parenting literature.

DISMISSIVE!

When these mothers do respond they don't always respond appropriately. They might grab a child without warning, or comfort a child who is not distressed, or laugh when a child is upset, or give them a toy to play with when the child wants comfort. Even while apparently interacting with their child, they are still so closely engaged with their own emotions that they fail to register how their child is feeling — and therefore don't respond to how their child is feeling. They might be occupying the same space, but there is a lack of emotional connection between them. That lack of empathy from a parent will prevent the child developing the ability to manage his own mood.[5]

This emotional mismatch usually leads to a child becoming increasingly distressed in an effort to 'break through' their mother's absorption. Even when the mother finally 'wakes up' to her child's emotions things don't improve. When these children actually receive the comfort they have been asking for, they don't calm down. Close proximity to Mum does not help them feel soothed after all, and sometimes it even further unbalances their flailing emotions. The body-to-body connection that is so much part of a secure attachment is missing from the relationship.[27]

The preoccupied parent

This is a fictional story that a parent still caught up in the events of her childhood while attempting to parent might tell:

'You know, she'd be so upset some days and she'd just fall apart. And so it fell to me to do lots of things: I cleaned the house, I brought up my siblings. She'd sort of come in now and then with them, and she'd often get it wrong, you know, come on too strong with us, miss what we were really on about.

'She didn't like me for doing her jobs — she could be a real bitch, actually. But someone had to do those things. And I was the eldest girl, so I kept on doing them, even though my brother was the favourite, because it was something I could do to make a difference. But he was the golden boy and he still is. He can't put a foot wrong.

'I'd have done the house from top to bottom and he'd have just stared at the TV all afternoon or gone out and kicked a football around some oval. He'd be the one to get the real thanks — I mean, she'd thank me, but the benefits always seemed to somehow land at his door. Now Golden Boy doesn't have full-time work because he's really slowly making an important documentary on early TV shows, but that's okay because he can stay with Mum rent-free and eat the food I cook and bring over for her. I get really angry with the pair of them, I can tell you.

'I shout at her and I say, "Mum, if you'd just spend a bit of your time with my kids that would be great. Golden Boy is actually an adult now, and you are missing out on my kids right now and they are so beautiful." My two younger sisters have just disappeared from our lives — perhaps they had the right idea?

'I've tried to limit what I do for my mother but I always come back in the end to the fact that she is my mother and she does actually need me.

'There are days when I want to fall apart too, just like her, but I don't. My kids aren't going to get turned into little caregivers like I was and get screwed up. I get angry lots of the time, and I just can't think straight when I'm angry either; it makes working out what to do with the kids so hard when they're difficult. But I hope they don't just disappear from my life like my sisters have from Mum's; even though it's so hard to cope, I don't know what I'd do without them. They're my life.

'Mum's not always so uptight, though. Sometimes we have great times together and we laugh and I can see the kids just basking in it, and they relax, you can see that, and I wish it could always be that way. They're my favourite times in the whole world. But they don't last. I can't keep it up and neither can she. I don't know why. The kids start whining and carrying on over absolutely nothing — except for Lloyd, he's my good boy, he helps me keep the others on track — and I lose my shirt and I whack them. I feel so guilty then, and I make it up to them by doing something special with them — but that is so tiring to keep up and I'm trying to look after Mum as well ...'

You might have noticed the role reversal — the fact that the daughter cared for her siblings and ran the house. This is a marker for *disorganisation as well as ambivalent attachment. Like everything else in parenting, this tends to travel down the generations, taking on a slightly different shape with each new generation.*

Children take on adult roles not because they want to, but in order to make themselves feel safe. It is not in a child's long-term interests to take on adult roles in childhood, no matter how remarkably 'mature' and special they seem to observers. I'm not suggesting children should not help in roles around the house, but that they should not take on the 'emotional' role of an adult. Taking on an adult role puts a child at risk of growing up to have borderline personality disorder.[28]

At the heart of this story lies every child's need for a secure attachment. Our storyteller is still looking for that from her mother. Her adult life has been a quest to receive that acknowledgment and approval — it was withheld in childhood and she's never got over doing without it. The tragedy is that a quest should always end with someone finding the grail — but in this case, the grail is a change to someone else's behaviour. Like love itself, a change to another person's behaviour is not something you get as a reward. The gates for change are within, and they open from the inside: only the person themself has the key.

Our storyteller's quest is fruitless, but she can't see that yet. Every now and then she has a moment of 'true connection' with her mother and, rewarded by this, she keeps on.

Other ways to create a 'clingy' child

At a recent conference I attended I was told that, while a mother being preoccupied with her past was the main reason for her children developing an 'ambivalent' attachment, there are also other reasons.[29] Plain old 'inconsistent' parenting was the first of these and I'd spotted that for myself. One of the hard things is that we are all busier these days. The kind of inconsistent on-and-off parenting that was once associated with parents with the 'preoccupied' psychological status is occurring in parents without this kind of personal history. We need to be very careful that this isn't a trap we fall into.

I've come to realise that it doesn't matter what we are preoccupied with, whether it's writing a book or something that happened to us, if we only inconsistently respond to our children we are going to see the same effects. I find it is difficult to stop in the middle of a train of thought to listen to Rafael tell me that his Bionicle now has a little brother or to Sam telling me that the water pressure at the bottom of the ocean is equivalent to so many jumbo jets sitting on top of my head, but, as I've become increasingly familiar with the attachment research and the consequences of preoccupied parenting, I do now stop and listen.

What else creates ambivalence in children?

Actually forbidding them to go out and explore has the same impact as inconsistency. Instead of a child sticking close to Mum in order to keep her up to the mark, we keep a child close ourselves. So if we feel that the world is a very dangerous place we will do this, and we will also do this if we 'need our children to need us'. In both cases, we are heightening our children's 'attachment system' — the part of them that needs a parent close to feel safe — so they don't feel able to go out and explore the world.

The children are the 'obviously in trouble' children by the time they reach school. Their intense emotionality puts them at immediate risk of being bullied. Having not been empathised with properly by their parents means that they cannot empathise well with others. They are the children who frequently behave inappropriately or 'out of tune', having missed the emotional cues of the other children.

The self-regulation skills that lead to resilience are also missing. In particular, good impulse control is not rewarded in this type of parenting. The children have learned to immediately turn their emotions 'up to eleven' in order to get what they want. And, with their focus on keeping Mum available through whingeing and clinging, these children are behind on their skill development. This puts them at immediate disadvantage when it comes to learning in the formal setting of school. Finally, the seesawing emotions, the difficulties reading other people and the leftover issues from childhood put these children on track to parent just as they have been parented.

But transmission of insecure attachment patterns is not set in stone because we can change. The human ability to metamorphose is phenomenal.

Chapter 4

Changing an attachment pattern

Had the ghosts of those long-ago boys moved on at
last, or was it simply that she was set free from her
own ghosts ... leaving her alive and free.

Margaret Mahy, *Dangerous Spaces*, 1991.[30]

A ny change in behaviour means a change in the brain itself. This
applies just as much to growing a new way of relating to other
people as it does to learning to interpret what you see. And, just as
there are 'critical periods' in our development for such things as
learning to see or learning to talk, there are critical periods in our
development for learning to relate.

The first is in the earliest years of our lives, from birth to three
years of age. The second great surge occurs, along with so much else,
in puberty. And then again (and this is a new discovery) it occurs in
mothers, from the third trimester of pregnancy and onwards until
the child is three years old. (In fact, anyone closely involved with
the baby — dads, grandparents — will also be affected to some
degree.)[31]

How motherhood remakes a woman's brain

*There is still some controversy over whether or not pregnancy makes
you dumber but there is very little doubt that, after delivery, motherhood*

makes you smarter. When a woman is pregnant her hormones, particularly the 'love hormone' oxytocin, rewire her brain.

Scientists have recorded improvements to memory, spatial skills, stress management skills and people-reading skills in pregnant women. And these changes stay with us for life. And the more babies we have, the stronger the effect grows.[31–35] Better stress management has inevitable repercussions for overall health. [36] So strong is the invigorating effect of pregnancy that women who give birth in their forties are four times more likely to survive to become a centenarian than women who gave birth earlier.[37]

One leading researcher on the subject is Dr Craig Kinsley, his attention initially caught by the way his wife, previously ambivalent about mothering, was transformed by both pregnancy and the early months of caring for their children.[31] The difference between a mother's brain and a non-mother's brain, he says, is 'like comparing a tree in the winter to one in full bloom in the spring, when it is much fuller and richer'.[38]

And it is not just the mother's brain that changes. An involved, and not necessarily biological, father's brain does also: a cocktail of hormones, but most particularly vasopressin (the monogamy hormone) turns men into better 'hunters' and protectors, making them both stable and vigilant, sharpening environmental and people-reading skills and making them as keen on cuddling as on sex.[37, 39]

The studies are just beginning into how being around a baby affects other carers. When I worked in nursing homes I would always take my babies with me, and so rejuvenating was the impact of a smiling, sociable baby that I have little doubt what researchers will find. For most people, interacting with a baby will lead to a surge of oxytocin — promoting brain activity with all the kick-on benefits from that you see at any age — and also improve physical health, showing up in such things as a drop in blood pressure and an improved mood.

Of course we can change at any time, but at those times particularly we are helped along by a bath of oxytocin, the love and learning hormone. One friend who read this part of an early draft of the book rang me to say how exactly this had been her own experience. She had been eighteen and there was a baby on the way.

> I knew I was too screwed up to do a good job. Dad was alcoholic and abusive. Mum didn't have any power to stop him. So, with my husband's support, I found a counsellor. It was a heavy two years, but I had my head straight by the time my daughter was eighteen months old.

Her nurturing and sociable teenage daughters are a testament to just how very straight she got her head.

It is the right side of the brain that transforms

It is one hemisphere of the brain that is particularly involved in our ability to transform ourselves to parent better — the right brain. In the 1980s there was a surge of interest in left and right brainedness, and then popular culture moved on, leaving us with an impression that there was nothing scientific in talking about the two hemispheres.

But while popular culture moved on, science didn't. We now know that the two hemispheres are very different and the right brain is the early developing side, remaining dominant until a child turns three. The left side, from which comes our verbal ability and our logical ability, is the prose. It is the left brain we test on our way to an IQ score. The right side is the place from which passion both flows, and is turned to good account in our lives.

The mother who glances at her child and knows something is wrong and calmly overrides the doctors until she is proven right is following the 'gut instinct' that comes from her right brain. The child who knows his parents aren't telling him something, by reading their micro-expressions — a skill he honed in infancy — is using his right brain. The mathematician who 'knows' his equation is not right because it doesn't yet appear beautiful or satisfying is using his right brain within a left brain task. The man who is transformed by a mentoring relationship, emerging with better coping and people skills, learning ability, memory and a happier mood, has just grown his right brain. The grieving woman who finds that weeks of making shirts has returned her to an engagement with life has begun healing her right brain, and thus her pain, through touch and texture and colour and movement.

In fact, the right brain cannot be reached through words and logic. Sensations and movement are what get through — the rueful expression on a father's face, the whimper of a tired baby, the crackly warmth of a fire, water flowing over a palm, the alerting bump of the median strip, the dying fall of a pop song, the tingle of wine, the smell of grass. From all of these sensations the right brain builds meaningful patterns that are stored as memory.

The right side of the brain is where autobiographical memory, spatial skills, regulation of emotions and body systems in the face of stress, and the ability to read other people and to empathise with them dwell. It is the part of our mind that we often think about as the 'unconcious' or 'subconsious'. And it is the right brain that your baby spends the first three years of her life growing.

This brain growth doesn't just 'happen', nor does it grow in response to 'intellectual stimulation', because this part of the brain is not about logic or words or facts. Your baby's right brain grows because of the passionate, intimate connection forged with you.[40]

And for you to grow this part of your baby's brain to its 'best possible', you need to have a well-developed right brain yourself. You need to have had a secure attachment relationship, whether in childhood or later on in your life, for this part of your brain to be strong enough to grow a strong right brain in your child.

The active ingredient is the same, whatever our age

So what can you do to grow or keep healthy your own right brain? The central message is that you cannot do it on your own. It requires a relationship. You might be like my friend and find a counsellor, but the relationship must be a reciprocal one to work as an attachment. Just as a baby cannot grow a right brain without a parent's strong right brain, an adult cannot 'imagine' a relationship and be transformed.

With that person's support you then need to learn to tell the story of your own childhood attachments coherently and meaningfully, and let go to a great degree the losses of your childhood. Once you are able to do that, you will find that you can both allow a child to explore and also be ready to comfort her when she needs it. These are the two halves of parenting.

If you are doing this work and you have childre
baby, remember that mother–child attachment is recι
for some people the best thing to grow their right brair.
All those things that support your baby's attachment
support your right brain growth. Smelling and looking an
and cradling and rocking your newborn is good for you   .vell as
your baby.

What else? You also need to be getting enough good, healthy food, because a rapidly growing brain, as yours will be as you do this work, is a great consumer of energy. Food is also part of our biological connection to the natural world — or, at least, it should be. And as well as food, we need to be out in that world as much as we can. Leaves, flickering and green, the sharp solids of rocks, the dash and dip of a small bird, and your own movement as you walk among it, will feed your growing right brain. Music (the heart loves a steady drumbeat), happy loving faces, rich stories (the right brain loves narrative), colour, play, laughter, dance, cooking, pets, making something, a feeling of being lovingly supported and appreciated for yourself — all of the things that make you feel good and give you that warm fuzzy feeling will help you to remake your pattern of attachment.

If that is what you need, then what don't you need? There are no surprises here. You need to *not* be fearful or traumatised or just plain 'stressed-out'. If you wish to deliberately regrow your brain, to learn a new story for yourself with an ending that leaves you and subsequent generations free of the past, you can do it any time. Feed your growing right brain, find your support crew and set out. You will find that your children will ride in your back pocket, learning the story along with you. (See Appendix II for more on the different attachment patterns and suggestions for changing a negative attachment pattern.)

Those of us who have been lucky enough to have inherited a secure attachment cannot become complacent. Patterns are broken in both directions: securely attached children can become parents of insecure children; insecurely attached children can become parents of securely attached children. A great deal depends on the people, the environment and the events surrounding mother and child.

The Bidi Bidi Project, Mt Magnet, Western Australia

How to grow the right brain is a huge interest for Mum and me, because we believe that this is the way forward for Aboriginal families where we work, in the remote communities of the Murchison in Western Australia. These are mostly Indigenous communities, with fly-in fly-out mine sites sprinkled throughout. Indigenous disadvantage is not just being passed on, but speeding up and widening as it travels down the generations. It is snowballing as poverty and rapid social change, trauma and passive welfare are interfering with the attachments people have to each other. For Aboriginal people in the Murchison the name of the game has been survival, which is a function of the right brain. Meeting the imperative of survival has meant that all other right brain functions have been co-opted to support that need alone.

The name 'Bidi Bidi' — 'butterfly' in local language — was coined by Mt Magnet elder Phyllis Thompson in reference to the metamorphosis she wants to see in people's lives. How does she see this change happening? She wants to see the young mothers better supported. And this isn't just 'helping by caring for their kids' but an intervention to directly grow their right brains. The Bidi Bidi Project has four 'wings': four interlinking sets of relationship-based programs. One of them is a right brain growth program for young mothers.

Seeing the ghosts in your nursery

Sometimes, when you are alone with your baby — perhaps you are the only two awake in the middle of the night, or perhaps you are deeply connecting with a smile — it can feel like you are the only two people in the world. And it may feel exhilarating or it may feel terrifying, but it is an illusion either way.

There are always ghosts walking the path with you — the memories of your own childhood. However, this approach — seeing the ghosts — doesn't ask us to deal with our past. It simply requires that we look right now at what we are doing with our children, and, in doing so, see the ghosts that are standing between us and our child.

There are a number of ways to go about this, but my attention was particularly caught by the revolutionary Circle of Security parenting approach. In this approach a group of parents are shown a beautiful ocean scene on a DVD. The sea is gentle and blue. There are birds flying above. The accompanying sound track is a piece of tranquil classical music.

And then the facilitators change the sound track. Instead of classical music the parents hear the accelerating 'da dump, da dump' of the *Jaws* theme music and they are asked to reflect on how quickly their internal switch was flicked from tranquillity to alarm. The scene had not changed, but their emotions had. Their emotions changed because of a historic association between a sound and their experience of an emotion — a vicarious emotion, because none of them were actually there in the water when the monster shark attacked.

The parents are asked how that change felt — to name it, to locate it in their bodies, to see how it changes how they want to treat others. Because it is that same feeling that we sometimes have as parents.

Have you ever seen a parent react to a child's actions or words in a way that looks 'over the top' to you? They might become furious with a child for crying or smack them for asking for food — to you, the child's behaviour looked normal, but to the child's parent it is obviously only a few steps away from the end of the world. The parent is hearing something that you cannot: shark music. Something about the child's behaviour set off a depth charge of emotion because of something that happened in the parent's past.

Sometimes, when our children do something, a switch is flicked in our brain that has more to do with our own past than anything that is happening in the present. Even though we feel great love for our children, in that moment we do not express it 'lovingly'. From our own childhood the message is sent — the child has done something dangerous and must be stopped from doing it again. So we might yell at him or turn away coldly from him or say by our behaviour, 'you are not allowed to have that emotion'. We are automatically responding to our child as our parents did to us, no matter how much we may have wanted to do things differently.

The Circle of Security trainers focus on teaching parents to hear the shark music, which is like a herald announcing, 'Here is a ghost.' Such ghosts tell lies: 'She only needs a good smack', 'She's just attention seeking', 'He's trying to manipulate you', 'She needs to learn that you won't pick her up every time she cries', 'Don't let her make you feel guilty', 'He's just trying to get out of doing it' or 'He shouldn't be running to you for every little cut and bruise'.

What do you do when you hear the music and spot the ghost? They are not hard to see once you have heard the 'da–dump da–dump' because they are standing directly between you and your child. At this point you need to identify what need or emotion in your child brought out the ghost. Did your baby want to be cuddled after a fright? Did your child want you to pay attention to him doing something? Was the emotion he was expressing allowed in your own childhood? Most likely it was not.

At this point you might be wondering how you should react?

That was certainly my thought, after I realised that the shark music started when my sons found something 'too hard' and would cry despairingly. And the thought that emerged in my mind was 'It isn't safe to advertise the fact that we are vulnerable, it puts us at risk.' Where had that come from? It may be because I am from 'pioneer stock' on both sides, Africa and Australia. A loudly crying child may attract the wrong sort of attention in both contexts. It may have been because I went to boarding school. To cry was to advertise vulnerability. I spent hours learning how to suppress tears. In fact, it was probably a combination of both and perhaps a bit more I still haven't seen. So my dismissive behaviour originated in a desire to protect my children, and I think this is pretty common.

It is so very loud, the shark music, that it drowns out thought. I found it very hard to think of a different way to react. And this is when I found Haim Ginott.

Ginott's strategies for a secure relationship

Dr Haim Ginott was originally a teacher and famously observed of his classroom, 'It is my daily mood that makes the weather.'[41] His books for parents and teachers were bestsellers, and his advice became a permanent influence on the way parents in the western world try to go about the business of parenting. If you recall, I was looking for advice on how to stop forbidding my children from showing despair. And that's exactly what Ginott's strategy offers.

First of all, and exactly in parallel with what is required to create a secure attachment, he says 'allow all feelings'. He says that if you find yourself saying to your child, 'Don't cry now' or 'Stop making that horrible noise' or 'You can't really mean that' or 'Toughen up' or 'Calm down' or 'You aren't stupid [or ugly or whatever it is he says of himself]' you are denying your child's right to feel a particular emotion. He writes, 'Strong feelings do not vanish by being banished: they do diminish in intensity and lose their sharp edges when the listener accepts them with sympathy and understanding.'[42]

So before offering anything else, offer understanding, says Ginott. This is the kind of story he tells in his books:

'I hate James,' says your seven year old. Instead of saying something like 'it's wrong to hate' or 'never mind James', you need to focus on the feeling your child is expressing, and empathise with it.

'He must have done something awful for you to say that.'

'He said that I couldn't be in his group because I wasn't eight and I didn't have an orange rubber like he and everyone else does.'

'That must have made you feel very upset.'

'I pushed him.' Instead of saying 'Oh no, you shouldn't push!' focus back on how your child was feeling.

'You were obviously very angry too,' you say.

'I wish I'd pushed him again, but the teacher came over.' Picking up on the fact that your child still has angry feelings towards James that weren't alleviated by pushing him, you say:

'You still feel angry with him.'

'I do feel angry still and I'm sad I wasn't in that group.'

'You had other friends in that group and you couldn't be with them.'

And at around this point, Ginott promises, there will be the dividends you are looking for. Your son's mood is softened by your understanding and he will begin thinking about his behaviour all by himself.

'I guess I shouldn't have pushed James though. The teacher won't put me in that group now until she's forgotten about it. I should just have ignored him.'

And at this point you could perhaps say, but gently, because you do know how he felt, 'So you could, and people are not for pushing.'

Making the rule (in this case not pushing) attached to a 'thing' (people) is a key feature of Ginott's way of enforcing limits. It takes the focus from the child and puts it on the behaviour. So you don't say 'You must not throw sand' but 'Sand is not for throwing'. In our house we have found ourselves saying things like, 'Soap is for washing, not for carving up with a knife' and 'Eggshells are for the vegetable garden, not for crushing up into tiny pieces and scattering throughout the kitchen.'

Prior to reading Ginott, a discussion with my son Sam might have gone something like this:

'I just can't,' Sam would cry, weeping bitterly. 'I'm stupid.' This was something Martin and I had been hearing from him for about a year and we couldn't understand why.

'You aren't stupid! Now stop, just stop.' The shark music was playing, and, rather than focusing on feelings I would focus on facts.

'I am, I know I am.'

'I can't understand why you would say that about yourself. You really aren't stupid at all. Look how well you are doing at school.' Another appeal to facts.

'I can't remember how to tell the time. And remember when I stabbed the milk cartons to get them out of the box and the milk went everywhere. That was a stupid thing to do.' The difficulty with facts is that they are rarely controvertible.

'That doesn't make you stupid. Now just stop crying. You need to stop. You can't just keep crying.' I was back to attempting to control his emotions.

'I can't stop. I can't stop because I can't stop thinking about being so stupid.'

And so it would go on, until eventually Martin or I would say that he was stupid if he thought he was stupid.

After reading Ginott we had just one discussion about being stupid, and Sam hasn't mentioned it since. It went something like this:

'I just can't,' Sam cried. 'I'm just stupid.'

His crying was setting off my shark music, but I had resolved to tolerate it and concentrate instead on Sam's emotions rather than mine.

'That doesn't sound like a nice feeling to have — that sounds like you are feeling awful.'

Instantly I saw him lift his head slightly. The tears gushed out with a bit more intensity at this sympathy.

'I am. I do feel awful.'

'You are feeling really unhappy having that thought about yourself,' I said in my best Ginott style, but feeling that I sounded artificial, despite sincerely wanting to understand him better.

'It makes me feel sick,' said Sam in response, but he had stopped crying. And then, to my astonishment, he said, 'I do some stupid things, but that doesn't make me stupid.'

And he proceeded to tell me about an incident a year earlier when he had been larking about with some other children and a fork had dropped on the floor. The only adult present had said to him aggressively, 'You are bloody stupid, Sam.' So we talked about that. But, in the end, he'd said it himself. Doing stupid things from time to time doesn't make us stupid.

His expression of his feelings had drawn us closer and we both felt the difference. Ghosts stand between us and our children. It was not the adult who'd spoken harshly to Sam that had caused the problem, it was my attempt to stop him from expressing that feeling of despair.

It had all happened just as Ginott promised. My empathy let Sam connect properly to his feelings and then use his reasoning skills to draw the poison out from the wound himself. Of course, after this I was a Ginott convert. So what else does he say?

It is of little use, says Ginott, to lecture a child about how he should have behaved after the event. And he's quite specific about the different forms this kind of commentary from parents can sometimes take. He advises against:

- Moralising — 'You only got what you deserved, you shouldn't have pushed.'
- Minimising — 'You can't hate someone just because they didn't want you in their group.'
- Attacking the child's personality — 'You are so stupid! How many times have I told you not to be rough with other kids? You never listen, and then you get into trouble.'
- Prophesising — 'Well, you won't get any friends that way, you'll end up being Mr No Mates for sure.'

If you have set firm limits, as he advises, your child will know your definitions of what is right and wrong already. It is better to use opportunities like 'pushing James' to hold up a mirror to our child so he can see how he feels. If it's just a matter of 'letting off steam safely' and acknowledging his emotions, then the job is done. If it is a matter of sorting out other ways he could have behaved, then, with his emotions softened, he can begin doing that too. And, instead of alienating your child with *your* opinion, you have communicated to him your love and your respect for *his* emotions and opinion. You have strengthened the relationship between the two of you.

Ginott writes directly about handling our own anger as parents, about recognising it, accepting it and expressing it safely. He advises against smacking because you are teaching the child that physically expressing anger is acceptable. He says not to tell a child off in front of his friends as it always makes him play up more: leading to parents becoming even angrier and the situation sliding out of control.

Instead, he says, express your angry feelings as long as personality and character assassinations aren't part of what you say. In fact, what he says next is now taught at every 'better communication' course around the world. It's the 'I–you' messages: I feel (emotion added here) when you (action added here)'. Begin with 'I feel angry', but if, after saying that, you still feel angry, you can amplify the message. 'I feel extremely angry.' And if you are still experiencing anger, Ginott suggests a third stage: saying what you'd like to do to release that anger. 'I feel so angry when you hit your little brother that I feel I'd like to hit something myself. And I feel terribly sad too. I just want to sit and cry.'

His warnings against harsh parenting have proved prescient: of all the 'everyday' parenting styles, excluding abuse and neglect, this is the one associated with the worst outcomes.[43, 44] If someone ever tells you that you are being 'too hard on your kids', it is always worth seriously evaluating what they mean. If they are talking about the limits you set, then this may not be a problem. However, if they mean that you mostly punish, praise rarely and make unpleasant remarks about a child's character, his abilities and his future, then change is required.

Whereas popular opinion holds that 'being hard' is a direction you

can safely err in ('I'd rather be too tough than too soft on my
research shows conclusively that it is not, if what you mean by
is being punitive and a denigrator. The attachment research, of co ˌᴜᴄ,
has shown the same thing in its research into 'frightening' parents
and the link through to disorganised children — this research comes
from people who study 'parenting style' — and it is worth looking
at this slightly different take on what happens when you frighten
children. **POSITIVE REINFORCEMENT**

In addition, recent neuroscience shows that children under eleven
don't have the neural circuits in place to learn anything at all from
criticism. They literally cannot adjust their behaviour based on
negative comments: in one study, eight- to nine-year-old children
performed disproportionally more inaccurately after receiving
negative feedback relative to positive feedback. If you want to change
your child's behaviour, you must tell him what you *like* about what
he is doing and exactly what it is that you want him to do.[45]

Am I too hard on my kids?

*Your eldest son has taken his smaller sister in a stranglehold: his fingers
are round her throat. She is obviously in some distress. Do you:*

*Accept the aggressive feelings, but not the behaviour and yell at the
top of your lungs: 'Stop! Let go of her! Other people are not for
hurting! I can't bear to see you hurting your little sister! I feel terribly
sad and anguished and upset when you do anything like that! Come
and see me when you are angry with her.' Or do you experience an
upswelling of negative feeling towards your son, coupled with anxiety
over his behaviour? Propelled by these violent emotions, you fly into
action, pulling your son off your daughter, and place your own hands
around his neck and squeeze hard, yelling, 'See what this is like? See
how scary this feels? You are such a horrible brother!'*

*Of the two of these, it is the second response that is the harshest.
Powered by parental fears for the child's social and emotional future, it
is every bit as aggressive as the behaviour originally shown by the child.
Research shows that rather than changing the child's behaviour, such*

an intervention only cements-in aggression. The child's idea of himself is shaped by the idea of himself that has taken root in his parent's mind: negative, aggressive, defiant. By the time a child has reached middle-primary school, customary ways of behaving may well have become 'traits'.[46]

So the concern that lies behind harsh parenting — that the child is aggressive, unpleasant and selfish, and that the parent has lost the power to influence this child — is eventually realised: the cumulative effect of negative words and harsh actions, including physical coercion and force, leads to the prophecy of a poor outcome being fulfilled.

If the harsh parent is Dad, the children with the worst outcomes are his sons. If the harsh parent is Mum, children of both sexes suffer equally.[43]

Are you at risk of becoming a harsh parent? In addition to having been harshly parented yourself, being a young mother and living in a dysfunctional family setting[44] are the factors that most often contribute to harshness in parenting.

You hold a negative opinion of your child

The biggest marker for harsh parenting is that parents feel their child is poorly behaved. If your child appears to you to be aggressive, disobedient, negative and defiant, then you need to consider that your parenting style might be responsible. A difficult temperament can contribute in the first place to a parent feeling they need to be harder, but sometimes what is perceived is difficult is simply a toddler working through the normal 18-month-old behaviours. You also need to consider whether you are seeing 'another person' in your child: a disliked or despised relative is the most frequent candidate.[46]

Your finances or marriage or both are in trouble

Families at risk for harsh parenting are those where Mum and Dad are stressed: where there is marital conflict, money troubles and so on. Flow-on effects include harsher, more negative parenting and can explain why at such times children so often seem to 'play up'. It is

*when parents are tired, stressed or unhappy that they find it ha[rd to]
manage their own emotions; when they are most likely to punish a
child in an emotional and impulsive manner.*

You have difficulty with impulse control in general

*The ability to stop yourself impulsively acting upon an emotion is a
key part of parenting. Our children have an unequalled ability to 'get
to us'. Their ability to disturb our equilibrium comes in part from the
fact that we know we are judged on their behaviour; and also because
children quite naturally move through different stages of behaviour,
some of them difficult. When a child's difficult behaviour is coupled
with a parent whose emotions escape from their control, a pattern of
punishing children in a highly charged atmosphere begins.*

*In the absence of good modelling of impulse control, children are
more likely to be defeated by their own impulses. Children with poor
impulse control are more likely to be aggressive, and struggle with peer
and sibling relationships, and these are the children far more likely to
then 'trigger' further aggression from you. It's a hard cycle to stop once
it has started.*[47]

Sadly, it is often fears that your child will take to drugs or become
a delinquent that drives parents to such harsh extremes. They are trying
to frighten their child into behaving properly. The same kind of
approach is taken in the 'scare them straight' education programs,
where children tour jails and meet inmates. Does it work? In fact, it
does the very reverse. A recent review of 16 such programs concluded
that they 'increase delinquency relative to doing nothing at all to the
same youths'[48] In other words, children exposed to such experiences
are far more likely to go on to offend themselves: the underlying
message is 'we think you are likely to do this, so we are showing you
how bad it will be'. And they proceed to live down to our evident
expectations of them.

Ginott was equally prescient when it came to praise. In recent years
there have been many studies showing just how destructive the wrong

kind of praise can be to children's motivation and esteem.[49, 50] Ginott was there well before them. He distinguishes between evaluative praise and appreciative praise. Evaluative praise carries a judgment: 'you are being good!' or 'what a helpful boy you are'. Such praise is loaded not just with our expectations but with the risk of the child becoming addicted to such praise, at the risk of losing his ability to evaluate himself and to take the risks that are necessary to learning.

He adds that no-one enjoys direct praise of their character. If you are told by another adult that 'you are such a wonderful, generous, good person' you are likely to wonder 'just what is it they want me to do?' Such praise can seem a bit creepy and insincere. When children are praised in such a manner, they may 'misbehave to set the adult straight' says Ginott.

Instead he recommends appreciative praise, where you comment on the task or the achievement. So say to your child, 'That was difficult' rather than 'You're so clever', and let the child infer his cleverness himself. This is far harder than it sounds to do.

I want to praise you like I should

When praise is delivered in the right way it has been shown to:
- *make children better at doing things for themselves*
- *enhance their feelings of mastery and independence*
- *make them happier*
- *motivate them to stay on task*
- *motivate them to try new ways of doing things*
- *help them keep their emotions from interfering with their ability to do something.*

But when praise is given for completing an easy task children infer that their ability must be low. And when a great deal of praise is given for accomplishment of something very difficult, children infer that this same standard is expected of them all the time. Both are difficult experiences for children to endure.

When evaluative praise such as 'good' is given — 'What a good kid! You got that right' — children are likely to infer that getting something wrong must mean that they are 'bad'.

Once children are over seven they tend to evaluate praise criti~~c~~ *Insincere praise is detected in a flash, often rightly perceived as* *attempt to manipulate and promptly discounted. Children then search* *for other reasons for the praise and may feel that it has been given to* *cover up for the fact that they are pitied or disliked. Insincere praise* *can be very damaging for this reason.*

Along the same lines, one American study indicated that older *children may actually consider praise for hard work as conveying the* *message, 'You are low in ability, and so I want you to work harder.'* *As older children over-price the value of 'natural ability', this can be* *very destructive.*

However, telling a child that he has a 'natural ability' seems to be *equally destructive: when the next, harder level of task inevitably arrives* *and he must struggle to master it, he is likely to conclude that the* *praiser was mistaken, and he does not have the natural ability after* *all. Consequently he is far less likely to keep trying.*

Boys and girls seem to respond differently to praise; children and *teenagers likewise. Girls are more likely to examine praise for* *insincerity; teenagers will experience praise in front of a group as* *negative, whereas younger children experience it as positive.*

Another great risk of praise is that children will become 'hooked' on *it, and not develop an internal set of motivators. Their 'feel goods' are* *not generated from within, but by the approval of others. This denies* *them the experience of 'flow', that wonderful sensation that occurs from* *being entirely caught up in a task. It denies them the ability to be the* *'captain of their soul', to determine for themselves their self-worth.*[49]

How then should we praise our children? Ginott puts it best. 'Our *words should state what we like and appreciate about his efforts,* *help, work and accomplishments.'*[41] *So rather than saying, 'You are* *Mummy's good helper!' try, 'I am so thrilled when I look at the tidy* *kitchen. It hasn't looked like this for days! The scrubbing you did on* *the benches has made all the difference.'*

Not 'You must be the best big brother in the world' but 'Thank *you for putting down your book to read to your little brother when I* *asked, I know how difficult that is sometimes.'*

> Not 'What a brilliant writer you are' but 'I like this sentence in your story particularly. It puts me in the hero's shoes.'
>
> The latest researcher to focus on praise is Dr Carol Dweck. She says that getting praise right encourages our children to have a 'growth mind-set' rather than a 'fixed mind-set'. She means simply that one child will keep trying, while the other one won't want to risk the shame of trying and failing. For the 'growth mind-set' child, failing is just a diagnosis of where more effort needs to be applied, an indication that something needs to be corrected. For the 'fixed mind-set' child it is a sign that he should give up.[51]

Ginott ends his book *Between Parent and Child* with yet more uncanny percipience, suggesting that a secure attachment allows children to not only learn to deal well with the challenges of their particular temperament, but to 'switch on' the more refined individual traits and abilities that too often lie hidden for a lifetime. (You will see how right he is in Chapter 11: Humans — the tallest trees.)

This is the same message that Dr Shonkoff has drawn from the last two decades of research. The active ingredient in our child's life is the relationship he has with us. Following Ginott's strategies does take you to a closer, happier relationship with your child, and it takes your child closer to the person he wants to be.

Chapter 5

Barriers to attachment?

'O my Hostess … a Wild Thing from the Wild Woods
is most beautifully playing with your Baby.'
'A blessing on that Wild Thing whoever he may be,'
said the Woman, straightening her back,
'for I was a busy woman this morning and he has
done me a service.'

Rudyard Kipling, *Animal Stories*, 1932.[52]

Childcare and postnatal depression are almost always associated with a discussion on attachment. Childcare is a heavily divisive issue, with some people feeling that parents should not place young children into centre-based care as it will negatively impact on attachment. Postnatal depression is also a divisive issue in terms of why it happens and how it is best handled. So here is an overview of the very latest research on both.

Childcare

The assumption many people tend to make about childcare is that it's 'bad for mother–child attachment'. But this is an assumption that is not currently supported by the research. Even the journal that is the bastion of attachment research has recently published papers which reveal a very different picture.

The pattern of attachment between a parent and child is so powerful in a child's development that attending or not-attending childcare pales into insignificance. A secure attachment is the most important thing.

To the question 'Is childcare good or bad for my child?' the answer is, 'That's not the question.' The question remains, 'What kind of attachment do I have with my child?' And also, 'What other kinds of attachments does my child have with other carers and loved ones?' Another relevant question is, 'What alternatives do I have?'

Often there are no alternatives. My belief is that 'childcare' is really 'mother's help' or 'cooperative care', and should be called so. This is what we once called the women who helped out other women in their homes, and then, as it is now, women needed that particular help.

The impact of non-maternal care on children

In a nutshell, the big finding from all the studies is that non-maternal care is not the significant factor in your child's development. The biggest predictor of all child outcomes overall comes from home: how stressed parents are, how good the marital relationship is, and, above all, the attachment type that exists between the parents and their child. Time away at work does not necessarily equate to children missing out on that same amount of time with you. Research shows that many women give up other activities, such as household tasks and leisure, to spend more time with their children when not at work.[53]

This research told Mum and me that trying to improve outcomes for Aboriginal children at risk in the Murchison by providing them with high quality daycare was not going to be 'the answer'. Although an enriched environment does help children, the best way to improve outcomes for children at risk is to improve the kind of relationship they have with their parents.

Rather than aiming to provide an 'enriching environment and learning experiences' alone, our goal for working with children at risk has changed. We now have a range of strategies that all aim at changing the emotional environment around parents and children so that their attachment patterns can change too. One of these strategies is to provide parents with a mentor who has their own head 'straight' regarding attachment, so that they can experience an intimate relationship with an adult who can help them become autonomous themselves. After that experience they will have the necessary 'right brain growth' to be able to create secure, organised relationships with their children. 'Time out' for these women to grow their right brains is also valuable, and to achieve this time out, we will be providing a top quality crèche for the children of participants.

Along the same lines, any women who need time alone to get enough fuel in their tanks to warmly and sensitively parent could also benefit from being able to access this kind of support. Once upon a time that help was provided by extended families, but extended families are now spreading across the globe, following opportunities rather than staying at home and supporting (or staying near) kin. If a woman doesn't have that kind of support available from family and friends, high quality childcare is all that is available. Often it is all that is available for a woman who needs to work. It is the quality of relationships that your child experiences that makes the biggest difference to her outcomes, and this is the thing to remember in reading the rest of this section.

The best known researcher into childcare in America is Professor Jay Belsky. In looking at his research you need to be aware that he personally feels children should not spend long hours in non-maternal care. In the very early days of the childcare debate he was a co-author on a report on how time away from parents in centre-based care impacts on a child's wellbeing in the short and longer term — and the message from this report was 'we don't know yet'. Unfortunately, this inconclusive position was 'spun' by the pro-childcare lobby. They announced that his work proved that there were no harmful consequences to children from daycare. Professor Belsky was infuriated by this disingenuous tailoring of his work and promptly waded into the public debate, not just in the United States but in other countries also.

In 2007 Belsky and others released a report from a well-designed, long study of 1300 American children from birth to 12 years on the impact of childcare. This report looks not just at specific effects from childcare (for example, maths skills) but also at when those effects appear — at two, at eight, at 12 — and whether or not they disappear over time or grow stronger. In addition to the finding that family life is a far better predictor of outcomes than childcare, they also found that, at younger ages, better quality care, including time with grandparents, predicted better language abilities than did poor quality care. However a 'sleeper effect' of subsequent poorer language abilities in children who had non-maternal care between three months and four and a half years of age was also found down the track. In other words, children in non-maternal care performed better initially than children who stayed at home, but they were later overtaken by these same children at around 10 years of age. Why? Is it a one-off finding? They aren't sure yet.

Secondly, the longer children had spent in centre-based care the greater the number of problem behaviours such as aggression, neediness and hostility were found at all ages. This related only to centre-based care. The interesting thing is that these effects were found in all children who'd spent time in centres, even those who were securely attached. The conclusion is that this is a very real and concerning issue for Americans, particularly when you add up the impact of all that increased aggression in schools.[54]

So how well do Belsky's findings apply to the Australian setting? The general feeling of researchers here is 'not that well'. The critical difference is that the care offered in Australia is of a much higher quality. Even in America, quality of care makes a significant difference.[55] The leading researcher in Australia is Dr Linda Harrison, who is crunching the data in this area from Australia's own (even bigger) child development study, *Growing Up In Australia*.

In her most recent paper on the subject she concludes that there isn't much difference in the social and emotional development of children who receive non-parental care and the children who do not. Children who are in childcare tend to develop better social skills, as these are required in such a setting. They may also, however, have more behaviour problems and less empathic skills with longer hours in care. But these effects are very small, particularly when set against the much more powerful impact of family life and the individual nature of the child.[56]

So what makes the care in Australia of higher quality? Dr Harrison calls it simply 'child-focus'. What does she mean, exactly? Smaller numbers of children in a group and carers who spend more time doing things with the children.

I would say that it is all about the relationship. The person caring for your child needs to be 'autonomous', to have the state of mind towards attachments that allows a secure, organised attachment to be formed. They need to have the energy and the time (and so a very low ratio of staff to children) and the commitment to your child individually for that to occur.

Dr Harrison does sound one warning related to childcare. In a

2000 paper she found that Australian children who'd moved between many different care settings had more behavioural problems. A meta-study (where the results from many different research papers are combined together to get the big picture) of American non-maternal care studies found this also. The conclusion that continuity of care is a big deal seems solid.[57]

Before we finish with Belsky, it's interesting to know that he has recently published a paper on temperament. Along with a number of other researchers he has identified a group of children who are 'temperamentally vulnerable'. These seem to be the same children who temperament theorists call 'highly sensitive' or 'difficult' or 'high reactives'. They are the children who are slow to adapt to changes, quick to respond negatively, highly active and very sensitive to their environments. These children, he suggests, may be unusually susceptible to both positive and negative environments. More often than not they are boys, who are, in general, more sensitive to environments anyway.[58]

Belsky has not yet explicitly linked centre-based childcare with very poor outcomes for the highly sensitive group of children, but it's a fair guess that he will. Certainly he is not alone in highlighting that temperament and gender may influence how childcare affects development.[59, 60]

And postnatal depression?

A baby and mother are nested inside the circle of close family, which is nested within a wider family and social circle, which is nested within a society, which is nested within a nation, which is nested within the world. The first circle is usually the one that impacts most on the pattern of attachment developed by a baby. There is the mother's attachment pattern, but there are other factors too, which both change and are changed by that pattern. Postnatal depression is, unfortunately, known to increase the likelihood that the baby will have an insecure attachment. A depressed mother who is 'autonomous', however, is far more likely to be able to create a secure attachment in her baby despite her depression.[61]

Postnatal depression, like any other illness, is greatly alleviated by the kind of care the ill person receives. In this case, the more supportive her partner is of her decisions in caring for the baby, the better the quality of the relationship and the more help she is given with practical tasks, the shorter the duration of her postnatal depression.[62, 63]

Why is the partner's support so very important? Is it because such support helps to prevent sleep deprivation? That seems a good explanation, given the link between sleep deprivation and postnatal depression.[64] Or is it perhaps because such support gives a woman more time to be with her baby, learning to read her cues, with a consequent improvement in her own faith in herself as a mother?[40]

Or is it because such support decreases stress, resulting in more oxytocin release, changing her right brain faster and making her feel happier and emotionally warmer? When women are stressed in late pregnancy, those brain-transforming oxytocin surges are absent: and the absence of increasing oxytocin predicts a decreased sense of connection to baby, which is very distressing to most mothers.[65]

Of course, each answer is valid. Common sense tells us that a new mother needs good support from those closest to her for every one of these reasons.

Depression, anxiety and fatigue: barriers to secure attachment

What makes parenting so hard is that it requires you to either call out of yourself forgotten aspects (for example, living at the very slow pace of the toddler) or grow in yourself whole new capacities, and your baby is always one step ahead, changing the dance as you change yourself. And while every parent really wants to throw themselves totally into the dance — passionately, absorbedly and consistently — sometimes it can be difficult. You know you should dance but between you and the dance floor lie anxiety or depression or fatigue. Sometimes you know you should be dancing, but no-one has told your baby! In each case 'knowing you should' becomes a burden to lie alongside everything else. You'll notice the word 'parents' is used here, rather than 'mother'. This is not mere political correctness but because, as we are increasingly recognising, fathers get postnatal depression too.

What postnatal illness seems to impair, above all else, is your ability to become obsessed to the right degree with your baby. What is the right degree? It is far more excessive than you can imagine before you actually have the baby. You are passionately preoccupied with the baby, almost to the exclusion of all else.

It is actually normal to have some horrid intrusive thoughts of what might go wrong with the baby. Revolting as some of these thoughts are, you do need to accept them as warnings that help keep your baby safe. They usually fade when the baby is about six months old.

Fighting the thoughts is exhausting, and usually causes them to throng in even greater numbers. What has worked well for me is saying simply, 'I'm listening, I'll be careful', and 'befriending' the anxiety and wrapping it in the same care with which you wrap your baby. However, if you really can't cope, even with the knowledge that most women actually have these thoughts, and they have grown too many for you to enjoy your baby, go to see your GP. If you are actually having difficulty thinking about the baby and you don't want to be holding the baby much of the time, go and see the doctor. Don't let anything get in the way of this time with your baby.

It is also normal to have difficulty being interested in anything else but the baby. If you have become boring company you will probably be a better parent for it. An obsessed mother, and an only marginally less obsessed father, is the right emotional environment for a baby.[66]

Try not to castigate yourself for any sense of insecurity. If you are feeling unsure of your ability to provide the kind of emotional environment you'd want for your children, you are hardly alone. In fact, in Australia parents are experiencing a growing lack of confidence in our ability to provide the emotional and financial family environment we would like for our children. In 2008 the Australian Institute of Family Studies reported that the dropping fertility rate in Australia is nothing to do with a 'lack of wanting to' have children. Poignantly, many Australians would like to have more children than they do. The choice not to have a child, or to have fewer children than they really want, appears to be one some Australians feel forced to take. Parents, write the authors of this report, 'require access to community resources, including family-friendly workplaces and the confidence that they have a strong, continuing commitment from the community. It is of the utmost importance that parents do not feel alone in raising the next generation of citizens.'[67]

Feeling alone: the crux of the matter

Children down the centuries and across cultures have been raised in cooperative family groups, usually with parents at the heart of their care, but we seem to have forgotten this and expect mums and dads to do and be it all. So parenthood often leaves us feeling alone: mothers at home with children by themselves, fathers of young babies marginalised in the workplace when they decide to put the hours in at home rather than with their mates, new parents distanced from their own parents by a very different world in which to parent. This aloneness straightaway puts us at risk of depression.

The latest research from beyondblue, Australia's national depression initiative, indicates that parents (and their partners and their friends and their families) still don't necessarily know when they are depressed. Fatigue and anxiety are equally insidious. How many of a certain kind of thought is too many? What is the difference between very tired is too tired? If you feel that fatigue, anxiety or distressing or depressing thoughts are limiting the degree to which you are enjoying your baby, then go and see your GP.

The other thought that struck me on reading the recommendations from beyondblue was their insistence that it is all family members who are affected. Is it useful any more to talk of a mother having 'postnatal depression'? Is it perhaps more helpful to see it as a whole family illness requiring a whole family approach to healing? (Or a whole society illness requiring a whole society approach to healing?)

I could have listed out risk factors and warning signs, but I've chosen not to. Why? The research is very clear about the fact that such lists cannot be used to diagnose or eliminate postnatal depression. You will often see the Edinburgh Depression Scale reproduced on brochures or in magazines, but now beyondblue is saying quite explicitly that the Edinburgh Depression Scale should not be used by itself. Reading through such a scale and thinking 'that's not me, really' is dangerous. Again, if you are not enjoying your baby — or only enjoying your baby occasionally, see your GP.

I also wonder if such scales contribute to 'stigmatising' people who do get depressed by encouraging 'us' and 'them' thinking. The truth is, anyone can get postnatal depression. Anyone can become anxious. Anyone can get too tired and from there slide into postnatal depression or anxiety.[64] It is in recognition of this that beyondblue is rolling out a new strategy for postnatal depression that includes 'universal application of a routine psychosocial assessment strategy as a population health initiative'.[68]

Let's follow the lead of this most informed group. Let's support every mother and every father and every baby and every family as if they have, or could easily develop, postnatal depression. This, of course, is what some cultures have always done. In Islamic cultures, all cooking is done for the new mother. She is brought high-protein snacks by friends and family. She is encouraged to rest and sleep as much as possible for the first 40 days after the birth of her child.[69] The time is designed to be as pleasant as possible for everyone, with lots of the warm fuzzy feelings that promote right brain growth. Mind you, Islamic women still get depressed, but usually for reasons other than fatigue. So insufficient sleep and rest are not the whole of the problem. Nonetheless, these rituals allow the new mother to be 'mothered' herself for a period of time after the birth, and may help with the transition to the mothering role, as well as protect against fatigue.[70]

If you are a father or a grandparent or a general support person to a new mother you might be thinking, 'I don't have much time, so what is the one best thing I could do to support attachment between this mother and child?' One study showed that the support most appreciated by women cross-culturally is practical support. Women put a higher value on being helped out in caring for the children rather than on help with the housework. All of these women said that an unequal division of childcare was more distressing than an unequal division in the housework.[71] By offering your time to help with caring for children, you are actually valuing the role of mother and appreciating how very hard it is. You are also offering her time for personal growth — right brain growth — which she can then pass on to her baby.

In the next part of the book you will see just how contagious strong right brain growth is, and what makes it happen. This is part of the research that utterly transformed my idea of who and what we human beings are.

Part Two:

The beginnings of self-regulation

Positive emotions are the key to early development, to growth, to not only positive psychological states but physical health …

Dr Allan N. Schore, psychotherapist and researcher, whose life's work has been the synthesis of attachment, neuroscience and psychobiological research.[1]

We are faced with having to learn again about interdependency and the need for rootedness after several centuries of having systematically — and proudly — dismantled our roots, ties, and traditions. We had grown so tall we thought we could afford to cut the roots that held us down, only to discover that the tallest trees need the most elaborate roots of all.

Paul L. Wachtel, 1993.[2]

Chapter 6

The beginnings of impulse control

Wombat hung his head, and hoped he wouldn't cry.

Mem Fox, *Wombat Divine*, 1995.[3]

I n Part One we focused on your state of mind regarding your own attachments and how very important it is that you are able to reflect usefully upon the big, deep relationships in your life. Those reflections, the support you have and the world around you create the frame in which your child develops. The focus was on you, the parent. From Part Two onwards we will focus on what happens within that frame, starting with the very small baby.

The work of attachment in these early weeks is largely invisible — the way it sinks through to our subconscious, alters our biochemistry and even the rhythms of our heart — but we see the impact most clearly in our baby's self-regulation skills. Empathy, impulse control and the other self-regulation skills are things baby begins learning from the very beginning. And he learns all of them through his relationship with you.

Impulse control

Impulse control is the ability to stop yourself doing something. To return to the analogy in 'About this book', in the small aircraft you are learning to fly, it is impulse control that allows you to stop your automatic tendency to drive the plane as you would a car. It is an ability that is central to success in all kinds of ways.

Impulse control is what allows us to wrest our attention from one train of thought to another, to correct an action before it has even happened, to stop ourselves saying something that we should not. Life in many ways is a long series of decisions about whether to do something or not do something — impulse control is what gives us some measure of ability to stop an impulse, to think and, having thought, to choose a course of action.

The ability to 'delay gratification' fits neatly in here too. It is the ability to wait for something you want: impulse control by another name. Like the ability to 'stop and think', the ability to 'delay gratification' is a big player in success in adult life. But impulse control is not just important for your child in the future: the child with better impulse control is a happier child throughout childhood.

Do you want your child to divert his attention to something else after an emotional upset so he can calm down? It is impulse control that gives us the chance to put something out of our mind — so it makes a big contribution to emotional wellbeing and self-management. The child with poor impulse control becomes an attractive mark for bullies because he is easy to upset and slow to soothe, which is a big boost for the ego of the bully.

Impulse control also is central to problem solving. It is what stops us 'jumping to conclusions' or getting distracted by unprofitable bypaths. It is strong impulse control that helps keep a child fixed upon his goals.[4]

Both the attachment and neurological research agree that good impulse control in children correlates with a secure, organised attachment.[5] To understand how that happens, we need to understand just how babies learn.

How babies learn so fast

A newborn baby can do some extraordinary things. Even though his eyes aren't yet working terribly well, a 12-hour-old baby can pick out which of two dummies he's sucked just by looking at it.[6] How is this possible? How can a baby link up information coming in from one sense with information coming in from another with such a very minute amount of life experience? It is scarcely credible — unless, of course, our brains have some kind of 'touchstone' that they can use to interpret the just-met world, and some kind of 'language' by which different parts of the brain communicate their findings.

I guess the underlying question is this: How do babies start making sense of the world around them so fast?

In fact, we are born with just such a 'touchstone' and language. The touchstone that we are born with is called the *amygdala*. And the language that the brain/body of the newborn speaks to itself is with us for life — it is the language of emotions.

Of baby's senses, balance and hearing are very developed; and touch (including pain), smell and taste are mostly developed.[7] All of that information is routed through the amygdala. And what the amygdala does then is transform it into emotion, and that emotion is transported around his body and brain by hormones or 'neurotransmitters'. In the case of the dummy, one is spiky and the other is smooth: one looks and feels 'pleasant' and the other does not.

But it's rather a rough-and-ready system at this stage. In your brain the 'black and white' or 'all or nothing' thinking that afflicts adults when we're stressed comes straight from the amygdala. But we have higher brain regions that work to refine and gentle those impulses. Even so, when we are very emotional we sometimes need to talk to a friend and borrow their 'higher brain centres' to help ourselves calm down enough to be able to reach our own.

Your baby doesn't have those higher regions available yet. He just has you. He cannot refine and gentle the impulses from his amygdala himself. That is your job for quite some months to come, and it is a vitally important one. The first thing your baby needs to learn is that you can settle him.

So if baby is feeling uncomfortable because of a dirty nappy, or lonely and frightened, or hungry, the amygdala uses that emotion to unleash a wave of response. Baby cries for help. Adrenalin and cortisol flood the little body. Baby's heart rate becomes more reactive, his breathing uneven. His tummy will feel yucky as his gut is stilled. The world suddenly seems bright and sharper and more intrusive. It is easy for us to empathise because this is how stress affects adults too and we know it as the flight-or-fight response.[8]

And, just like us, babies can't separate out the emotion from what is happening in their bodies: they are simultaneous and felt together. And, what's worse, emotion and sensation compound each other in a positive feedback loop, like the ever-increasing *screeeech* that comes from the speaker when the microphone is too close. The experience of the emotions increases the unpleasant sensations, which increase the unpleasant emotion … and so on.

Always go to your baby

The faster you get to him the better. In those times when the brain is swamped by stress there is no neural growth. Leave him long enough and neural connections made will be burnt away by catecholamines, one of the neurotransmitters that rides under the black banner with cortisol.[9] A newborn who is only very rarely comforted (and the latest research is showing that neglect is every bit as damaging as abuse) will find it very hard to grow those higher brain connections, which give him access not just to the upper regions of his own mind but to the minds of others, from where life gains much of its meaning and wealth.

But there is a value to those dark times for your newborn, if they are kept as brief as possible. He calls for help and you are there directly. Perhaps he has only made a fussing noise, but you are there. And because you have come he is able to move on from his state of despair. He has communicated his distress and you are closing the loop by doing something about it.

Parents' sleep versus baby's needs

In reading this you may well be thinking, 'So what about "controlled crying"? Does leaving baby to cry at night do damage?' In fact, once you start thinking about sleeping decisions you then come to a great many other interconnected issues, such as temperament, other siblings, baby's health, breastfeeding, dummies, birth, parents' mental health, work and life balance … So complex and individual are these links that only a parent can trace out and balance the full implications of a decision made in one sphere for another. Well-informed parents can be the only arbiter of such decisions for their baby.

In making this decision, though, you need to bear in mind a baby's need for consistency. Once babies are about seven months old they begin to worry that you will go and never come back. This is separation anxiety, and it must be the nastiest feeling in the world. That beloved face and smell and feel that makes him feel better than anything else can do: knowing where it is and when he will see it again is his whole sense of security. When your child resists being 'put down' to sleep anytime from seven months on, do start wondering if he is worried that you won't come back.

A kind and consistent set of rules so baby can predict just where you are and when you will come is required. It is the hardest thing in the world, to be consistent, but so important. Inconsistent parenting creates an insecure attachment — a baby who must 'up' his signals of neediness so that you come. It is not a path you want to take.

Does it matter if you can't stop your baby fussing or crying straightaway? What if you change his nappy and he still cries? Then you check to see if he wants a top-up feed, but he doesn't. And then you think that he might like to be rocked on your shoulder, but that's not it either. Do the many attempts you've made before solving the problem somehow damage your baby? No. In fact, mothers get it wrong 60 per cent of the time.

Don't be distressed by this. 'Getting it wrong' some of the time is just as valuable to your baby as when you get it right first time around. From being on the other end of your care your baby is learning that people won't always understand you straightaway. You have to keep trying to 'repair' the misunderstanding and eventually you will be able to 'reconnect' with the other person. In our relationships as adults we see this same pattern of rupture, reconnection and repair.

And because you come as soon as he calls, he'll soon learn to anticipate your arrival. He will be able to call, and wait, knowing that you will come. He has put a moment between the urgency of his feeling and his behaviour. This is the beginning of impulse control. Your baby is growing that moment in which he can say to himself, 'Wait a moment.' This waited moment grows into 'impulse control'. Research from both the temperament and the attachment research shows that impulse control is positively correlated with warm, sensitive parenting.[5] Studies also show a clear link between time spent 'delighting' in your baby and your baby's ability to delay gratification as a toddler.[10] The researchers have not traced out exactly why, but it seems likely that being taught to wait — which lies at the heart of delayed gratification — is something we teach by 'waiting' for a response from our baby to our own actions. It is the give and take of 'delighting in' that sows the seeds of waiting. When you play with your baby — perhaps making a funny noise that always amuses him and looking hopefully for the pay-off of his belly-deep 'ha ha' — you are demonstrating waiting.

In baby's brain various circuits are being switched 'on' or 'off' depending on his experiences. When he experiences the joy of reconnecting with you after his despair, the resulting surges in the 'good' neurotransmitters in his brain switch on the circuits that will help him stay calm in times of difficulty for the rest of his life.[11]

If that sounds to you like baby should be getting easier and easier to manage the more he is responded to, you'd be right. But *not* in the first six weeks. Those weeks are simply not easy at all, because during this time babies all around the world hit a crying peak at six weeks. Afterwards baby will cry less, and just how much less depends partly on temperament and partly on parenting style. In general, western culture babies cry for longer than those from other cultures, not more frequently, but for a longer time once they have started.[12] The reason for the shorter duration of crying in other cultures is that the first response mothers make to their crying baby is to offer the breast.

Building impulse control in the high needs baby

We will revisit impulse control later in the book — how to build it in older children, and also in regards to attention deficit disorders, where a lack of impulse control is a core deficit. But now we are going to turn our attention to the baby who doesn't easily calm down when comforted: the colicky or fussy baby.

I became particularly interested in researching colic when my friend Katie was struggling to deal with a difficult-to-soothe baby. Alexis was Katie's seventh baby, and, while she looked exactly like her beautiful siblings, on the inside she was evidently quite different. She fitted exactly into the description of the typical colicky baby. A colicky baby is, generally speaking, growing well and larger than the average baby *but* all of a sudden begins to cry as per the 'rule of three': three hours of crying, about three times a week, for more than three weeks.

What is so horrible for parents is that the colicky baby cries *inconsolably*. There you are, trying to 'close the loop' with your warm and responsive parenting, but your love and care just do not seem to get through during a bout of colic. As a parent of such a baby you may find yourself wondering at how such traits have remained in the human genome to the present day. 'Whose little bundle of joy are you meant to be?' remarked my exhausted father to me at two o'clock one morning. (Perhaps I was also so interested in colic because I was a very colicky baby too.)

Doctors exclude for such things as an allergy to milk protein, constipation, infection, reflux or a sore neck, and, lacking all of those, a baby is diagnosed with colic. So what is colic? And did Alexis have it?

Current research seems to be going in circles. After years of researchers saying 'it's not gas', a 2005 study found an association between colic and later problems with allergies and gastrointestinal issues.[13] After initially repudiating the psychosocial status of mothers as part of the cause, one very large study showed that a demanding work situation predisposes women to having babies with colic.[14] Another study suggested that maternal depression may cause colic.[15] There is also an indication in research that looks at the interface between environments and temperament that a hard to soothe temperament develops in babies when their mothers have an iron deficiency.[16]

I found one 2007 article drawing together all the different strands of medical thinking on colic. Despite the medical standpoint of colic being a 'diagnosis of exclusion' (in other words, there is no detectable medical cause) you'll notice that this article still has a focus on treatment. Here is the list from the article:

- colicky babies are often hungrier than other babies
- colicky babies also show 'disorganised' feeding behaviours, and this is linked to difficulties self-regulating later on
- stick to breastfeeding baby rather than putting him on formula, but do drop all dairy products yourself. You might also like to remove eggs, wheat and nuts

- probiotics for baby and Mum seem to help colicky breastfed babies, which indicates there is indeed a problem with 'wind' caused by an imbalance of gut flora
- there are both medications and herbs that can help, but some medications and herbs can also be dangerous
- gripe water has been shown to be of no assistance
- some studies have shown that relationship problems between parent and child are part of the picture, and other studies have shown that they are not.[17]

This didn't help Katie much as Alexis was breastfed, on probiotics and Katie herself had given up dairy. So things were better, but not easy. Katie certainly related to the iron deficiency, the demanding work situation and the hungrier baby — but none of this was knowledge that was particularly useful to her right then.

Is colic a 'heads-up' for a 'highly susceptible' temperament?

Katie was much more interested in the research which places colicky babies on one end of the temperament spectrum. The children who find it hardest to self-soothe *initially* are the babies who are described as 'high reactives'. They are not exactly the same as the 'difficult' child, typically described as slow to adapt to changes, easily and often distressed, intensely emotional and also unpredictable in terms of biological rhythms. But there is a great deal of crossover there: easily upset and intensely emotional are features of the highly reactive child.

Plus there is a neurological basis for that emotionality and reactivity. Highly reactive children have a more responsive amygdala.[18] Because of the extra responsivity in their amygdala they startle more frequently and grow up to be more sensitive to the world around them.[19] Highly reactive babies are frequently 'colicky', with a pattern of early starting colic, within the first two weeks.

Being more upset by sensory stimuli is also the central diagnostic of the 'sensorily defensive' child (see Appendix IV), and it is likely that these children are one and the same group. The 'highly sensitive' child identified by Elaine Aron in her work on sensitive people is perhaps also the same group again.[20] Sensory defensiveness and intense emotionality are features of her diagnostic criteria also. In addition, children with autism spectrum disorders display some of these behaviours; as do some, but not all, gifted and creative children. This same group has been renamed just recently after a new characteristic was identified. These highly reactive or highly sensitive children have been followed in long-term studies and a new pattern has emerged.

When these children are parented well (that is, with a secure and organised attachment) they outperform their other well-parented peers, but when they are poorly parented (a disorganised or insecure attachment) they perform less well than their poorly parented peers.[21, 22] These children are now called 'highly susceptible' because they are the children for whom parenting makes the most difference. They are currently one of the 'hot spots' in child development research. Perhaps the very susceptible children are so fascinating to researchers because they amplify what happens between mother and child?

When the highly susceptible child has a parent with an insecure or disorganised parenting pattern, he becomes ever more challenging and demanding, stressing out a mother who is already not coping. The poor mother, doing her best though she is, parents far worse under these circumstances, and it shows in a child who performs worse than other children who are poorly parented. The mismatch widens over time. It's a 'positive' feedback loop where the worse the parenting, the worse the behaviour, so the worse the parenting.

But put one of these highly reactive children into the hands of a parent with the capacity to create a secure attachment and the very opposite occurs. The sensitive parent responds to the challenge of the very difficult child by providing an environment that is a very good match for his needs. So close is the fit that this baby spends far more time learning than the average child. It's another positive feedback loop but one where the outcomes are actually positive.

The importance of the parents' beliefs about colic

Colic throws a spotlight on the relationship between parent and child. The central question is: How do parents interpret their baby's cries? If they believe baby is crying to manipulate them, and the crying does not cease despite their efforts, then their parenting becomes less and less sensitive. They believe their baby could help it if he would only try: a thought process that leads straight to anger and perhaps to hurting the baby. Less sensitive parenting leads straight to toddlers and older children who cry more in general. Less sensitive parenting of the susceptible child results in a child with worse outcomes than occurs in their less susceptible peers.

When parents interpret their child's cries as 'distress calls' (as Katie does with Alexis) then the relationship unfolds very differently. When parents believe that baby can't help it, and that their role is simply to be there and endure it with the baby, they parent far more sensitively. With the highly susceptible child this leads to better outcomes across the board than for other sensitively parented children.

In fact, common wisdom holds both that 'the colicky baby is brighter than average and will be talking sooner' and that 'colic is just the start of the trouble'. The research on highly susceptible children suggests that both of these statements are true, and it is parenting that determines just which pathway a baby will take.

So the message is clear. Even though it feels as if your caring is not getting through to your baby, those longitudinal studies make it very clear that it is. It may take some time to show, but it is likely to be your colicky, difficult baby who gets the most out of your parenting. When you respond fully to those difficult behaviours, and persist in trying to soothe an apparently inconsolable baby, the pay-off down the track will be a child with strong self-regulation skills.

So how is Alexis now? The statement about 'later problems with allergies and gastrointestinal issues' seems to have been prophetic in her case. Katie is still working hard to find out the right things for her little girl to eat and continuing to breastfeed Alexis into her second year. And Alexis, outside the times when her tummy hurts her quite dreadfully, is a happy, affectionate little girl and spot-on developmentally. I have watched her sit and play patiently with a nesting toy — quite a test of a baby's impulse control — and try and try again to fit it back together. This is very typical behaviour of securely attached colicky babies in general. Somehow all that time spent screaming doesn't delay development when the attachment is secure.

Katie begs readers with colicky babies to trust their mother's instinct. Even if you are told it is 'just colic' and to wait it out — as she was — and you feel that there is something else, then trust that feeling. It can be difficult to get someone to listen, even if this is your seventh child and you can be expected to know what you are talking about, and Katie eventually said to her paediatrician, 'I'm not leaving your office until you run some tests.' The tests have now been run and action beyond the 'wait it out' advice is now under way.

Tips for sensitively parenting your colicky baby

The most useful writer on colic for parents who wish to sensitively parent their colicky child is Dr Sears. He also suggests that colic sits on the temperament continuum as part of the overall 'high needs' and 'sensorily defensive' child (in a book that was written before the theory of the highly susceptible child was developed). If you have a baby with colic he offers the following tips:

- *Evening is often when baby, utterly exhausted by reigning in his unusually emotional temperament, suddenly loses it. So prepare for that time. Have dinner cooked long before dinnertime. Instead of preparing food in the late afternoon, lie down at that time and nurse baby off to sleep.*
- *Keep baby in a sling (not a carrier) much of the time, even when he is not asleep.*
- *Find a movement pattern that helps baby relax. Usually this is a rocking dance accompanied by humming.*
- *Bear in mind that this little person has a much greater chance of becoming a more sensitive person, so get a head start on helping him cope with the world by providing 'more' in this very sensitive period: more touch, more help to deal with surprises, more help in transitions like going to bed or having a bath.*
- *'Putting them down' to sleep never works with these children, says Dr Sears. The 'parenting to sleep' approach is required for these children who have more difficulty self-soothing.[23] Waltz around the house with baby in a sling until he is heavily asleep, nestle down next to him, and keep him near you at night.*

Chapter 7

Building attention, concentration and perceptual skills

Slowly the baby opened her eyes and looked at him.
He maintained for ever afterwards, against great
scepticism, that for a full three minutes her great
violet eyes were not unfocused, but looked straight in
his. All his exhaustion and lethargy left him as he
gazed down into those astonishing eyes.

Elizabeth Goudge, *The Heart of the Family*, 1953.[24]

Attention and concentration skills begin in infancy. Parents have become very aware of their importance with the increasing incidence of attention deficit disorder, which is often highlighted in the mainstream press. Our children need to be able to *switch the focus* of their attention at will, to choose what they will attend to and illuminate with their attention. We all have a 'spotlight', and the important thing is the ability to direct it at will. But that skill is not of much use all by itself. We also need the ability to keep the spotlight in that place while drawing simultaneously from our inner knowledge to make sense of what we are seeing. This is *concentration*: the ability to persist for a span of time in switching back and forth between existing knowledge and information coming in from the outside world.

Babies have a long way to go in developing these skills. Your newborn can look only fleetingly at any one thing: her attention is pulled from one thing to the next by movement, by sound, by touch. It is hard work for your baby to learn to look and keep looking longer each time. But she does it. Within just days she is able to keep looking at your face: each glance seeming to be that bit stickier, more adhering, connecting ever more deeply through that brief shared gaze. In making these strides she needs your help to take control over the three different sets of brain circuitry that create our attention skills.

The first of these is the 'emergency override' switch called the startle or the Moro reflex. It forces your baby into a whole-body alerting response in the face of possible danger. And while most babies will never need it, it is part of our genetic endowment and every baby should have it at birth.

The startle reflex is an in-built alerting system which focuses a baby's attention on a threat and helps her survive it. Just how sensitive your baby's senses are is revealed by how easily she startles. Babies startle in response to movement, particularly a 'dropping' movement, or an unexpected sight or sound or pain. To the 'fight-flight' hormonal bath is added a violent, automatic physical response. Baby's arms and legs make a clasping movement, baby breathes in and then screams.[7, 25]

In the first eight weeks to four months your baby learns that she has no need to startle at a door banging, or upon being laid down for her nappy change or at a sudden movement near her head. She is safe, she is loved, you are with her. As soon as something is unpleasant or upsetting, you are right there, your presence and care providing the reassurance her own brain cannot supply.

Every time you lovingly kiss her forehead or her hands and feet; every time you reassure her after a fright; every time your face says to her, 'You are safe and I am here', you make a new connection. Over time her startle reflex pathway is swamped and diluted by a mass of new connections; no longer simply a road in to the amygdala, but a road out to other parts of the brain. And, as we startle in response to sensory information coming through all of the different senses, the startle reflex helps link the different senses together even further.[7]

Imagine a piece of string, held tight, down which a drop of water can easily run. That is the startle reflex at birth, easily triggered as there is nothing to interfere with the 'run' from beginning to end. Now, imagine that string with many new connections tied on. The drop of water slows, is diverted and sent down a number of different bypaths. As your baby slowly 'integrates' her startle reflex, this is what is happening in her brain. The startle alarm system is still there throughout life, and we remain able to respond in the blink of an eye to such events as nearly stepping on a snake, but only when the trigger is a very large one.[25, 26]

At four months of age, when that the startle reflex is no longer dominating your baby's alerting and attending control circuits, she begins to be able to direct her attention. And, because the startle reflex operates partly through the muscles of the neck, jerking baby's head backwards, as it disappears your baby is able to begin working on the massive project of controlling her head. Because the startle reflex ensures baby is vigilant in looking for danger through her as yet not properly working eyes, as it resolves she is able to start attending to fine details. Not the broad outline of Mum's face, but her eyes and eyelashes, her mouth and nose, the texture of her skin.[27]

Although the primitive startle reflex has effectively disappeared by the time we are four months old, enough of the system remains to create what is called 'reflexive attention'. It is always operating, but we are unaware of it much of the time. Every now and then it will say to us, 'Look at this, right now, it's more important than anything else'.

The next piece of the puzzle

You might recall the brief snippet on the children who had left Mum and me so puzzled in Chapter 2. Without a clear explanation for just why these children's eye development was so very delayed, Mum had begun to spend the occasional lunchtime watching them. One day she was watching a group of children playing a ball game. Her attention was caught by the odd behaviour of two of the little boys in the game.

Every time a bird flew overhead or a car went past or a voice called out they would be distracted from the ball and the game. And Mum was riveted because, first of all, this is hardly a normal way for little boys to behave and, secondly, because she knew these two children very well. Both had every single one of the behavioural problems reported by teachers and every single one of the physical delays we had found in these children.

What Mum found so unusual about their behaviour during the ball game was that it looked as though it was involuntary. It looked reflexive. And that is what it turned out to be — the same startle reflex that a newborn has usually resolved by four months of age.

So these children were not able to direct their attention as they wished. They were still involuntarily 'startling' in response to sound and movement and touch like newborns. Why?

It is feeling safe that allows a baby to resolve the 'override emergency switch' of the startle reflex. But these children lived in overcrowded houses where alcohol and other drug abuse was common, and feuding and family violence happened regularly. Of course, the children who experience abuse and neglect are affected more adversely than other children — they know for sure they are not safe — but all babies growing up in such a setting will find it harder to integrate their startle reflex. The same finding has been made in war zones and after natural disasters.[28, 29, 30]

But this is not the whole story. Babies are made to feel safe by their mothers, when the attachment is both secure and organised. Although the mothers of these boys loved their children, they were not able to express that love in a way that created a secure and organised attachment. Of course, this comes from that chaotic, impoverished environment, and from not having had that secure, organised attachment themselves as children.

In the body of this chapter is a description of how integrating the startle reflex means that the child is no longer forced to look at the broad outlines of shapes to detect potential threat. Now fine details such as Mum's eyelashes and smile lines can be pored over intently by the fascinated baby. When the time comes for reading, the fine differences between letters such as 'p' and 'q' can be detected. The very reverse is true for highly stressed children.

The two little boys Mum had been observing were simply not able to pick up fine details. So these two little boys were among the most severely affected and were not able to learn to read. Other children, less severely affected, were definitely on the pathway to reading. With the teachers we began to track the impact of trouble in the community upon reading skills. After an outbreak of violence or feuding whole classes would be unable to read on Monday as they had on Friday. The primitive startle reflex is 'potentiated' (in other words, the neurons are 'primed' to fire) by emotion — distress, fear, anger — and it is far easier to trigger afterwards. As a result, whole groups of children distressed by an event would have their primitive startle 'retriggered' and be unable to focus on the small details that we need to be aware of in reading.

Children need to be safe. They need to be free of fear. If they are not, then they will continue to need the 'override emergency switch' of the startle on a regular basis — and the need for survival overrides the need for optimum development.

If your baby is studying the details of your face, you know that she has begun to develop the second part of attention: the ability to orientate to particular information. In other words, to choose the things she wants to attend to and to wield her attention like a spotlight upon the things she wants to illuminate and magnify and explore. You will also note that her eyes are now 'yoked' together, rather than crossing and diverging. Her eye movements match. This has happened as you gently rock your baby while her eyes are fixed upon the ever-fascinating details of your face.

And finally she must develop her concentration span, that part of us which allows us to maintain our attention on a task, despite the 'reflexive' part of our attention saying, 'But look over here, a fluttering leaf, and, say, aren't you hot, and what about that niggle in your back?'

It is those children who have 'long play sessions' with Mum and

Dad who have the longest attention spans. There is some evidence that babies who begin life temperamentally difficult, like Katie's little Alexis, end up with the best deal here. In doing everything they can to keep a difficult child happy, their mothers play with them for longer. In the process they build better language skills, better play skills, and better attention skills. There is a belief that children are difficult because they are clever but perhaps difficult children *become* clever as a result of all that extra play! The human brain is frequently described as a 'use dependent organ' in the neuroscience research — and by this researchers mean that the brain is shaped by the uses it is put to.[30] If a baby spends more time stretching their concentration span in joyful play, their brain will grow a longer concentration span.[31]

What if my baby is still startling after four months?

This is a developmental milestone you need to watch out for. Some children are still startling later if Mum and Dad have noticed the startle and decided to eliminate all the things that make the baby startle. If the door bangs, they stop it. If it is the noise of other siblings, then they are told to be quiet. In fact, this approach prevents babies learning they are safe, so let the door bang and reassure the baby every time. Do vacuum, do let siblings play in normal voices, because baby needs to learn that none of these noises presents a threat. Startling for longer and more frequently is also a marker of the highly susceptible child.

Remember the first part of this book. Make sure that you or another person involved with the baby are not frightening her. It is important that play with your baby is gentle and sensitive and that she is in charge. Don't let people loom in at your baby or put their fingers around the baby's neck — you will see this kind of behaviour sometimes in other children for a number of reasons. Always reassure your baby after startling and remember that the reflex feels like the very big fright you would get if you pulled back a lounge chair and found a large snake on your carpet.

Building attention and concentration in your newborn

One of the biggest surprises for me in the parenting literature was the importance of 'low intensity' activities for good attention and concentration. Reading, completing a jigsaw, walking, listening to a story or nursery rhymes, warm baths, being sung to, just talking with Mum and snuggling up, all of these are *low intensity* pleasures. The children who enjoy low intensity experiences are more likely to show strong self-regulation skills as toddlers and as school-age children.[32] It's obviously terrifically important, but just why is not so clear.

I believe that it has to do with the fact that a low intensity activity does not compel a child's interest. Television, computer games and exciting physical games compel our attention. Low intensity activities require us to attend more to get something out of them. They are rewarding only when we bring our attention to bear upon them.

For parents of newborns and young babies the message is that you need a range of play. There should be some of the high octane tickling and chasing games and playing peek-a-boo, but there should also be singing nursery rhymes and talking and just being together quietly. Some babies need to be intrigued by your high intensity manner into the low intensity pleasures initially, but over time you can decrease the 'hook' into the activity. For example, with a little baby you begin reading in a 'highly intense manner': when you encounter a duck in a book you will quack like a duck. You might jump off the chair and be a duck. You might go get the toy duck from the bathroom. Next time you see a duck with your baby you will say, 'Like your book, a *duck*!' You will probably quack some more. Over time a lot less intensity is required to engage your child in the book because her own motivation is supplying it. You are steadily hooking your child into one of the best value low intensity pleasures to be had. When she is eight years old you can mumble your way dog-tired through story books, and your child will be utterly riveted despite your low energy manner.

Perceptual sensitivity in the newborn

Perceptual sensitivity refers to how well your child detects changes in the world around him. And it requires not just 'working senses' but the ability to combine new impressions with those taken and stored earlier, and work out what is happening in the world around him.

Perceptual sensitivity is a key link in learning and also a 'self-regulation' skill. When our senses provide just the right amount of information, neither too little nor too much, we can navigate with skill. Too little information and we miss vital information. Too much and we are unable to distinguish what is really important in the barrage.

The best start for your children's sensory skills is a secure attachment to you. But there are some securely attached children who still have sensory difficulties as part of their temperament. For some babies the world is brighter, louder, busier, harder, sharper, steeper and smellier. These are the 'sensorily defensive' babies who research is now linking to the 'highly susceptible' group of children.

Recognising your newborn's sensory sensitivities — how much he reacts to things and what he likes and dislikes — is a very important part of getting to know him.

Reading baby's cues: some places to begin

We tend to focus very much on faces in our culture, but our babies are not yet fully 'enculturated' and so they have more diverse ways of expressing themselves. So watch your baby's expressions but also check his skin colour changes, movement quality and movement frequency and listen to his voice tone. For example, some babies begin a blurry hum when they are tired, others may pull at their ears, others will get a little pale, and their movements may become less deliberate and more fidgety.

Observe your baby with the dedication of a naturalist, learn his habits, compare notes with your partner and with older children, who can be brilliant interpreters of younger siblings' signs. It's worth doing, as these cues tend to remain in place throughout life. The teenagers of habitually observant parents are often convinced that 'the folks have a sixth sense'.

When your baby is hungry his suck and rooting reflexes grow more pronounced, if he is sucking a finger or blanket when he is hungry. The hands and mouth are on the same 'neurological loop', so if the palm curling around your finger seems to be tighter and 'grabbier', consider that baby might be hungry.

People often think that a whingeing baby simply needs to go to sleep. I believe that many babies need to relate a little, to play a little, to actually get tired before they are expected to go to sleep. So how can you tell when baby wants to play?

The little face is open and alert, the big eyes bright and expressive. Take time to note the exact expression in those eyes. A very little baby may look mischievous or delighted or bashful or amused or just about anything else, and often it is an early indication of an aspect of their character. There is a 'waiting for action' quality to the arm and leg movements. Vocalisations will be pitched directly to you. Baby is inviting you to play. And you play until baby has had enough. Babies will differ here too in their signs. There are some babies who want to keep playing even though they are getting too excited and go from excitement to screaming all at once. Parents soon learn to put an end to the game before this happens, although it is just about impossible for the non-parent to spot the flashpoint. Other babies will look away, grimace, stretch, flush or get pale. And that's it, baby needs to be soothed and calmed.

Start thinking in terms of rhythms. Some babies have stronger biological rhythms than others, but they all do have some kind of pattern to their sleeping, playing and waking. Knowing your baby's rhythms gives you a big headstart in reading the cues.

Early sensory games

There are a couple of constants in playing with babies. The first is imitation, or back and forth. The other is anticipating a surprise. From very early in life (as early as three days) babies begin to respond with decreases in heart rate variability when they are trying to invite more surprises from the adult with whom they are playing. Babies enjoy surprises.

Surprise games with newborns are very gentle, and have a stop-start or a 'pause-burst'. It takes baby a remarkably short time to see the pattern, and at that point the surprise comes when you vary it just a little. Wait until your baby is staring alertly up at you, his body movements are 'quiet' and his little face is bright, then try playing some of these games.

Sing a nursery rhyme one time the whole way through, and on the second time pause before singing the last line:

'Round and 'round the cobbler's bench
The monkey chased the weasel
The monkey stopped to pick up his socks
POP goes the weasel.

Can you spot a reaction? Does baby begin to suck in rhythm? You might also like to notice how you are singing. There is a measurable difference in the way we sing to infants. It is more emotional and you will find that you take a breath in different places. Every baby is likely to show a reaction to singing, even if it is simply a change in heart rate.

Now try swinging your head in and out of baby's field of view in a rhythmic pattern, and then pausing for a moment, and then doing it again. Is the reaction more or less than the one garnered by the paused nursery rhyme?

Another game is placing a cloth — velvet or silk — on baby's forehead and gently rubbing it back and forward. Stop the movement to see if baby reacts, or even tries to turn his head a little to recapture the sensation.

Pick up your little one and gently rock him. What happens when you stop rocking him?

The other great game is copycat. It's well known that newborns can copy facial expressions, and, later on, arm movements and so on. Just why this is so has been the subject of dispute for many years. In recent times many researchers have come to accept the existence of 'mirror neurons'. Their opinion is that a newborn baby's ability to instantly read a face and body (and an adult's ability for that matter) is created by the magic of the 'mirror system' or 'mirror neurons'. Effectively, this system causes a 'mirror' effect in your brain when you are watching someone. The neurons that are fired when the other person moves also go off in your brain. So, if you are watching a tennis player on television belt the ball to the back of the court, the same parts of the brain are busy in both you and the player, courtesy of the mirror system.[33]

Just what this means is still disputed. Some researchers feel it is simply automatic and means nothing. Other researchers see it as one of the foundations for empathy. The viewpoint which fits best with the rest of the neuroscience is that baby is born ready to communicate with another person.[34] If baby is born ready to communicate in this way, parents are more likely to see their baby as a person. And when parents see their babies as people right from the beginning, they are going to care for them more sensitively. Being ready to connect and communicate is a powerful survival strategy.

When we are imitated it tells us that 'here is another being just like me'. It warms us through and through. This is why the salespeople who are best at mirroring are also the salespeople best at selling.

Baby copying you is just one half of the game. The full game occurs when you copy baby … and he knows you are copying him. As baby learns that he can cause you to do something, he is becoming aware that he has a self and you have a self. How early does this particular penny drop? Certainly by two months of age.[35]

So copy your baby. If he yawns, yawn exaggeratedly yourself. If he is looking at you, look back and widen your eyes and smile. If you feel that your newborn is demonstrating an awareness of himself and you as different selves, you are hardly alone. Parents for generations have thought this, and while some scientists remain sceptical, many more believe this too.

Watch your baby closely for some kind of response. Your baby will show you the kind of games he likes by turning his head, sucking harder, grasping, opening his mouth, sticking out his tongue, making a noise, looking at you more intensely or even smiling a little, kicking his feet or waving. He might also signal that he's had enough by looking away, moving uncomfortably, arching his back, grimacing, yawning or fidgeting agitatedly. Babies are only too willing to give their parents some feedback.

Something else to look for

This is also a good time to observe how your newborn is reacting to hospital and the world in general. People differ greatly in how intensely they experience things. Life in the hospital is overstimulating for some babies. Watch and see how your baby copes with all the bangs and rumbles, the bright lights, the hospital smells, the sudden movements of those around him. If he is fretful, startling often and changing colour frequently, it is likely that he is highly sensitive to the world around him. If either you or your partner is highly sensitive to sensory information, consider that your baby is likely to be the same. Even if you were not considering rooming-in for all the advantages it confers in terms of attachment, consider it as a matter of kindness to your sensitive baby.

Conversely, a newborn who remains completely placid no matter what happens may well be under-responsive to sensory information. He may need special help 'wakening' his senses, just as the hypersensitive child will for sensory overload. You will find more about these issues and ideas to help in Appendix IV.

The importance of playtime with Dad

The role of Mum is so vital, and compared to dads, mothers seem overwhelmingly more important to newborns. But researchers are uncovering more all the time about the importance of that early social play with Dad, and also the enormous importance of babies having both a man and a woman in their lives.[36]

When Dad is interacting with his baby son, the degree of synchrony is that little bit higher than baby achieves with Mum; and it is the same for mothers and daughters. The natural biological rhythms of each sex are just that little bit different, allowing a closer match with the same sex parent. Baby boys find it easier to 'get into sync' with their dads, and the benefits to them are enormous.[37]

But the different kind of play that both Dad and Mum bring to the equation for both baby girls and boys is also valuable. Researchers have found that a father's play is more physical than a mother's, and often also involves a physical object. What this means is that baby learns there is more than one kind of relationship possible in this world: this doesn't just help in relating to others, but also becomes important in the development of thinking skills.[35]

If you are a dad and feeling a bit lost when it comes to interacting with your new baby, check through your memories of your own father. Look for one where he was comfortable with your vulnerability, where you felt trust and admiration for this much bigger and stronger person. If you are lacking such a memory, try to find another memory with the same kind of emotional feeling.

Keep that memory in mind: once you were the vulnerable one, now you are the big, strong, wise person. Martin's tip is that it is easier to do this when you remember that the baby desperately *wants* to be picked up by you, to hear you talk and sing, to look at your face.

Spend time watching your baby and you will begin to notice movements he makes in response to your face. Baby will look at the broad outlines of your face, and his little arms will wave with just a bit more excitement. Coupled with an alert expression, this means 'pick me up'. You need to respond to this. Pick up your baby, supporting his neck. Then start talking and watch for any movements (wriggles, kicks and waves) that correlate to the pitch and length of your words. I think that babies respond more physically to dads from the get-go. See what you think, see if the wriggles of arms and legs are larger in a conversation with you. You will, of course, see the most movement from a baby before a feed.

Look for those beckoning movements and then add a little movement in return for your baby to digest. It's the same kind of give and take, reading the play, adding your bit and watching for a lead that occurs in any social interaction or even in a sporting game. Until a baby is four or five months old he can't grab things, so the give and take of social exchange is all he has.

Consider that you want your child, particularly your son, to develop all his emotional competencies. If you want him to be resilient, this is achieved not by withholding comfort but by giving comfort. If you want him to be independent in his thinking, neither a bully nor a victim, comfort him when he cries. What's the link? By withholding comfort as a parent you are actually being a bully and placing him in the role of victim, giving him one of two pathways to follow later. But by comforting him, you are teaching him to regulate his own emotions, to become his own 'man', neither requiring him to gain more energy and power by bullying another nor creating in him that need for outside reassurance.

I have tended to refer throughout to mums — I am one, after all — but a very involved dad as well as a mum adds another dimension to development again. Baby has two brains to grow from rather than one, conferring life-long advantages. If you are a single parent, the message is to ensure your baby regularly interacts with another adult who loves them.

Chapter 8

Empathy and your baby's sense of self

That night he was almost too happy to sleep, and so much love stirred in his little sawdust heart that it almost burst. And into his boot-button eyes, that had long ago lost their polish, there came a look of wisdom and beauty …

Margery Williams, *The Velveteeen Rabbit*, 1922.[38]

The splitting up of the 'human control system' into different self-regulation tools is, of course, a completely artificial thing. They develop together. They never work in isolation from each other. We split them up to understand them better and that is all.

So impulse control doesn't solely develop from the 'waited moment'. It also develops as a consequence of our knowledge that another way of looking at things is likely to emerge if we wait that moment. We might be furious at a friend, but still appreciate that she's not seeing things the way we are and that waiting to find out her perspective on the situation is going to be helpful. Even without knowing exactly what feelings, knowledge and perspective she has that differs from ours, we know that there will be 'another way to look at things'. We are able to think about thinking, and to think (and feel) about feelings. These are two vital skills for children to develop, and they begin developing very early.

These skills have separate names. Recognising and thoughtfully responding to the emotions of ourselves and others is called empathy. Less well-known is the term that describes 'thinking about thinking', including the ability to wonder about what other people might know or think. The term for this is skill is 'theory of mind'. Again, this is one of those purely artificial divisions, but it is useful because these two different parts of knowing, interrelated though they are, develop at different rates. It is important to understand that your baby knows from a very early age that she is not you and your emotions aren't hers, and that she also knows that she isn't able to predict what you do and don't know.

Empathy starts with the heart

It is empathy, or heart knowledge, that comes first. And it really does come from the heart. This was, for me, a transformative piece of knowledge, because, like many people with a western medicine background, I had believed that 'I' was located behind my eyes. I had also believed that empathy was mostly created by baby being treated empathically and then later taught at a 'thinking' level: for example, 'And how would you feel if that was you?' I was right but I was missing out the vital first step. The groundwork for empathy is put in place from very early, beginning in the womb.

It begins when a baby's heart speeds and slows in imitation of her mother's. Even at birth, the ebb and flow of baby's heart is not yet properly regulated by her own control systems. Cradled to Mum's left side, baby's heart learns to echo the changing and 'environmentally responsive' beat of the loving heart next door.[39]

The way our hearts vary their beats is critically important. The more variable your heart rate, the better your health, your empathic skills and your concentration skills. The words 'high' attached to the word 'heart' tend to freak us out a little, as we associate them with 'high blood pressure'. Not in this case. You want to know that your heart is 'highly variable'. In fact, the words 'low heart rate variability' are a red flag for all kinds of health issues: panic disorder, psychopathology, difficulties with glucose regulation, problems coping with stress, and also heart disease.[40-44]

I find it just fascinating that it is not until we are six weeks old that vision, the most important tool for learning we have, comes into regular use. Why does our vision come online so relatively late in development? I think it is because, once seen, your face becomes baby's favourite thing in the world: nothing can compete with the sheer joy of Mum smiling. For the whole of the rest of our lives another person's gaze is the most powerful emotional stimulus in the world. Perhaps the delay is because babies need to be protected from it for a little while so they have more time to detect and internalise the subtler cues of their mother's body: her heart rate, respiration rate and muscle tension.

Keeping baby close to you while you are talking to another person or concentrating hard on a complex task or walking briskly or resting peacefully means that baby's heart can learn to detect all these variations of heart rate. Having learned to 'echo the changing beat' of your heart in the first six weeks, down the track baby will begin to match facial expressions to different heart rates.

Of course, the more congruency between your emotions, your facial expressions and your heart rate, the better the match your baby can grow between her own emotions and body systems. That close match between her emotions and body systems helps your child understand and manage her own emotions. It also gives her a head start in recognising and responding to the emotions of others, which is the basis of empathy and social skill.[11, 35, 36, 45]

When you go to pick up your crying baby, you'll find, if you listen, that your heart slows in anticipation of her need for a soothing heartbeat. A lovely encasement of calm can descend upon you as you hold her close; and in calming her, your slower heartbeat calms you too. You pick up your baby and hold her close, very frequently to your left side and with her right ear pressed close to your chest, and you slowly rock from side to side. Your dropped heart rate coupled with the slow rocking says to your baby 'all is well', and her heart rate drops also, no longer pounding out a raggedy, incoherent rhythm that sends out powerful messages of distress to her body and brain.

We are used to thinking that heart rate is controlled by the brain, but that's not quite right. The heart and the amygdala are in constant dialogue, and sometimes it is the heart that is the boss. When we are very stressed our heart begins a raggedy, incoherent beat. It also secretes stress hormones (it turns out the heart is a gland as well as a pump) and this is a double whammy emergency gong for the brain and body. The heart, which has its own 'little brain', sends the powerful message to the amygdala, 'Turn off higher thought. Instinct must rule if we are to survive.'

And this is what happens. The amygdala promptly concurs and we can't reach those higher brain regions anymore: we simply react. You can imagine how useful this was on the African savanna when faced with a giant sabre-toothed cat, but it's a poor match for modern life, which calls for us to be able to think flexibly most of the time.

Unfortunately, our heads are no match for our hearts in this situation. We are simply not able to calm ourselves down by 'thinking' once our heart believes it is in an emergency situation. Trying to think usually means that we get stuck, thinking the same thoughts over and over again (a feature of depression and anxiety disorders), waiting nervously for disaster to strike (panic attacks) and defending ourselves against a world that has become too much.

So what happens if we pick up our crying baby and our heart beat 'takes off' under these circumstances rather than slowing down? What if we pick up our crying baby and our heart slows initially but then begins to race under the stress of dealing with a colicky or difficult-to-soothe baby?

The HeartMath Institute has pioneered the use of biofeedback to help people see what is happening in their hearts: this incoherent rhythm shows up as a ragged line. Clients are then taught how to calm their wildly beating hearts.[43]

One of their techniques goes like this: you are instructed to put a 'freeze frame' around what you are feeling. Then you are asked to place your hands on your heart and breathe in and out from there. The next instruction is to 'Find a memory of a time when you felt good — not the event, simply the emotion. If you can't feel that emotion, try and find the appreciation or the attitude that went with it. Aim for neutral if you can't find positive.'

I've found that this technique works well for me and my friends even without a screen to watch. Once you feel that you are able to access those high brain regions again so you are not having looping thoughts, 'He shouldn't be crying, I must be such a bad mother' or doom thoughts, 'I can't cope', then check through to see what thoughts you are having about the baby.

Make sure you are *not* thinking that baby is attempting to manipulate you or that baby is rejecting you or that baby is angry with you. Remember that these are distress calls and that always responding pays big dividends. The messages of the first part of the book are important here too: listen for shark music and look for ghosts (see pages 38-40).

The take home message for parents is that heart rate variability is a vital component for empathy, and that it is created as much by the heart as the brain. And it begins in infancy. Babies with a secure, organised attachment partly get a good head start in life because their deep physical connection to you, heart to heart, helps them develop a more variable heart rate. So keep them close.

The heart research has altered how I think about myself and my children, and how I deal with illness and sadness and learning issues. It has altered the kind of programs I write for parents. More than anything, it has said to me that 'the relationship with your children is what is paramount'.

I have always tried to write programs that would be fun for mother and child to do together, but now that has become the central goal for any therapy program. I aim to strengthen the relationship between parent and child, because that will improve every single outcome for the child.

No, this does not mean that I believe that learning difficulties are necessarily or only relationship difficulties. But every relationship can become stronger. If one of my boys is having a 'catching everything' patch or a 'sad patch', I now say to myself, 'more time needed there'. More listening time, more cuddle time and more fun. Build the connection deeper.

Gaze and growing your baby's sense of self

When baby is about two months old the time for just gazing at each other has arrived. So enjoyable is this that parents often continue to gaze after baby has gone to sleep — and there is nothing like catching the sparkle growing in a just-awakened baby's eyes either. It is hard not to just sit and look at them, waiting for them to wake up and look back at you. And so often, in these next few months, baby will wake and you will see quite clearly that there is more looking back at you from behind those eyes than there was when baby went to sleep. More comprehension, more curiosity, more humour ... more of the person altogether. Professor Schore, the great synthesist of neurology and psychology, calls this utterly addictive mutual gazing the 'face-to-face joy interactions', and notes that they trigger off a new pattern of growth in both your brain and your baby's.[11, 46]

Gaze when baby is born early

One of the difficulties for parents of the premature or near-term baby is connected to gaze. A premature baby is easily overstimulated and the gaze of another person gets to be too much very quickly, so baby looks away. The risk is that this will continue past the time when gaze is overstimulating to baby, and researchers have indeed found that this pattern of only briefly meeting each other's eyes continues past infancy. And it is not just the child who holds a gaze for less time, the mothers also show the same pattern of looking away after a few seconds. This is not just a risk factor for being able to reconnect and repair, but for less time spent in the face-to-face joy interactions.

How can we correct such a thing? Can it be corrected? Should it be corrected? Or is it perhaps a maternal response to ongoing sensitivities in the child?

It does need to be corrected, and the only way to correct it is by increasing your awareness of what is happening. If your baby is still little and you are not already doing it, switch to kangaroo care or loads of skin-to-skin contact. It is difficult to accept, but some hospitals still promote incubators over kangaroo care despite the overwhelming evidence in favour of it, for everything from more responsive temperature control and better weight gain to improved synchrony between mother and child. So hold your baby and touch him with love. But make sure you tell him what you are doing, give him warning of your presence and your actions, and move slowly. The beginnings of gaze are supported by loads of skin-to-skin contact.[47]

Talking is also important. Copy the smallest of your baby's happy vocalisations (the gurgles, small exploratory sounds, coos) back to him, whether he is looking at you or not. Focus yourself on getting that sound back like the most faithful of echoes, mixed in with the love you feel. And, of course, always respond instantly to cries with soothing and the warmth and steadiness of your body.

As many times a day as possible, banish all the world you can and immerse yourself utterly in your baby. This means that you put all else from your mind — the emotional difficulties of an early birth, any *accompanying fear that may still be rearing multiple heads — to just be in the moment with your baby. Keep baby curled up, his little legs over his tummy, his head absolutely supported but free to look away. Watch your baby with every bit of dedication and 'in the moment' that you can muster: let the task become a moving meditation, as if you were watching the flickering flame of a candle, mentally itemising baby's cues. Pull back gently if there is a hint of disengagement — a premature baby has far more subtle signs that require much more skilled reading. Be patient and keep your baby's corrected age in mind. It is not until a baby is two months old that the face-to-face joy interactions even begin.*

In parenting literature, one researcher has used the word 'moist' to describe early gaze, in an attempt to characterise the very gentle 'adhering' quality of gaze between a baby and mother. Without intruding or imposing on your baby, try to keep gaze going longer with that very subtle stickiness. You will find that your face is opening and brightening as you hold baby's gaze, and your body is softening. Relax into that exchanged gaze and your baby will learn to do so also. See if you can build the amount of time and increase the elasticity and length of gaze. Play little stretching games: slowly turn your face sideways while smiling and holding eye contact with just one eye, and then come back to full face. These stretching games are the mutual limbering up for more complicated games like peek-a-boo. For example, when your baby is sad, your face empathically reflects back that sadness, but not *only* the sadness. You automatically mix in other messages too: your loving concern, your patience derived of your knowledge that 'this too shall pass' and even a hint of 'you are gorgeous even when you are crying'.

How reassuring this is to your baby.[46] Each of those messages is read, and the feeling that prompted them in you is caught by him as his 'mirror system' picks up those fine gradations in your expression and matches them to changes in your heart rate and breathing. It is in this way that he discovers that a 'let's play' smile is matched with an increasing heart rate; a look of focus with a steady slow heart rate;

surprise with a sudden freezing in the gut (the 'swoop' we all feel); an open-mouthed smile with a feeling of openness and 'lift' through the body.[48, 49]

How especially important those joyous moments are! From them comes our drive to explore and discover, our motivation to master, our curiosity and, most of all, our desire to relate well to other people. The 'ah-ha' moment beloved of the student and scientist, the moment of recognition in our love stories, the satisfaction of a completed project. All are moments of joy.

The 'lift' mentioned, the one that seems to roll outwards from our hearts through our bodies at such times, is no illusion either. When you smile in response to your baby's smile, and talk back in response to his talk, joy rolls like an express train through his whole body, leaving a trail of good in its wake. The 'joy express' is the vagus nerve. In babyhood this is the carrier of messages from the heart to the amygdala; as we grow up it links through to the right brain. Vagus means 'wanderer' and this nerve wanders from brain to colon, taking in the throat and the heart on the way.

So what happens in that smiling moment when your eyes meet in mutual delight? The vagus nerve releases oxytocin (the love, learning and anti-stress hormone), relaxing your baby, coaxing his heart to match the moment and simultaneously dropping his blood pressure. At the same time, the oxytocin release increases his immunity by increasing the production of white blood cells and decreasing the production of corticosteroids. If something is hurting him, the oxytocin surge will make it feel a bit better. On reaching his tummy, the oxytocin makes it feel 'warm' and helps along digestion of food. And for an encore, oxytocin prods along the release of growth hormone and helps your baby grow.[50, 51, 52]

These social interactions have a long term effect too. In the 1960s, attachment theorist Dr Daniel Stern said that every social interaction between mother and child was a mini-narrative or a 'micro-story'. There is a beginning — baby catches mother's eye; a middle with some tension, some build-up — 'Is Mum going to tickle me? She is! Oh oh!'; and an end — the game winds down, or baby is beginning to get too excited and must be soothed, or a different game starts.[53] In the 2000s Dr Schore synthesised those stories with the underlying biology. Baby and mother's heart rate speeds up in synchrony as the game gets going. Oxytocin is released in both brains — it is not just the love but the learning hormone — and both brains are primed to learn. Learning is a biological process — if someone has learned something, their brain has changed.

What is baby actually about to learn? He's going to learn about keeping the game going longer through building concentration span and paying attention to one thing. He's going to learn about reading the most fleeting expressions on Mum's face and guess when the gentle fingers will poke him next, thus building his social skills by predicting what is going to happen. He's going to practise his burgeoning communication skills by giggling and gurgling in anticipation. By matching his mum's body systems' changes he's going to learn more about controlling his own heart rate and hormone release so that he can keep playing and keep that positive feeling going longer.[11, 46]

And what is happening in Mum's brain? Is she just going through the motions? No. If baby is learning then Mum is fully engaged in the game too. Creating synchrony is an emotional process, and if the adult isn't fully present it can't happen. Mum is growing not just her right brain, but the identical part of the right brain to her baby. She doesn't just monitor her baby's but also her own emotions, and learns when to turn off the stressful emotions in both of them. This is multitasking at a most refined level. A mother's brain keeps growing to keep up with the job as the social interactions with her child become ever more complex.

Dr Schore concludes one of his papers with the extraordinary suggestion that the baby grows his conciousness of himself as different to other selves because his mother has also grown a map of who he is in her brain.[11] Faithfully copying her brain growth as he has throughout, why should his idea of himself not have begun in her mind and then taken root in his? And can a person develop 'self-hood' without being a self in someone else's mind first? I don't think they can. I believe it is not 'I think therefore I am', but 'I am loved, therefore I am'.

Perhaps the strongest support for this comes from those who work with troubled youth. Youth workers often comment on these children's and teenagers' lack of *a sense of self*. So pronounced is this missing sense of self that it is not possible to deliver self-esteem or self-confidence programs because there is 'no-one there' to deliver it to. But, say the youth workers, it is possible to help these troubled kids develop that sense of self. They often note, in passing, that when that has been achieved, they find that they keep that relationship forever. Those kids never fully leave their lives.

I believe what has happened is that the youth worker has been the first person to ever 'attune' to that child. And the first person to ever grow a map of that individual in their own brain. And in doing both those things, they trigger in the teenager's brain the process of building a 'core self'. They know who they are now because someone else does too. No wonder they never want to lose touch with that person.

In the light of this research I've been left to wonder just what happens when a person is transformed by a spiritual experience. It is quite definitely their right brain that is involved in that experience, the emotional, pattern detecting, non-verbal right. Can a person 'imagine' such a powerfully transformative experience? I believe they cannot. I believe that the evidence suggests we cannot claim that right brain growth in a baby requires an 'other' but that right brain growth in adults does not. This last bit, of course, would be considered simply speculation by scientists, and I'm just sharing it with you as part of my journey through the research as promised. It is taking some courage!

Chapter 9

Learning how to talk and think

It is more fun to talk with someone who doesn't use long, difficult words but rather short, easy words like 'What about lunch?'.

A.A. Milne, *The House at Pooh Corner*, 1926.[54]

Your baby has been listening attentively from before birth. She is born knowing her mother's voice and the shout of each sibling; able to recognise often-read stories and her mother's language against those of other cultures. Researchers have found that when a newborn baby is interested in what she can hear her heart rate slows — as does that of an adult who is concentrating. At birth, baby responds to the sound of her mother's voice by looking for the source of the sound, and so finds her mother's face. That gentle connection, a face to go with the voice and the smell and the comfort and love, grows in richness and significance for the baby in the early weeks of infancy. Eventually it becomes the heart of learning how to talk and how to think.

One of the strongest findings for securely attached children is that their language skills and IQs as a group (although there are always children with genetically based difficulties) are a great deal better than those of insecurely attached children. It's no accident.

The gift of a secure attachment
A secure attachment means that a baby starts on the pathway to communication earlier. This is because her more subtle signals are

recognised more quickly by the more sensitive parent. Empowered by this, baby begins to experiment with more and varied speech sounds. Her parents respond by making those sounds right back at her. All she is getting is 'go' signals.

Let's look at the same baby, but with a preoccupied parent. Sometimes a cry brings Mum and Dad running, but sometimes baby is left to cry. There's no clear pattern of response for baby to build on. Puzzlingly, crying sometimes works as a communication, but sometimes it doesn't. Her more subtle signals, like waves of her little hands and soft gurgling noises, are only sometimes heeded. The mix of 'stop' and 'go' signals keep this baby hesitating a long time before she steps onto the pathway of building language.

One of the great misconceptions people have about responsive and sensitive parenting is that it will result in a more dependent child. 'You'll be training her to run to you for everything,' is one of the criticisms parents hear. Of course, what studies show is that securely attached children are both more resilient and more competent than insecurely attached peers. And this is due partly to their more advanced language and thinking skills. Siblings who can negotiate with each other are far less likely to be requiring frequent interventions from their parents. Children who know and can express clearly what they want experience less frustration and far more self-efficacy.

So first of all you do indeed respond to just about everything: every whimper (if you are quick enough baby won't need to cry and experience the cascade of anti-learning stress hormones), every coo, every indication of interest. You talk and you sing and you watch for a response, except when baby is feeding. All mothers say very little then. If baby can't talk back because her mouth is full, it seems that we don't feel the urge to speak to her. After all, this is a *relationship* where normal social rules still apply. There are, however, some key differences to a social interaction with an infant.

First of all, you have a new voice. It is time to change a nappy, and you talk baby through the process in the special new voice that arrived with your baby, the slowed down, high-pitched, very modulated voice. Babies love motherese; until they don't and then it just fades from a parent's speech. Secondly, you are talking to someone who doesn't know the language. The regular routines of bathing and feeding and changing nappies offer a chance to show that words have specific meanings. Interestingly, in the well-known disposable versus cloth nappy environmental impact debate, far less attention has been paid to one clear failing of disposable nappies. Babies in disposable nappies are changed far less often, and with that, many opportunities for language and interaction are lost.[55] If you stick to the same words more or less each time (but don't anguish over them being exact) you are giving baby words to peg to the routine.

Also in the interests of learning the language, babies need lots of language directed right at them to 'crunch out' basic rules, and they've done this by nine months of age. They learn nothing if the language is on the television or on the radio or directed to someone else. They need to watch your lips as you slowly speak straight to them; not in an unceasing stream, but in response to their indications of interest.

If you are feeling concerned that you didn't sufficiently respond in your baby's early life, please don't despair. It is what is happening now that counts most. Studies have shown that secure attachment can be created later in a child's life also, with concomitant improvements to their competency in language. In fact, outcomes for toddlers who were treated insensitively as babies but are now sensitively responded to are better than for toddlers who were sensitively responded to as babies but are now treated insensitively. What is happening now counts for a great deal.[56])

So there you are with your little baby. You talk and then wait attentively for a response. You sing, and see if she is interested in more singing. Perhaps from having listened to the give and take of conversation in the womb, your baby knows that space you have made is for her to take a turn. Perhaps it is something she learns in the first month simply because you keep offering it to her. (The research is not yet clear on this.) Whatever the reason, in the second month of life baby starts to talk back to you.

Your repertoire of imitation and surprise games will immediately grow to include more 'goo, gurgle and giggle' sounds. From around two to three months of age, babies enjoy 'echo' games: they make a sound, you make a related sound back, they make another.

Baby (invitingly): 'Aaaah!'
You (sounding impressed): 'Ah-ga!'

Baby (trickily reversing the sounds): 'Ga-ah!'

You (acknowledging this as a hit): 'Ooh! Aaaa-gaaaa' (on a deep intonation).

Baby giggles and so do you.

A surprise game such as this is effectively a science experiment conducted by your baby. She is working towards understanding 'me' and 'not me'. Like all the best science experiments, these ones have just one variable.

In a copying game, the actions are the same and the one variable is the person performing the action. 'I do it, then you do it. You do it, then I do it. If it's the same thing, but we aren't doing it at the same time, we are obviously different.'

In a surprise game, baby learns that she isn't in charge of exactly when that surprise comes. The variable is time. 'You surprised me! The thing you did isn't quite the thing that I expected you to do. If you can surprise me then we aren't the same thing.'

Both games lead to a baby knowing 'we aren't the same'. This is the first step towards theory of mind: appreciating that other people are things with minds and with different knowledge and intention to yours. This in turn becomes the basis for thinking skills.

Baby is learning about emotions too. When you reflect back to baby your recognition of her emotion — that she has a sore tummy and you are sorry about that — she catches not only her feeling returned by you but also your empathy. Something the same, and a little bit more. She sees that emotions can be shared, but that you are adding something to the exchange. She begins to appreciate that you can see what she feels, but you feel something a little different. Slowly and steadily, through the rich emotional games played with you, babies piece together that your perspective and your emotions are not the same as their own. Amazingly, basic empathy and the beginnings of theory of mind (the ability to predict what someone knows) are things babies have nailed by six months of age.[35]

How baby teaches you to teach her to talk

Speech pathologists have been saying 'follow your child's lead' for years now. They have always believed that a baby can actively shape the language experiences provided by adults if given the chance. Oddly enough, that's something that language researchers are only just beginning to look at; and not so surprisingly, they are finding plenty of evidence for this proposal.

By their coos, their gaze and their movements babies charm the sensitive, responsive parent into providing more of the interaction they most enjoy. Perhaps the strongest evidence for this commonsensical idea that babies need to be 'active agents' for good language development comes if you couple two findings together. Firstly, that babies learn language fastest when talking is coupled with lots of eye contact and social interaction.[57] And secondly, that better language development goes with secure attachment.[58] Both pieces of evidence support the notion that when babies are sensitively and predictably responded to they can 'shape' the learning experience and so get loads more out of it.

Early and late talkers

Just as early walking doesn't mean that a child does or does not have a gift for movement, early talking doesn't necessarily tell you much about a child's eventual language skills either. The vast quantity of research shows that how well a child acquires language cannot be predicted by studying the child alone. The most reliable indicator of language skills is how responsive a parent is to their child's attempts to communicate.[59]

And there are other, linked indicators. For example, the best predictor for a large vocabulary at three and a half is not 'early words', but the quantity of items that a baby gestured to. Complexity of sentences at three and a half was not predicted by early speech either, but by how well a child linked together both gesture and speech. The key here is you.

If you are consistent in observing and responding to your baby, when baby points, you will supply the desired word. The reward of your interest and attention means that your baby will point more, you'll provide more words, and so it goes on. Toddlers string together words and gestures to make sentences — if you are paying good attention you'll put it all together verbally for them, which will encourage them to continue trying to sequence ideas and emotions. For example, my friend Chandra's two-year-old son Lachlan pointed at the clothes line, opened and shut one hand and said 'sock'. She promptly put it together for him — "you were looking at the clothesline and you saw a butterfly on Daddy's sock".

So if your gesturing or 'signing' baby doesn't say a word for months, as in the case of the well-known 'late talkers' who suddenly catch-up, she is still learning. (Investing in a 'baby signing' book or classes can also be a good idea.) This research into the importance of gesture also suggests a solution to the great conundrum of which late talkers will suddenly catch up and which won't.

About 14 per cent of children are 'late bloomers' with language. Imagine a toddler is approaching two years, and, while it is apparent she understands everything that is said to her, she still isn't saying a word. She approaches three, and has a vocabulary similar to that of an 18 month old. At this point the 'late talker' group splits roughly in half and the children develop in one of two ways. Either at four or five years they've caught right up and may have even overtaken some of their peers, or they are still delayed. At the moment there is no way of predicting which group a child will fall into. This new research might mean that speech pathologists will be able to add gesture and parental responsiveness and know which child is going to have difficulty talking.

The puzzle of helping your baby to good language development is unlocked when you start thinking of her as an active participant rather than a passive recipient of your knowledge. I will never forget my anxiety over whether or not to use different words to describe something with a six-month-old Tim. Should I say 'cat' every time, or was it permissible to sometimes say 'puss' or 'pussy-cat'? Was it important that the sofa always be 'the sofa' or could it also be called the 'lounge' or the 'settee'? It was quite paralysing. It was when I realised that I simply had to be guided by him that I finally relaxed. When I began to think about him as 'shaping me into the teacher he wanted' I realised that if your baby seems interested in a range of words, then you'll use them. If your baby looks lost, you will find yourself stopping.

To begin with, you need to give your baby as much material to work with as you can. Talk, sing, talk while always pausing for her comment or approval. If she makes a noise, seize the moment and make it back. 'Un! Did you say "un"? Was that because you like Mum to pick you up?' Note especially your new voice: modulated, higher than usual, with the words spaced widely and drawn out. Do not resist the urge to talk this way. Your babytalk gives your baby the best chance to learn, particularly if she watches you as you speak. Each slowed down, well-spaced word is shown in production so baby can see the shape of each sound as it emerges from your mouth. When baby no longer needs you to speak like this, you will just naturally stop. Remember, baby is 'shaping' you into the language teacher she needs you to be.

Develop a patter for routines like nappy changes. Say mostly the same thing each time, which will give baby a head start in pegging words to events. 'Off with the stinky nappy, freshen up the little bum ...' Use blank verse, rhyming verse, and sing a little. You will soon find that a baby can be the most rewarding audience in the world.

Chapter 10

Breastfeeding

Soon he forgot his embarrassment and became
mesmerized by the slow rhythmic sucking.

Michelle Magorian, *Goodnight Mr Tom*, 1981.[60]

Just as I was on the last edit of this book, a study of 2500 Western
Australian children followed over 14 years found that those who
were breastfed for more than six months had lower rates of aggression,
depression and anxiety than those who were not.[61] All of this adds
up to significantly better mental health — happier kids, in other
words. So why does breastfeeding make such a big contribution to a
child's self-regulation skills? No-one has come out with a definite
answer. I'd like to speculate here and say, beyond being the right food
for babies, these mothers and babies often have more body-to-body
contact, which (as we saw in Chapter 8: Empathy and your baby's
sense of self) develops into stronger empathic skills.

So I knew I had to talk about breastfeeding but I discovered I had
a tremendous aversion to doing so because, unlike most other aspects
of parenting, breastfeeding is something that it seems not everyone
can do. Once upon a time nearly every Australian woman could
breastfeed, of course, just like they currently do in Russia and Norway.
But not now. I didn't want to make anyone feel guilty!

And yet, I do believe passionately that women need every bit of
good information they can find. Perhaps I believe this so passionately
because, despite looking very hard, I wasn't able to find that good
information when it came to giving birth. It took me 55 hours of
full-blown labour to give birth to Tim and only right at the end was
I given syntocin. I took a year to recover from giving birth to him —
not mentally, but physically. So I was wary when it came to birthing

Sam and wondered if, perhaps, a Caesarean would be better. 'Oh yes!' was the response from the doctors. None of the risk factors of a Caesarean in terms of later births or for the babies themselves were discussed.

It took me about eight months to recover from that Caesarean. Later I found more information on the risk factors to babies of Caesareans too. So when it came to Rafael I thought that I would try for a normal birth. I could try, I was told, but I would not be allowed to use syntocin as the Caesarean scar could rupture. Without that help, though, I wasn't able to labour properly and I had another Caesarean. Just two months after he was born I heard that only *some* doctors won't allow use of syntocin in the case of a vaginal birth after Caesarean. You can imagine the grief I felt at hearing that. I am very good at ferreting out information, but despite reading, researching and talking to other medical people I hadn't found several critical pieces of information in time.

So I hope no reader is reading this chapter and feeling guilty. Guilt implies that something was your fault. Our society makes it very hard for women to breastfeed, so this is not a matter for guilt. But sorrow and grief: these, too, are hard emotions to live with.

So why is breastfeeding something that fewer and fewer Australian women are able to maintain, despite the fact that 90 per cent of us initiate breastfeeding with our newborns? Along with much of the other knowledge about child-rearing, breastfeeding wisdom has disappeared from the community as a whole and is held only by a few professionals. And, on top of that, breastfeeding is very tricky, especially at first.

For the very first feed, if possible, encourage baby to crawl up your body to find the breast. If a newborn baby is placed on his mother's stomach he will 'crawl' using the stepping, rooting and sucking reflexes to find the nipple and attach. For the first 15 minutes or so he will just lie there, but before an hour has passed he will find his way to the nipple all by himself.[62] Continue to lie baby next to your bare skin as much as possible, and get him to do some of the latching-on himself — but have that attachment carefully checked by a midwife.

Having your baby latched on correctly is utterly critical to successful breastfeeding. I recommend that you ask for help attaching baby from an *experienced* midwife at least a few times every day for the first few days. This is especially important if you've had a C-section. Even if you've breastfed successfully before, don't be shy of asking for assistance. Even with Rafael, where I had four plus years of successful breastfeeding experience, I still insisted on help for those first days with getting him properly attached. (My friend Kate advises you to look for the older midwives to help: breastfeeding skills are not necessarily something that younger midwives have had a chance to develop, with fewer and fewer women breastfeeding and shorter and shorter hospital stays.)

When your baby isn't 'on' properly it leads straight to blisters and cracks of the nipple. (Some great advice on healing such injuries can be found on the KellyMom website.) Cracked nipples are apparently (I've never had one due to my insistence that the midwives attach my sons to my breast) terrifically painful, so it is really worth the embarrassment of refusing to attach your baby yourself for a few days after he's born. Both you and the baby learn what a good attachment feel like this way.

I have, however, plenty of experience with both thrush and mastitis to share with you. If latching on is terrifically painful, but after the first few sucks that pain disappears (until next time) you and the baby have thrush. Anti-fungals for both you and your baby are required — and they work very quickly. Just a day later the pain is a distant memory.

I associate mastitis with bras that are either too tight or too loose. If you are having repeated incidences of mastitis, get a new bra. Occasionally I've felt 'fluey' and missed that it was the beginning of mastitis — if you are breastfeeding and start to feel very unwell, always suspect mastitis as a possibility. Check your breasts for streaks, lumps and hot patches — and get to a doctor immediately if you feel it could be mastitis. You need to obtain antibiotics urgently as mastitis develops and worsens very rapidly. (Cabbage leaves will help here too.) Many women I know say that mastitis becomes more of a problem with successive babies.

If anything at all is bothering you, just ask for help. In fact, assume that you are going to need help. Breastfeeding is not something you will innately know how to do. Perhaps once, when we grew up with breastfeeding all around us, we might have known, but today, where the dominant image is of a baby sucking on a bottle, we are a long way removed from that.

Breastfeeding is also very time-consuming initially. A breastfed newborn may feed up to twelve times in twenty-four hours — and each feed may take quite some time. You and your partner need to be clear that getting breastfeeding well established is a great deal of what you will be doing for some months after the baby is born.

My sister Stephanie has struggled with breastfeeding with each of her three sons. With the two eldest boys (now eight and four) everything went well at first, and then, at about three months old they were diagnosed as failing to thrive. She now says that she realises that they had been somewhat underweight from very early on but that the situation became far worse at this point. She feels that this was when she began pushing herself to 'do more', coupled with the first round of immunisations, which led to them sleeping more and feeding less. Breasts are very sensitive to demand — if it decreases, they promptly produce less.

Her decreasing milk supply was also distressing for Steph, and that distress caused her milk supply to drop further. (I remember one day when Declan spat milk back up: 'there's not enough of it for you to do that' she said sadly to him.) Breastfeeding is a confidence game.[63] Milk supply is a key to confidence. When there's less, you feel less confident. Less confidence means more stress and less supply. The way to reverse this is to spend all your time with your baby either nestled up to you, skin to skin, or feeding. If they aren't feeding enough to build up supply, then you need to use a breastpump to tell your breasts to produce more milk.

Put simply, for those first three months, women who want to breastfeed need to spend the majority of their time doing just that. To support a friend or partner who is struggling to breastfeed, do her dishes for her. Play with her toddler. In this way she can let go of all other concerns and simply have loads of skin-to-skin contact with her baby.

In addition to being very time consuming and 'technically challenging', breastfeeding is difficult for other reasons too.

We haven't just lost a lot of breastfeeding knowledge out of the community, we also have replaced that knowledge with disinformation. Even the phrase 'breast is best' gives the wrong message. It sounds as if breast milk has added extras and formula is normal. Breastmilk is normal. Another of the classic pieces of disinformation is that women are told they shouldn't feed their babies off to sleep, and that for 'good' deep sleep for both themselves and their child a bottle of formula works better than a breast. In fact, you don't want your baby to have the same kind of 'deep sleep' you see in older children and adults. Feeding babies formula (quite apart from all the other risks) increases their risk for sudden infant death syndrome because they are 'sleeping deeper'.

Parents worry terribly about getting enough sleep. This is entirely reasonable, as getting too tired puts you at risk for postnatal depression among other things. But why then are women told that they shouldn't feed their babies off to sleep? It is an extraordinary statement, particularly considering the fact that breast milk is full of sleep-inducing hormones.

And does breastfeeding really mean that mothers get less sleep? No. In fact, research shows that breastfeeding *increases* sleep in parents by 40 to 45 minutes. The writers of the report on breastfeeding conclude, 'parents who supplement their infant feeding with formula under the impression that they will get more sleep should be encouraged to continue breast-feeding because sleep loss of more than 30 minutes each night can begin to affect daytime functioning, particularly in those parents who return to work'.[64] Breastfeeding parents get more sleep.

Another disincentive to breastfeeding is the fact that women who breastfeed in public can be harassed. I remember feeding Rafael at a road house and two middle-aged men walking past with one saying to the other, 'Tits a fine day'. What did I do? Nothing. I was so overtaken by rage and shame that I did not respond, although many responses have occurred to me since.

Part of 'breastfeeding confidence' is knowing that it is okay to breastfeed anywhere, anytime. Unfortunately, this is not what happens in the media at the moment. Instead, women as individuals are pilloried for the decision not to breastfeed. And it's very wrong reasoning. If women are harassed for breastfeeding in public, the blame lies with the society that allows this harassment.

So why is there such a level of disinformation in the community? Why don't we better support women to breastfeed? There are two reasons.

The first is that in Australia commercial interests have shaped our ideas of how babies should be fed. The bottle has become the symbol used by pharmacies and supermarkets to indicate their interest in being seen as 'family friendly'. This has become so ubiquitous that it is not something I even noticed until blogger Lauredhel (whose various writings have provided much of the material for this chapter) pointed it out to me. Over the last 50 years Australians have come to regard formula feeding as 'normal' and breastfeeding as 'extra'. This is a triumph of marketing. The reverse is true: breastfeeding is normal. In fact, feeding babies infant formula is very far from being either normal or benign. A range of serious health consequences flow from feeding babies infant formula. The best known of these are the greater risks for cot death, diabetes and obesity. There are other risks also, including greater risk of developing allergies and asthma later on, and more illnesses in infancy.[65, 66]

The World Health Organization has developed a code of practice for infant formula manufacturers. It bans them from advertising and claiming health benefits for formula, and also from giving free samples to women able to breastfeed. Australia has signed this code, but has not enforced it in legislation. Instead, there is a 'voluntary code of practice' which is co-signed by formula companies.

Every infant formula advertisement acts as disinformation to the women who read it. The manufacturers continue to present formula as an equivalent alternative — not the best option, they say, but close — when the two are worlds apart. So while the WHO code of practice bans companies from using labelling that 'idealises' the use of breast milk replacements, it still is occurring. You will see phrases like 'keeps little tummies happy'. Imagine the distress of the mother of a baby with colic who weans her baby, only to discover after two weeks on formula that her child's colic is worse! This is human suffering for commercial gain, and needs to be clearly seen as such and legislated against.

The second reason why women are not better supported to breastfeed is that we, as a society, don't offer them any alternative to returning to work as soon as possible after they have given birth. Where women have long paid maternity leave — for example, in Norway — sustained breastfeeding rates are over 90 per cent. In Norway, maternity leave is either ten months on full pay or 12 months on 80 per cent pay. There, when women return to work they are allocated two hours extra on top of normal breaks to breastfeed their child.

So when Stephie's milk supply all but dried up in the third month and I watched her struggle — the baby getting thinner, her distress when the paediatrician told her that in another baby he'd diagnose 'failure to thrive and neglect' — I knew utterly that the wrong thing to say would be, 'Well, why don't you just switch to formula?' I knew how much she feared having to go through the grief of knowing her baby was missing out on breast milk and losing the breastfeeding relationship she had so wanted to share.

If a woman wants desperately to breastfeed her baby and she is having difficulty doing so, telling her that it is not that big a deal is not going to bring her any comfort. She needs to be supported to find solutions, rather than have her mind changed. And there was a solution for Stephie with her first two babies — it came in a pill and she was able to wean herself off it after a month or so without compromising her milk supply. With her third son she's managed things very differently.

Callum was a sleepy jaundiced newborn who didn't suck enough for Steph's supply to increase commensurate with his increasing needs. And, as my friend Cindy says, newborns 'don't know what they are missing' — they don't demand that you feed them. So Steph compensated for that missing sucking with the breast pump. After every feed she would pump, so that when Callum returned to the breast there was more milk available than there had been at the last feed. With this happening he was able to 'feed through' his jaundice and is now, despite this unpromising start, the plumpest of the brothers at four months of age.

Rather than the usual 'go on to formula', Steph recommends that women see what happens if they try pumping to boost supply, and, perhaps in addition to this, ask for a prescription of the travel medicine that also boosts supply. Unfortunately it can be hard to access this kind of support. It seems that women are more likely to have their determination to breastfeed undermined in Australia at the moment. Blogger Lauredhel writes:

When your kidneys fail, it's a medical drama. You get hundreds of thousands of dollars of medical care, there are kidney associations, there are research foundations and telethons. You get time off work and specialist appointments and medications and dialysis.

When your breasts aren't working quite as they should?

'Here, have formula.'[67]

Ninety-nine per cent of Australian women wean their babies well before the recommended two years. What keeps some of us going? One study of 100 women (many of whom struggled with breastfeeding initially) who breastfed for that time found there were three interconnected reasons. Firstly, these women were hearing and reading enough information about the benefits of sustained breastfeeding to counter the classic Australian belief that 'they are too old once they can help themselves'. Secondly, they had support from other breastfeeding women. And thirdly, they had joined the Australian Breastfeeding Association, which provided support and connection with other mothers.[68]

The right information, support and connection to other breastfeeding women made all the difference for Steph and Callum. I went to both the Australian Breastfeeding Association website and the KellyMom website to find information for Steph as she battled to return Callum to his birthweight. More information came from my friend Cindy, who just months before had won the battle to breastfeed her premature, jaundiced son Casey. Steph's local Child Health Nurse was also a tremendous support to her, recommending and providing her with a breastpump and celebrating with her as Callum went from below the twentieth percentile for weight up to the seventy-fifth. Hurrah!

Chapter 11

Humans — the tallest trees

We now have the twin crises of deteriorating health
and deteriorating environments that threaten our
quality of life. These crises are intrinsically
interlinked.

Brian Goodwin, *How The Leopard Changed Its Spots:
The Evolution of Complexity,* 1994.[69]

In the last few years a new set of research has been threaded amongst
the existing strands of child development research. It is research
that is particularly useful for parents to be aware of, for both personal
and political reasons. At a personal level, it helps us value how
important our mental health is to our children's health. At a political
level it makes even stronger the case that Australia needs to focus more
on the needs of children and young people. This new set of research
is called 'epigenetics'.

What is 'epigenetics'?

Scientists had just begun cheerfully sequencing the human genome
and confidently expecting answers to all kinds of mysteries as a result,
when they were blind-sided by the discovery of an unexpected third
evolutionary force. (Not unexpected by Darwin, mind you: 200 years
ago he documented his suspicions that it existed.) The epigenome
contains the mechanisms that turn our genes on and off throughout
our lives. These 'epigenetic marks' are the 'software' operating the
hardware of our DNA, and this software can be just as heritable as
the 'hardware' of the DNA.

The thing to remember in epigenetics is that the DNA sequence
itself does not change but just which genes are switched on and off

does. The epigenome picks what it feels are the most useful genes for survival in the current environment. I remember reading in early high school a novel about nuclear war. Among other things, the new generation of survivors were covered with a fine fur which assisted somehow in coping with radiation. The author insisted that this was not a 'mutation' but a possibility that had been waiting in human DNA, switched on by the demands of the environment. This change was then inherited by the next generation. Epigenetics in action, in rather a hopeful interpretation of what our DNA might contain. But research is actually suggesting the opposite: that our DNA and epigenome are so ancient that they cannot find a way of usefully responding to many aspects of the Western lifestyle: sitting indoors for long periods of time, processed food, pollution and so on.

At the time that story was written the epigenetic knowledge was confined to some of the historical medical research. Epigenetic effects were found from population-wide events quite some time ago. The most famous of these are the grandchildren of the survivors of the Dutch famine. The children born during this famine were, not surprisingly, small. What was surprising was that *their* children were equally small, even though food was plentiful. So the epigenetic response of one generation to the famine had been inherited by the next. Researchers are now looking at — through studying rats, mice and monkeys — such things as how gene expression of ageing in the heart muscle is switched on and off by such events as calorie restriction in middle age.[70] They are looking at cancer as well and studying how an epigenetic mark can turn on or off the expression of cancer.[71]

The relevance to parents of all this is, of course, that the environment in which we parent, and parenting itself, have epigenetic effects. The stress we feel when pregnant, the food we eat when pregnant, the kind of relationship we have with our children — all of these have epigenetic effects.

'Genome wide' (that is, affecting everything) epigenetic changes occur in both 'germ cell' development (eggs and sperm, in other words) and in the early embryo.[72] What are those changes based upon? Our diet is one factor. And another, for the embryo at least, seems to be the degree of stress felt by the mother.

This is how it works. Imagine a place where life is tough and Mum is worried about survival all the time. This might mean a famine or a war, but it also might mean Mum is in an abusive relationship or living in intergenerational poverty. It might mean a great grief or loss afflicts her. All are different situations, but with the same *emotional signature*. The important thing to remember is that emotion is the language the brain/body speaks to itself. Researchers have added a third factor to the list of how emotions shape the body. The first was that emotional messages shape the architecture of the brain, the second that they alter the neurochemistry that underlies temperament. The third is this: from early conception and throughout life, these emotional messages are used to choose between different genetic possibilities.

A baby conceived in a harsh environment picks up her mother's distress (the message is carried by such things as high cortisol) and makes the necessary genetic adjustments to ensure survival. Baby gears up to reproduce fast and survive in an impoverished setting. These genetic changes are seen instantly as low birth weight. The epigenetic software has selected for less muscle and bone tissue, fewer kidney cells (nephrons) and fewer brain cells (neurons). The child will hit puberty early in order to meet the goal of early reproduction. The child behaves differently — a trigger reaction to stress (the primitive startle reflex is wired to remain 'on' to a greater degree) leading to quite a different emotional profile: far more easily stressed and far less able to deal with stress due to the rapid triggering of stress hormones.

This emotional profile also carries with it long term consequences. Highly stressed children grow into adults with far more 'inflammatory markers' in their blood.[73] Research into 'inflammatory markers' is growing in intensity all the time, uncovering deeper and wider consequences in an avalanche of related research. Inflammatory markers are now viewed as causal in heart disease.[74] But there are strong indications that they also contribute to depression and diabetes.[75, 76]

As well as 'inflammatory markers' in the blood contributing to diabetes, there is another epigenetic mechanism involved. High stress also says to the human genome, 'Not enough food'. This switches on the 'thrifty gene' (this gene is linked to poverty and marginalisation rather than race) so that these children are predisposed to gain weight more easily and be insulin resistant. If the outside world has plenty of food, including cheap food full of trans-fatty acids, the result is early diabetes.

Now, let's go back and imagine the same child being conceived in an 'optimum' environment. Mum isn't worried about food supply or floods or bombs, she is not submerged in uresolved grief and nor does she live in a violent home. All this is detected by baby in the womb. Rather than everything happening early, baby 'invests for longevity'. The epigenome switches on genes for higher birth weight, bigger bones and muscles, more neurons and nephrons. Same genes but different environment, leading to different epigentic events.[77]

The active ingredient

So what is the connection between relationships and epigenetics? How does the 'active ingredient' of the relationship impact on epigenetic changes?

It happens in two ways. First of all, in our society, where famine is unlikely, it is the kind of relationships that a pregnant woman has that are going to mostly impact on the stress she experiences. This, as we've seen, directly affects the epigenome of the growing baby.

After baby is born it is the kind of relationship the baby has with the parent that produces epigenetic changes. Scientists have found that both abuse and affection alter 'epigenetic marks' — the off or on switch upon a gene — in both rats and people. A stressed mother rat produces baby rats with epigenetic marks that 'switch off' the production of feel-good hormones. If those same baby rats are given extra affection, those epigenetic marks are 'switched off' once more.[78]

A very similar mechanism is found in humans: abuse in childhood leads to epigenetic changes that go on to make the individual far more responsive to stress. Again, the important thing to remember is that these 'epigenetic marks' are reversible.[79] There is a very strong message here for anyone who was very stressed during pregnancy — perhaps you lost your last baby and you are worried sick about this one. When this baby is born she will need every bit of affection you can give her.

Our babies need affection, they need to be delighted in. Every moment of shared delight, of loving touch, is 'switching on' the genes that give babies extra help with all the self-regulation skills, not to mention their health.

The nature versus nurture debate is long gone. Nature and nurture work together to produce your baby. Genes (nature) provide a number of different opportunities for development, but which of these opportunities is selected is down to the kind of nurture your baby receives.[80]

The great lesson of epigenetics is not just for parents but for society. For years we have thought that changes in medicine are going to deal with our modern epidemics of diabetes, heart disease and cancer. But genetic engineering isn't going to be able to 'fix' our epidemics of diabetes or heart disease because there is no single gene associated with either one. What scientists are discovering is that instead of 'a gene' being responsible for one of these diseases, the epigenome is flicking on a whole array of switches in response to the environment. While the search is on for medicines that exploit epigenetic knowledge on the way to various cures, we might also need to look straight at the fact that it is our environment and lifestyles that need to change, to create a world that our ancient genome and epigenome can understand.

Adding together the epigenetic, heart and right brain research
The epigenetic research astounded me every bit as much as the heart and right brain research, altering again my idea of what it means to be human. In fact, just as dividing up the self-regulation skills into interlinking components is artificial, so is dividing the epigenetic research from the heart–brain research and the right brain research. So what did I get when I put them all together?

I completely dropped the idea that we, and especially our children, are resilient in that 'oh she'll get over it' dismissive sense of the word. Everything that happens to us counts, because everything that happens changes us. Not just our ideas and our memories, in other words our neurons, but our biochemistry and even what parts of our DNA are active and which ones are silenced. Children are *not* resilient, says Dr Bruce Perry, who specialises in working with traumatised children. They are *malleable*.[81] And so are we all.

In fact we are extraordinarily malleable. With our pattern-detecting right brains we connect to other people and to our environment: and this connection is so very finely tuned that we can even 'catch' a new idea of ourselves from someone else. The right brain is just part of a body–mind connection, constantly communicating in the emotional, chemical language of the body. A new pattern of being washes throughout the body, and so deeply is it felt that it can switch on or off different genetic possibilities: disease or not disease, coping or not coping. 'Malleable' sounds as though the end result is 'moulded', and that is true; and yet 'moulded' implies that it is only the outside form of us that has changed. The truth is that we are transformed.

And we are transformed on a daily basis. The kind of relationships we have with our children, whether secure or insecure, organised or disorganised are transforming them, and us too. Every day with them is a day where we are remaking them and remaking ourselves. I think, too, that it is this ability to be tranformed by each other that connects us all together. We cannot be separate if we can change each other so radically, and nor can we be separate from the world around us.

I find many of the implications of epigenetics not just compelling but distressing. The finding that the environment we are making is leaving marks upon our genes for the next generation does, at least, have one hopeful aspect. I hope that it will assist us to find the political will to change our way of life to reflect our utter interdependence with our environment.

Raising kids in Australia

People have been kind enough to read drafts of this book as I write and rewrite. My friend and colleague Brendin read all the information on epigenetics and found it very disturbing. He said it was not the epigenetic effects themselves that disturbed him — and indeed, I would be surprised if that had been truly news to him because he is a farmer's son and has carried his childhood into his community work as an unyielding belief in the interconnectedness of people and place — but that a wider appreciation of epigenetic effects will become yet another weapon in the war of 'you must' waged upon Australian parents.

You must, says Brendin, be a wonderful parent and partner. You must have a clean house and nice garden, a suitable car and other possessions. You must have well-presented children, and provide them with a good education and relevant after-school activities, have good food upon the table, ensure your children behave properly, keep up with your friends, be a productive employee, put aside savings for your retirement … and so it goes on.

I don't live in a suburb or town, but on a pastoral property in the outback where neighbours are many kilometres away, so this was a very different perspective for me to consider. So I read further, talked to other friends and concluded that he was right. With this new information there is every chance that what will happen is that the pressure on parents will grow even greater. By the time this book is printed most of our politicians will have heard of the epigenome and understood its significance for society. But can we reasonably ask more of parents?

We cannot. Australians are already working some of the longest hours in the world. Society cannot have it both ways. Parents actually need to do less of everything else if they are to do more with their children. The parenting research tells us that when parents are fighting for survival, it is extremely difficult to parent sensitively (see Chapter 4: Am I too hard on my kids?). Many Australian parents are fighting for economic survival. And, although some of those who are fighting have drafted themselves into working longer hours (having let the wolf of 'more' in through the door), they have done so in response to societal pressure. And there is a tremendous mismatch between meeting societal pressures and the needs of children.

Children need parents who have time and energy. Time, in our culture at least, is money. Income splitting, where the wage earned by one parent is split between two and therefore taxed less, is one legislative option that would give parents back time. Paid parental leave needs not just to be paid to 'working' parents but to all families. All of us who work would rather share in a community than simply live in a suburb, and this is what many 'stay at home' mothers are engaged in creating. This endeavour needs to be honoured.

Children need parents who are well supported. One example of this is the fact that mothers need fathers to be involved. The research on postnatal depression suggests that one of the most powerful ways to help a depressed mother is for her partner to pitch in with childcare. Yet the pressure in most workplaces for parents to demonstrate an 'over and above' commitment to the job and to their colleagues socially is prevalent.

Children need parents who are allowed to put them first. Unfortunately, this is not where Australian society is at the moment. We have a list of national living treasures, but it does not begin with our most treasured citizens, our children. We have an environment policy which, despite the special sensitivities of children, barely acknowledges their needs.[82] We still allow the media to use sexualised images of children and young people, despite the harm we know it does. Most people on the coalface of trying to improve services to children, including me, can tell you stories about how jobs and reputations are prioritised above putting programs in place that actually work. There is a culture of dishonesty on this subject in Australia. It is for this reason that Dr Fiona Stanley has recently called for the pay packets of senior bureaucrats to be cut where programs aren't working.[83]

If we want women to breastfeed in order that our children are healthier, then we need to make that possible: paid leave for the first ten months of a child's life, workplaces that commit to supporting a breastfeeding relationship and the banning of all advertising of infant formula and bottles for children up to the age of six. If we want parents to develop a secure and organised attachment with their children then we need to ensure the practical and emotional help is there so that it can happen. At the moment our demands on parents make it very difficult to avoid that 'stop-start', 'on-off' inconsistent parenting that leads straight to an insecure attachment, and from there to a whole host of less desirable behaviours.

Society seems to have accepted that 'empty calories and the wrong kinds of chemicals' are capable of rewriting the expression of a child's genes, but this is seen as the problem of parents, not society. It appears we would rather honour the right of business to market any kind of food ahead of the right of parents and children to find safe food without being required to wade through realms of misinformation.

As a society we have not yet looked straight at the fact that empty hours and the wrong kinds of attachment relationships are also capable of rewriting the expression of a child's genes. Undoubtedly, as Brendin feels, every attempt will be made by society and business to make this the problem of parents; not society and not business. And yet, if we want children whose epigenetic marks are going to allow them to express their 'best possible self', we need a society that makes that possible: parental leave, income splitting, supportive workplaces and more flexible childcare.

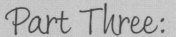

Part Three:

Now add movement

A child's experience of movement will play a pivotal role in shaping his personality, his feelings and achievements.

Sally Goddard Blythe, research pioneer in the development and significance of movement.[1]

Chapter 12

The importance of movement

The sheer ecstasy with which her booted feet came down in each puddle told of the depth of her capacity for happiness.

Elizabeth Goudge, *The Heart of the Family*, 1953.[2]

The thing to remember as you read this part of the book is that as your child moves from not walking to walking, and from there to running and jumping and hopping and skipping, this is not just a physical journey. It is an inward journey as well. The early movement milestones are a journey upward, not just to walking but to the higher parts of your baby's brain.

The better the foundations that are laid now, the stronger will be the brain that grows from these foundations. Your child's right brain — the empathic, pattern-detecting, body-system managing, spatially aware hemisphere — is what is growing in these first three years. At the end of this time the left brain will take over. The message is that we need to make sure children have a strong right brain as they enter their fourth year.

Although not as important as attachment security, movement remains a very important part of growing a strong right brain. This is something increasingly appreciated by therapists, as we have watched Australian babies, toddlers and children move less and less, and then go on to perform correspondingly worse as a group at school. From schools and from society the appreciation of the value of movement for human development seems to have been lost.

The tools for self-regulation — shifting attention, impulse control, empathy, theory of mind, perceptual sensitivity and concentration span — are creations of an integrated body and mind. Both body and mind learn by moving. Movement skills make a huge contribution to perceptual sensitivity, and vice versa. Better movement skills mean that children use ever finer movements, indicating that sensation is more precise. Of course, more precise sensation means that movements can be better controlled. It is an upward spiral of development that continues into adulthood.

Movement skills also contribute to concentration span and the ability to shift attention at will. In the absence of the right movement experiences, children continue to have their movements and their attention dominated by primitive movement patterns. Your child needs to be in charge of his body to also be in charge of his attention and concentration.

Control over our bodies is also a big contributor to the *feeling* of mastery, which is compounded of the bone-deep joy in having a body that does as we want plus the delightful knowledge that we have done something better than we did it yesterday. That feeling of mastery is what gives ballast to a child's esteem, which in turn helps his impulse control. With an anchored sense of self, your child will be better able to suppress his first, emotional impulses.

Attachment and movement skills

The addition of new skills to your baby's repertoire means that a secure, organised attachment will look different as your baby gets older. Where with a very little baby it is you, the parent, who moves to and away from him, in a sensitive reflection of his need of you, with a child who is able to do the moving away and back, it is his movement patterns that tell you how secure and organised that attachment is.

Simply, the toddler with an insecure attachment is less likely to explore properly. The disorganised child does not focus on exploring but on firmly controlling the parent. The secure, organised child moves away from and back to his mother, in ever expanding loops as he grows older and more confident.

'Mum, watch this. Mum, look at this! Mum, I found this. Mum, watch as I go down the slide! Mum, I'm hurt and need to be kissed better … and I'm off once more!'

How moving shapes behaving

And there is another reason for parents to think about movement skills. The journey to movement and self-regulation skills impacts on a child's behaviour. In the 1960s the Gesell Institute researchers systematically tracked just how children feel and behave during the struggle to develop a skill, the time it takes to consolidate that skill and finally to take that skill for granted.[3]

It is a pattern adults can relate to as well. Imagine you are working towards mastering a new set of skills. The greater frustration you are feeling as a result of having not finished climbing that particular mountain spills over into the rest of your life, making it harder to manage your mood and certainly to remember the feelings of others. As a consequence, self-regulation can be harder work at those times. You may find that you've focused more in on yourself as you internalise the new skills and ideas. But once you have mastered the challenge, self-regulation is easier. Now, confident of your new skills, or having reshaped yourself to fit your new ideas, you once more engage with the wider world. (I think this is partly what we go through as a new parent. Subsequent babies are always much easier.)

When your child has suddenly started a new and bewildering behaviour, such as the fake hyena laughing of the four year old or the terrifying complaints that his eyes or ears don't work at three and a half, the Gesell Institute's research is an excellent place to begin looking. This is not to say that you must simply accept the behaviour and allow it to continue, but it can help to discover that lots of children at around your child's age display the same behaviour.

A brief summary of the researchers' findings for age groups up to three years old follows. Bear in mind that the age groups are just an average and your child might hit this period of development earlier or later than average. Do note that the writers have implicitly assumed that baby is securely attached: from the steadying of baby's heart rate in the first four weeks to the way in which their sample children express a full range of emotions. (You will find the rest of Gesell's Ages and Stages in Chapters 18 and 22.)

Birth to one year

In the first four weeks your baby works towards the beginnings of managing his body without the support of the womb. Such things as regular breathing, steadier heart rate, and clearer sleep and wake cycles all appear. He is beginning to respond by deliberately communicating his needs and bracing a little as you pick him up. And he is smiling!

In contrast to the current view that crying peaks at six weeks, these researchers believe that it peaks at around three months. But at four months behaviour smoothes out once more and baby seems to recognise his own hunger signals better, feeds better and settles faster.

At five months he is unsettled again as he works to master passing objects from one hand to the other, keeping his head up while he is on his tummy, and rolling. Usually, by seven months he has overcome this new set of frustrations. In the afterglow of these achievements he is delightful company, beaming upon family and strangers alike. At eight months he has become determined to crawl but cannot, and he is unsettled once more. And so it goes on until he reaches one year, which is usually, the researchers say, a serene and delightful time, marked by a child who is crawling and possibly walking and feeling very pleased to be 'locomoting'. Your child might be walking at one year, but it could have been two months earlier or eight months later: the sunny patch will arrive accordingly.

One to two years

As your baby gets older the pattern of struggle crowned with success has stretched out. As well as being able to move, your child can speak a few words, knows and helps in all his routines, and can understand a breathtaking amount of what is said to him. It is often a harmonious time, until your toddler is about 15 months old.

Suddenly he is no longer so interested in helping Mummy. He is no longer so responsive to your gentle 'no'. He longs to conquer the world with his ever-growing skill-set — to touch, finger, throw, grab, stuff and dump — regardless of what Mummy forbids. Your serene baby will vanish, to reappear again at about 17 months, but only briefly. Eighteen months is when your baby learns to say 'no'.

And not just to say it, but to express 'no' too, by doing precisely the opposite of what you have asked. This is the age at which temper tantrums begin as well. At this point a temper tantrum is not about 'controlling Mum', it is simply about the frustration of not being able to convey the wonderful ideas he has to the people who can make them happen.

At 21 months children become a great deal more discriminating: 'fussy' is the word commonly used by parents. They are far more sensitive to smell, texture and taste, and this shows itself in the choices they start making about clothes, food and routines. This heightened awareness is not yet matched by the communication skills needed to say just what detail Mummy and Daddy have failed to produce. So there are more tantrums!

Two to three years

At two years of age communication skills are a lot better. Speech pathologists like to see 'two word sentences' by this age, and with these telegrammatic utterances your baby can convey a great deal. (See more on speech norms in Chapter 15.) Movement skills have come together too: and this age is characterised by an acceptance of limits of all kinds. The ability to 'put a moment' between the impulse and the action is on its way. Your baby still cannot be reasonably asked to share, but he can find toys for other children. The 'empathic' part of self-regulation appears in kindly actions taken towards others.

But at two and a half the story is very different. This is an age at which frustration peaks. The limits that were accepted by the two year old are challenged at two and a half. He starts by wresting the control for smoothing his moods from you. For two years you have sweetened, soothed and softened his moods, but now, if he wants to feel cranky then he jolly well will. There is little he will let you do about it.

His empire of domination expands at the same time as attempting to control you. And let's face it, we'd all find it a lot easier to manage our moods if the world did just as we wanted. This has never been put better than by A. A. Milne in his poem 'Disobedience', where it is the parent who has not obeyed the child: "'Mother", he said, said he, "you must never go down to the end of the town if you don't go down with me!"'[4]

The two and a half year old attempts to enforce rules about how food is to be offered, in what order the stories are to be told, and even just what facial expressions are allowed: 'Don't smile at me', 'I don't like you singing'. The best strategy is to direct his drive for mastery into acceptable routes, such as housework, puzzles and independent skills.

But perhaps the most difficult to live with of all is the rapid changes of mind that afflicts two and a half year olds. They want it desperately, then they don't want it at all, and then they want it desperately again. It's the beginning of decision making: the beginning of thinking through to the different consequences of different choices.

Putting this cycle of struggle, skill consolidation and success into emotional language helps us see every bit of development as important in appreciating how our child feels. Like attachment theory, it is a useful tool to strengthen our empathic skills, and the stronger our empathy, the better we become at helping our child through this cycle. Of course, knowing the nuts and bolts of movement development is also important: this is the focus in the following chapters.

The gatekeeper

There was only one mention of movement skills in Part Two of the book but it was a highly significant one: 'And, because the startle reflex operates partly through the muscles of the neck, jerking baby's head backwards, as it disappears your baby is able to begin working on the massive project of controlling her head.' The startle reflex is present at birth in all babies. It is the one that causes your baby to seem to leap out of her skin with fright, scream, and then cling desperately to you, needing unstinting reassurance that all is well, that you are there and she is safe. It should be gone by the time she is four months old.

Controlling her head so she can look where she wants to is the very first of the steps your baby takes on her journey to moving independently. And the integration of the startle reflex is just as important in the development of good movement skills as it is for eye movements and the ability to attend. It is for this reason that some researchers have suggested that it is the 'gatekeeper reflex'.[5] Where it remains active in its primitive form it bars the way to further development, not just for attention and eye movement skills and a strong immune system, as discussed in Chapter 7, but also for the development of the movement skills that underlie formal learning.

How does this happen?

As you will have noticed, your baby's startle (or Moro) reflex can be triggered by an unexpected sight, touch, sound or movement; it is most notably triggered by a rapid backwards drop of the head. If a baby is not soothed and reassured and taught that she is safe, her neck receptors continue to be linked to the startle reflex. If this link continues, those neck receptors will not be able to be trained to detect finer gradations in movement, particularly movement where the head tips backwards, because that will set off a startle response. As the neck receptors play an important role in the development of physical skills, an active startle reflex interferes directly with your baby's ability to make her body do as she wishes.

Just as we make distinctions between mind and body, so we think of the physical and emotional continuums as separate. They are not. It is only on the cusp between the first and second years of life that the emotional and movement circuits in the brain become disentangled from each other.[7] So before birth and in that first year there is a critical intersection between the two: the ability to self-regulate and the integration of the primitive startle reflex.

More on the children of the Murchison

In Chapter 7 I discussed the children we see in the Murchison of Western Australia who have kept their their primitive startle response well past four months of age. You'll note that above this text box I've said that body movements are affected by an active startle reflex. So do these children also show problems with movements in addition to attention and learning skills? They do.

And this is a finding that has been made in many different places where children live under great stress. Therapists and researchers living in war-torn countries or working in the more dysfunctional and impoverished communities in countries like America have often found that social disadvantage correlates with poor motor skills. For example, in 2007 Irish psychologist Martin McPhillips released a study showing that social disadvantage puts children at risk of neuro-developmental delay, including delayed motor skills.[6] These gaps in movement skills make learning difficult — you need good movement skills to learn letter and number shapes, for example.

When we introduced a program in 2001 to address these skill deficits it only worked to a degree. Murchison teachers began recording a 'year's growth in a year' for some children on educational tests: but this was not sufficient for the majority of these children to catch up with the rest of Australia. Children on a therapy program usually catch-up 'multiple months for every calendar month'. (The appendices contain all the knowledge we share with teachers and parents so you can develop your own programs for your child if required.) Why was that rapid catch-up not happening for these children?

The answer was a simple one. The active startle reflex was acting as a gatekeeper and blocking further development. So our program made very little difference for the 40 to 50 per cent of children from the most dysfunctional homes who still needed to be able to 'startle' for survival. Some children made gains, and the class as a whole was a little calmer, but we weren't helping the children who most needed help. These children needed to feel safe, and for this to happen we needed a program that helped parents help children to feel safe — one of the roles of the Bidi Bidi project.

Both continuums grow out of the quality of the relationships children have with the adults in their lives. For children to get a good start along both the emotional and movement continuums they need to feel safe. They need warm, responsive, predictable care: the kind of care provided by an adult who is described as 'free' or 'autonomous' in Part One (see page 10).

The point of primitive reflexes

My friend Emma phoned me last night to ask about reflexes. She is taking her little girl — who is doing everything a 14 month old should but with the absence of crawling — to the physiotherapist. Having played with little Pearl the physiotherapist told Emma that Pearl hasn't yet developed a reflex she needs for crawling, and gave her some exercises. So Emma is doing the exercises, but, being Emma, she wanted to understand a great deal more about what reflexes were and what the point of them was in the first place. We have discussed the startle or Moro reflex fairly extensively — it is the only primitive movement pattern linked also to an emotional response and consequent hormone release — but there are others that simply cause our bodies to involuntarily carry out a movement.

Newborns, as most baby books will tell you, are a 'bundle of primitive reflexes'. Where this book is going to diverge from the standard baby book is that while those books say the reflexes disappear in the early months of life, I say that they only disappear or integrate in the early months of life *under the right circumstances.* And to that I add, if reflexes continue to be active past that time they block the emergence of the adult reflexes, like the one little Pearl needs for crawling, and go on to disrupt normal development in ways beyond movement.

Pearl hasn't yet developed her 'amphibian' reflex. This adult reflex causes our knee to bend as soon as our hip bends. If you stand up and bend your hip as though you are about to take a step, you'll note that your knee automatically bends. You can keep it straight if you want but the automatic response is the reflex in action.

There are heaps of adult reflexes. A sneeze is a reflex! In our child development workshops for teachers and parents, Mum and I always ask people to stand up, wrap their hands around their neck with their fingers reaching around to their spine and then lean from the waist from side to side. If you do this you will feel little 'flickers' of muscle activity that are reflexive in nature — an adult reflex which keeps adjusting your head position relative to your body position. It means that you can keep your eye on a particular visual target while your body is in motion. This reflex is vital for success in sport, among other things.

So what is the point of primitive reflexes and why are our babies not born with the adult reflexes ready to go? The primitive reflexes have a number of roles in early development. The first is survival. In addition to the 'alarm' of the startle reflex there are reflexes which assist a child in the passage through the birth canal, in paddling up the body to the breast at birth, in finding the breast and in sucking.

Beyond survival, though, the reflexes also link movement and sensation tightly together, paving the way for perceptual sensitivity and precise movement later. As each reflex is repeated over and over and over again, baby eventually grows enough neural or brain connections to 'take over' the movement herself. This is 'integrating' the reflex: making it an integral part of her body movements rather than an automatically executed movement pattern. When one reflex is 'integrated' and the movement pattern is performed by the baby, another 'automatic' pattern emerges to take the baby to the next stage of development. This in turn is integrated and the baby is led, step by step, into the higher regions of her brain. Eventually, all that remains are the automated movement patterns that are useful in the long term: the amphibian reflex and its kin.

The successive appearance and integration of the reflexes is also the journey to each of the movement milestones: rolling, crawling, sitting, grasping and walking. We tend to obsess as a society over 'when' a child has reached a milestone when what we should care about is 'if' a child has taken a particular journey. So the achievement of crawling is important because it demonstrates that a child has integrated a set of the primitive reflexes and developed adult ones. And that in turn is important because it puts a child on track for her 'best possible self': with a body that is hers to command, rather than one still dominated by the forces of primitive reflex patterns.[8]

In the following chapters each journey will be traced out, along with ideas to help your child move through each primitive reflex and develop each of the adult reflexes.

Helping your baby to integrate her startle reflex

As well as always reassuring your baby when she does startle, being consistent and warm and responsive so she knows she is safe, there are other things that will help your baby integrate this reflex.

Exploit the hand-neck feedback loop
There is an ingenious feedback loop between the neck muscles and the Palmar reflex, the one responsible for newborns grabbing and holding tightly any object placed in their palm. Any pressure to the palm in babies activates the neck muscles, simultaneously increasing their strength and sensitivity. Remember that a common trigger for the startle reflex is the baby's head falling backwards. Pressure to the palms

activates the neck muscles, and as the neck muscles are activated they send back information saying 'hey, we can handle this'. This feeling of safety and competence is the natural counter to a startle reflex.

All the games that parents have played with their babies for countless generations — like 'Round and round the garden', 'Can you keep a secret' and 'Pat-a-cake pat-a-cake' — which are played while rubbing a finger around baby's palm or clapping her hands together, actually 'switch off' the startle reflex by growing neck muscle sensitivity and strength. We never quite lose this link, I believe. Just consider the way we 'wring our hands' when we are anxious, and the reassurance some people receive from squeezing a rubber stress ball.

Another great game is pull-to-sit, where parents encourage baby to grasp the parent's thumb and wrap their own fingers around her wrists and pull her up into a sitting position, and then lean baby back as far as possible and sing something like, 'London Bridge is falling down, falling down, falling down, build it up'. This game directly uses this hand–neck feedback loop. Start playing it with baby lying down, very gently, from about one month of age.

The hand-foot-mouth link

Intersecting with the link between hands and neck is the link between hands, feet and mouth. You might have noticed that, just like lambs wriggling their tails, babies wriggle their fingers and toes as they feed. This is another reflexive feedback loop (hand-foot-mouth) that has all sorts of benefits for little babies — and all sorts of disadvantages for older children if it is kept longer than necessary.

So any game you play involving your baby's mouth or hands or feet will contribute to the development of sensitivity and strength in those other, linked, parts of the body. Foot games like 'This little piggy' also help hands and mouth, and therefore neck muscle sensitivity. Sucking on a breast, which is much harder work than sucking on a bottle, helps develop fine motor precision. Finger play games like those described above also improve facial sensitivity, so the benefits of these games have a domino effect.

The benefits of massage

Babies love massage! The relevance to integrating the startle reflex is that the release of oxytocin during massage counters the stress hormones, and the less stressed your baby, the less likely the startle is to fire. Infant massage courses are not so much about teaching different massage techniques, but about teaching parents how to read their baby's cues. The emphasis is on following your child's lead rather than imposing a set pattern of touch upon her.

Kissing

The startle reflex is triggered partly by a sudden movement near the head. By kissing your baby on her forehead she learns that such movements are safe. Kissing her on her little palms is also recommended.

Chapter 13

Learning to roll and grasp

'In the bliss of perfect health he is striking out with his little arms and kicking about with his chubby feet. Your instinct tells you that he is seeking an object against which he may measure his strength, and by measuring increase and enjoy it. To the need indicated by his lively movements your motherly love promptly responds, and you hold your hands so that the little feet may alternately strike against them.'

Friedrich Froebel, *Mother Play*, 1895.[9]

Even though rolling is one of the first things your baby learns to do, it comes at the end of a long learning journey. Along the way to rolling your baby:

- straightens out of his lovely newborn curled-up posture
- learns to resist gravity
- develops sensitivity in his neck muscle receptors
- integrates primitive reflexes and develops adult reflexes
- discovers that he can move his whole body where he wants to go.

Straightening out

That 'newborn curl' reflects the fact that it is the flexor or 'curling-up' muscles that are strongest at birth. In other words, there isn't an equal balance between the muscles on the front and the back of baby's body — the muscles on the front are much stronger.

So how does a baby 'straighten out'? Not by you helping him — you'll find that to comfort your newborn you 'curl him up' again.

The straightening role is actually taken by one of the primitive neck reflexes, in this case it is the tonic labyrinthine reflex. And yes, all the names of the reflexes are just as discouraging but if we unpack each word the meaning becomes relatively clear. 'Tonic' means that it alters the tone of muscles by tightening them up or loosening them. 'Labyrinthine' means that it is the labyrinths of the ear that are the sensors involved here, in this case detecting a changed head position. In fact, in response to a changed head position, either when it is bent forward or backwards, your baby's body is swept by a wave of muscle contraction that changes muscle tone throughout.

If your baby's head tips forward then the muscles on the front of his body tighten and he curls up. If your baby's head tips backwards then the muscles on the back of his body tighten and he straightens out.

I first noticed this reflex in action when Tim was two weeks old. He had discovered that by tipping his head forward and backwards he could flip fish-like across the bed, and I would find him reattached to the breast shortly after I'd placed him some distance away. You might like to try it: head back, straighten out — head forwards, curl up — head back, straighten out. When you are lying on your side it does allow some movement.

Over time your baby loses that lovely curled-up posture because the muscle tone on the back of his body is now sufficient to balance that on the front.

Resisting gravity
Gravity in the womb is greatly softened. There's enough of an effect to train the labyrinths of the ears to respond to up and down, but that is about all. So when your baby comes out of the womb, your loving arms will be what cushion him from gravity early on. He experiences anti-gravity movement first of all by being carried around by you, feeling your body shift against his as you move. This is a multi-sensory treat for your baby: touch sensation and movement sensation while his balance sense absorbs the feeling of resisting gravity, accompanied by lovely mummy smell, comforting body warmth, quick visual shifts and the string of interesting sounds in his favourite voice in the whole world; alerting, comforting and teaching him.

Setting the scene for good movement skills

I remember being stunned when a friend procured the Choice list of the best baby equipment and systematically proceeded to ensure she had every item: the best pram, the best backpack carrier, the best cot, the best rocker. While something may be regarded as the best of its kind, it doesn't mean that you need to have it. Indeed, for good movement skills, less stuff is better.

To grow good movement skills your baby needs to spend time on his tummy on a flat surface and on his back, and he needs to have you there with him to make it fun. He also needs to be carried as much as possible, so a sling where he is cradled against your chest and turned in towards your face is useful.

Such things as prams and baby carriers, like the plastic slot-in-and-out of the car seat things, rob a baby of some of these important movement experiences. Apart from missing the warmth and smell sensations that create the feeling of safety in which a baby learns best, in a carrier he can't learn from the steady repositioning of your body about how you move against gravity. Nor can he hear your heartbeat changing, or yoke together his eyes by watching your face as he is carried in your arms.

Rolling is led by the head so, as well as a sign that your baby is engaging with the world, head turning is a very important step on the pathway to rolling. Babies don't turn their heads initially to roll or even to look, but to find the nipple. This is another of the primitive reflexes in action — the rooting reflex. Simply, baby responds to a touch on the cheek by turning his head in search of the nipple. As he grows, a touch to the cheek also encourages a baby to open his mouth in a smile. (A surprising number of politicians know this.) Of course, in turning his head your baby will be moving *against gravity*.

So baby is straightening out. He's turning his head but he also needs his neck muscles to be quite a lot stronger and working together more cooperatively to convert a head turn into a roll. How does this happen?

There are three compounding processes happening here. The first is simply a conditioning process: baby fights gravity and in doing so he gets stronger. A lovely game to play to help this process along is 'flying' baby through the air and this is a good game from around two months old. 'Up, down, flying around': babies who are flown through the air will arch their little backs and lift their heads, defying gravity just as bravely as the marvellous men in their flying machines. This activity also inhibits the tonic labyrinthine reflex, allowing your baby to develop more advanced movement patterns.

Second, your baby is developing an adult reflex, and it should be in place by four months of age. It was the one I had you feel on yourself in the last chapter when wrapping your hands around your neck, thumbs to the front, and leaning from the waist. This is the oculo-headrighting reflex in action. This reflex lets you fix on and follow a ball in flight, it lets you fix on a line of text and follow it to the end, and it is something you definitely want your baby to develop.

Third, your baby's neck receptors are becoming increasingly sensitive as the startle reflex integrates.

Neck muscle receptor sensitivity

The neck muscles have more nerve receptors than any other muscles in the body. One researcher conducted a very simple experiment to see just how important the information provided by these nerves is. He anaesthetised one side of a man's neck and watched what happened. The man toppled over on the opposite side of his body and couldn't right himself.[10] As you might imagine, the more sensitive the neck receptors are, the better coordinated our whole body movements will be. So how do you increase the sensitivity and accuracy of the nerves in your child's neck?

Give him opportunities for movement by carrying him in your arms or a sling, lying him on his back and tummy, and lying down and putting him on your tummy. In this way he will be able to curl and uncurl his body (the tonic labyrinthine reflex in action) and in doing so link movement to sensation. As your baby experiences over and over the feeling of head going forward and body curling up, head going backwards and body straightening out, he links the balance information from his neck to the positional information coming in from the labyrinths of his ears.

Tummy time

Every parent is told that tummy time is important, but many babies absolutely loathe being placed on their tummies. Before the connection between stomach sleeping and SIDS was made, most babies slept on their stomachs. And all that sleeping on the stomach must have conditioned them to the sensation, because Mum tells me that the large numbers of babies who hate being placed on their 'tummy for play' is a very recent phenomenon.

This is not to suggest that you sleep your baby on his stomach. The incidence of cot death has dropped by more than 50 per cent since the 'back for sleep, tummy for play' recommendations were made.

Instead, slowly build up the time your baby spends on his tummy, starting on the very first day of his life. Every day he will lift his head higher, building up his anti-gravity muscles and the sensitivity in the nerves of his neck.

If lying down on the floor on your tummy with him is painful for you, lie him on a table on his tummy and talk to him. Or lie him on your tummy. If you are constructed to allow it, breastfeed your baby with him lying on your tummy and 'sucking uphill'. Roll a towel into a crescent shape and place it under his chest, and put something interesting for him to look at that he'll be able to see if he lifts his head.

Basically, remember that tummy time means that he is on his tummy. It does not mean that he is left lying on the floor by himself, on his tummy. Come up with ways to make it enjoyable for both of you.

So your baby has developed the sensitive strong neck muscles that are required to get up the velocity to roll, but this is still not everything. We need to look more closely at the reflexes that are involved.

Reflexes and rolling

We've already met several of the primitive reflexes that are part of this journey: the rooting, palmar and tonic labyrinthine reflexes, and one of the mature reflexes, the oculo–headrighting reflex. Just two more reflexes for you to meet: one primitive and one mature.

Have you noticed how when a very new baby is lying on their side and their head is turned that their whole body follows in a 'log roll'? This lasts until baby is around six months old, at which point you can help your baby roll by simply pushing one leg to the front of her body when she is lying on her side. Straightaway, she rolls.

This is, of course, yet more reflexive behaviour. Both of these early rolling behaviours are called 'reactions' and lead straight to the development of a reflex called the 'segmental rolling reflex', which develops at around six months of age and should remain active throughout life. This reflex simply ensures that the body smoothly follows the lead given by the head or the feet. Once the shoulders or hips become involved, the rest of the body just flows in the right direction. The occasional adult you see with 'blocky' movements as they dance or run has not properly developed this reflex. It gives grace to our dancers and fluidity to our athletes: lots of rolling in childhood is vital to grace in adulthood.

Strong neck muscles, a body that he can uncurl at will, a developed segmental rolling reflex, the desire to turn over fed by lots of rolling play … and there is one more thing required for baby to be able to roll when he feels like it. He needs to have integrated another of the reflexes: the asymmetrical tonic neck reflex or ATNR.

This reflex makes the sides of the body *asymmetric*: shortening the muscles on one side of the body and lengthening them on the other. When baby turns his head to the side it activates the reflex. On the 'face side' the muscles lengthen, leading to the straightening out of the arm and leg. On the 'back of head side', the arm and leg bend.

A 'funny roll' is a warning sign

The ability to roll or not roll is a strong indicator of a baby's development. Research indicating that a baby who rolls late and who rolls 'despite' a still active asymmetrical tonic neck reflex (by arching his back and flipping in the opposite direction to the way he is looking) is at risk for a number of disorders, including autism.[11] If you see that 'flip in the opposite direction' roll, remember that it may well be a very early marker for later difficulties, so consider taking your baby to a paediatrician.

So what will happen if baby tries to roll with an active asymmetrical tonic neck reflex? As baby turns his head his hand will shoot out straight in front of him, becoming a barrier to rolling in that direction. So this reflex must be integrated for the baby to roll successfully. When it is gone, baby can turn his head, twist his shoulders and, by George! He's rolled.

Learning to grasp

When Tim was born I did everything I could to get him to grasp. I encouraged him to grab my hair, spectacles and nose. I wasn't so reckless with Sam. I had learned by then that a baby can grasp and hold long before he can voluntarily release!

Learning to grasp requires baby to see, to want, to judge how far away the object is, to reach and to open the fingers at the right moment and close them at the right moment and finally to let go. It sounds complicated, and it is even more complicated than it sounds. As well as being the journey to grasp it also:

- integrates primitive reflexes
- links balance and vision
- expands the journey to understanding
- builds eye-muscle skills
- is a critical step in your baby connecting to the world.

When teaching a sporting technique often the teacher will take the pupil's arm and move it for her. In this way she 'knows it from the inside'. The primitive reflexes perform this teaching also. The first 'feel' of grasp is provided by the Palmar reflex.

You see this reflex in action when you touch a newborn's palm with your finger: her tiny fingers will close tightly around your finger. You will notice that her thumb, which is so critical for the grasp later on, barely participates in this early grasp. From the first day baby enjoys the gentlest of tug of wars, pitting her tiny strength against yours. To release your finger you can gently stroke the back of her hand, and her grip will loosen (this does not always work, however).

What helps the Palmar reflex integrate into your baby's growing brain? It is the same movements that activate the neck muscle receptors: round and round the garden and pull-to-sit.

Baby first of all grasps reflexively, and then slowly begins to grasp deliberately by around three months of age. Being able to 'release' when she wants to comes a little later, and most babies will resort to the trick of flicking their hand backwards to pull open their fingers to drop an object. Once they've 'got the feel' of release, they can make the movement voluntary.

Why you should avoid 'prop-feeding' but consider using a dummy

The Palmar reflex is also integrated through the hand-foot-mouth link. Babies have a 'suck' reflex at birth that teaches them how to suck, and the reflex is integrated by lots and lots of sucking. But all that sucking doesn't just integrate the suck reflex. Because of that hand-foot-mouth link, sucking also assists in making grasp voluntary rather than reflexive. The work of sucking improves strength and voluntary control of the muscles of the head and neck, and also of muscles in the hand.

Babies who are breastfed are at an advantage here because breastfeeding is harder work, but care and attention to how baby is bottle-fed does help. At all costs, avoid 'prop-feeding': when the milk simply runs out of a teat a baby barely has to suck. Mum and I, among other therapists, frequently find that babies who are 'prop-fed' by bottle become children with both a sucking reflex and Palmar reflex. These children are characterised in schoolrooms by 'sucking' on their hair, or clothes or a pencil, poor fine motor skills and unclear speech.

But this is just one sort of child who needs to suck well past infancy. In my experience there are actually two sorts.

Whereas the first group, who didn't have enough sucking in infancy, keep both the Palmar and sucking reflexes, the second group did have sufficient sucking. What sets them apart is a very high level of interest in fine motor tasks. This places constant pressure on their fine motor skills, which they then ratchet up to more and more precision by activating the hand-mouth feedback loop, which is called the Babkin response. So, like the artist who purses his mouth (the beginning of a sucking movement) when adding a very fine final touch with his brush, these children increase sensitivity and precision of their hands through that hand-mouth loop.

The first group of children need extra assistance in all fine motor tasks, and my recommendation is to let them suck as it will help them develop fine motor precision. The second group of children will only be sucking when they are challenging themselves in more difficult fine motor tasks.

If your child fits into either group of children, and if you've chosen to give her a dummy which she is now using past a 'socially acceptable' age, think very carefully before weaning her off her dummy. You don't have to keep the dummy available in public, but why not continue to allow her private use?

Linking balance and vision and making sense of what baby sees

At the same time as baby is learning to grasp and release, she is learning to rely more and more on her vision. The development of vision is far more complex than we might think. To begin with, it needs to be linked to other sensory information to be really useful. Imagine that you can see a dog. It doesn't look friendly. How big is it? This is critical information: a very small unfriendly dog is not the same degree of threat as a very large unfriendly dog. So how do you judge its size?

The tonic labyrinthine reflex, where if a newborn nods her head forward her whole body curls up and if she tips her head back it straightens out, also trains the baby's vision. Both parts of this reflex work together to fine-tune the baby's sight to her balance. The baby begins to link what up and down *look* like with what up and down *feel* like. In other words, the activity of this reflex joins together the existing internal balance information with the brand new visual external information. It also links positional information coming in from the neck muscle receptors with the balance information coming in from the ears.

Baby is learning to recognise that her head has moved partly due to changes in her neck muscles and partly because of the change to what she sees. Balance becomes the foundation for vision, and shortly afterwards, vision begins to affect balance. This feedback loop becomes the basis for decoding visual information: we know how big the growling dog is because we know where the dog is in relation to us. It also becomes the basis for eye movement: we know how much to move our eyes because we know where we are in relation to the place we want to look. This is the beginning of depth perception. Of course, this skill will become a lot more refined when baby is able to crawl and find out how 'deep' a space is for herself.

But for the time being, through the early action of the tonic labyrinthine reflex, baby is able to begin linking together what she can see with how far away something is. And now another reflex comes into play: the asymmetric tonic neck reflex. This is the one that stops a child rolling and we very briefly mentioned it in the previous chapter. This reflex is also the one, however, that trains in the link between hand and eyes.

Linking hands and eyes and ears
If we unpack the name, 'asymmetrical' tells us that the two sides of the body take up different positions. 'Tonic' tells us it works by altering the tone in muscles, and 'neck' tells us that it is triggered by head movement. In fact, when your baby turns her head to the side this reflex causes the muscles throughout her body to respond. The muscles on the side of the body the baby is looking toward lengthen, causing the arm and leg on that side to straighten. On the other side of the body the muscles shorten and contract, pulling the arm and leg into a bent position.

This reflex has a number of critical roles. It helps baby wriggle down the birth canal and it ensures a good supply of air, moving the potential hazard of the baby's own hand away from mouth and nose. There is also good evidence that it helps baby turn her head to help her breathe if she's face down on a soft surface. And, as mentioned, it is crucial in the development of both vision and grasp.

The reflex gives the baby something to look at: her own hand, at just the right distance for baby to see. This is the beginning of intentional reach and grasp and, of course, of hand-eye coordination. And often it is a sound that has caused baby to turn her head, so this reflex also links the ability of the baby to look and touch in response to sound, 'tuning' those senses to each other. To begin with, of course, they need to be linked, but being tethered together permanently is very limiting. For one thing, it will stop her being able to close her hand around the object she is looking at. For another, it will stop her being able to look at an object held in the hand at the end of a bent arm, such as a pencil, and block the development of attention and concentration skills. (More on this later, in Chapter 16.)

The importance of 'back' time

Your baby needs to spend hours 'playing' with her asymmetrical tonic neck reflex to lose it. And to do this she needs to spend some awake time lying on her back. If you have a colicky baby, don't put her on a flat surface, but in a 'bouncinette' or on a wedge cushion. Not, perhaps, as a newborn (though mine had tummy and back time from day one), but certainly once she is a month old. This is not something babies can do in a 'sit-up' pram, so try to limit the use of the pram to sleeping only.

This reflex should be gone by the time a baby is six months old, but occupational therapists frequently find it in older children who haven't had enough floor time as babies, where it wreaks great destruction on their attention and fine-motor skills.

What do I mean by playing with the reflex? I mean that a baby will deliberately attempt movements that the reflex prevents. She'll go to the very limits of what she can do, and just keep stretching that envelope. Bear in mind that what this reflex does is cause a change in the arm and leg position based on the head position. So what your baby does is set up a confrontation between the action of the reflex and what she wants to happen.

For example, she'll lie on her back with her head in 'middle position', turned neither to the right nor left. Her attention is fixed on an outstretched hand that she turns into a fist and steadily brings down towards her face. Making a fist is significant as the action of the reflex is to open it up. Then her head turns a little and she loses control of the fist. Depending on the direction in which she turns her head, it will shoot off into space or hit her face above the eye.

She'll start bringing her hands together and keeping them there, despite turning her head from side to side. She'll grab her foot and watch it as she passes it from hand to hand. She'll pass a rattle from hand to hand. She loves clapping games (bringing both hands together) and 'boo' games where Mum suddenly pops up in a new place, taking her focus away from her outstretched hand.

Back time also builds visual skills

She is not just integrating this reflex and practising reach, but working towards adult visual skills. Watching her hand is teaching her to 'converge' (focus both eyes on a single near point, which is vital for reading) and 'accommodate' (switch focus between near and far) and generally yoking both eyes together to allow 'binocular vision'. Binocular vision means that the brain takes the slightly different images from each eye and uses them to judge distance and movement and speed. She needs that information to be able to grasp an object.

Soon, playing with the ATNR and reaching to grasp are indistinguishable from one another. At four to five months babies become dedicated graspers, or maybe 'grabbers' is a better word. Hair, noses, glasses, chest hair, nipples; and the more parents yell 'Ow!' the more dedicated they become. The more she can look at what she is grabbing, and watch it go into her mouth to 'taste', the more confident you can become that she has integrated her asymmetric tonic neck reflex. Being able to roll, of course, is another sign that it has been integrated.

Finally, all that time lying on the back and grabbing things integrates another reflex called the spinal galant, which should be gone *by the time baby is nine months old. If you have a baby you might like to experiment and see if it still there. When baby is lying on her tummy, stroke down her back near her spine on one side. Does she arch her back away to that side? If she does, the spinal galant is still active. More time playing on her back and kicking her legs is required: it will make a big difference down the track for such things as walking, sitting still in class and toilet training.*

It is such an emotional moment when our newborn grasps our finger. The thing to remember is that this is a much more emotional moment for us than it is for our baby. For her, that grasp is a reflexive response. Just a few months (three to six) later, your baby hears your voice, turns her head to look, and reaches out a hand to grasp yours. When that happens your baby is saying, 'I know you are here with me and that I am here with you and we are together'. This moment is a shared one.

Chapter 14

Sitting, crawling and walking

Pat a cake pat a cake baker's man
Bake me a cake as fast as you can
Pat it and prick it and mark it with B
And put it in the oven for Baby and me.

A traditional nursery rhyme that comes into its own in these months.

From very early in his life you will have been sitting your baby on your knee. As he's sat there he's felt your body shift subtly to maintain sitting balance and to lean forward and back and he's gained a good 'feel' for sitting, like the golfer holding the stick while the coach swings it. You might have propped him up in corners with pillows. And, of course, he's probably sat in prams and car seats, but hopefully not for more than an hour a day while awake.

The journey to independent sitting
Independent sitting is a bit different. In developing the balance required for the job your baby is also:
- training near and far vision
- starting on the important project of developing hand dominance
- integrating primitive reflexes and developing adult reflexes (how *did* you guess?)
- achieving that very desirable state of having *both hands* free to play.

Reflexes and sitting

As you sit your baby up on your knee, with a hand around his tummy and his head and neck prevented from dropping backwards by your body or a cradling hand, you'll notice that his head drops forward. If your hand is touching his tummy muscles at that time you'll feel a flicker of activity: his head has dropped forward and his whole body curls forward to match. We tend to say 'weak neck muscles', and although the muscles are indeed still learning to cope with gravity, part of the problem is that the tonic labyrinthine reflex is still active. As soon as his head drops past a certain point the tonic labyrinthine forward reflex is tripped. At about four months of age, if your baby has been carried a lot and spent time on his tummy and back, the forwards part of that reflex will integrate.

The 'backwards' half of the reflex, however, is still active, and this will prevent your baby being able to sit independently until it is integrated. Right now he can put out a hand to stop himself falling forwards in an adult equilibrium reaction. He can tilt his head back to compensate for his body moving forwards, which is an adult head-righting reflex. But the key word in these sentences is 'forwards'. Your baby can't yet stop himself 'straightening out' when his head tips backwards.

So a four-month-old baby, propped up with cushions or pillows or in a doughnut (an inflated ring inside which your baby sits), will play until his head tips backwards. At this point his arms, legs and trunk straighten and he 'slides' out of sitting, onto the floor. The tonic labyrinthine *backwards* is still active. It needs to be 'turned off' if he is going to sit — with it on he won't be able to develop that 'bend at the hips' he needs for sitting, or for crawling.

This is a tricky reflex to shift — in fact, baby must turn it off in sitting, then cruising (when baby walks by holding onto pieces of furniture) and finally in walking. It is not really gone until baby has been walking for a couple of years. The children who 'trip over' their own feet are frequently babies who didn't spend enough time rolling and crawling to fully transform the tonic labyrinthine backwards. (See Appendix III for details of how this can happen.)

So what does finally 'shift' the tonic labyrinthine reflex backwards? Another reflex. A 'transitional' reflex emerges from the brain to create a new opposing movement pattern that cancels it out. So just as the backwards half of the tonic labyrinthine cancels out the forwards half, the symmetrical tonic neck reflex neutralises the tonic labyrinthine backwards.

'Symmetrical' in this case means that both arms and both legs are affected in the same way by this reflex. 'Tonic' means that the reflex will change muscle tone, causing muscles to contract or lengthen. 'Neck' means that neck movement, by altering head position, will be the trigger for this reflex. The nerve receptors in the neck muscles are by now exquisitely sensitive to head movement. And, like the tonic labyrinthine, the symmetrical tonic neck reflex is triggered by the head going forwards or backwards — it is a reflex in two halves.

You see the reflex most clearly when babies are on their tummies and getting up onto all fours. When they look down, you'll notice their bottom rises into the air as their legs have straightened and their arms bent: it is a head down, bottom up position. When they look up you'll notice that their arms straighten and their legs bend: head up, bottom down. Baby has experienced a 'bend at the hips' before because you have arranged and held him in a seated position on your lap or in a pram, but this is the first time he is able to experience *himself* causing a bend at the hips.

Near and far

This reflex also continues the work of training your baby's vision. How? As your baby, lying propped on his tummy, lifts his head to look up at you, his arms will straighten and his legs bend. And when he looks down, his arms bend and his legs straighten. His little back 'seesaws' up and down with the movement, and he is forced to look from near to far, over and over again. This is training your baby to develop close-up vision quickly followed by far-away vision followed by a close-up yet again. So when your baby is a teenager on the basketball court and the ball comes whizzing through the air from the far end, he will be able to watch it into his hands with ease.

Finally, this reflex represents a huge advance in your baby's war against gravity: he's up off the floor for the first time. The symmetrical tonic neck reflex allows your baby to push his body up from the floor with his arms and also bend his legs and sit on his bottom.

By the time he can do this he has already had enough practice sitting supported on your knee or by cushions to have learned how to shift his weight to stay upright. He probably puts out a hand to save himself from falling forward because although he has integrated the tonic labyrinthine reflexes he is still top-heavy and at risk of falling. He possibly also puts a hand to the side and pushes himself back up when that heavy head leans too far that way.

All those things can be learned while sitting supported. Only when he's not supported can he learn the last skill of all: how not to fall over backwards in sitting.

Building sitting balance

Avoiding falling over backwards is what therapists call 'intrinsically motivating'. No-one likes falling over backwards, particularly when it involves a banged head, so your baby will be working hard to stop it happening. But if you watch your baby you will notice that he is still not too scared to experiment.

You will see him deliberately nodding his head up and down and shifting his centre of gravity in reaction to his nodding head. In fact, from about four months you will find your baby loves games where you rock him in sitting, encouraging him to put a hand out to stop him going too far. And if you tell the story as you go along (what speech pathologists call being a 'sportscaster parent') he'll love it even more. 'And Baby is leaning to the left, he's leaning to the right. Has he gone too far? No, no, he's put out a hand and, clever boy, he's on his way back up again!'

As your baby builds up these adult balance reactions, which will be automatic by the end of the first year, he is also reining in the symmetrical tonic reflex. A lack of reliable balance reactions in children indicates that a reflex is still dominating: in other words, the head position is determining where their limbs go, rather than the need to protect themselves by throwing out a hand.

Developing hand dominance

You do want to see your child develop these balance reactions. Unfortunately, some babies find another way to cope with their heavy head and the invariable wobbles that accompany early sitting. Rather than develop their balance reactions and integrate the tonic labyrinthine backwards, they will W-sit. The baby spreads both legs out and bends them behind himself, in a W shape, and has a much wider base of support. In this position there's no need to worry about developing righting reactions because baby is saved by 'the legs' every time.

Don't let your baby W-sit. Physically put him in the right position (legs in front, perhaps crossed) and praise him for 'big boy' sitting. It may take months or years for this behaviour to disappear, but stick at it.

Why am I so concerned by children W-sitting? There are a few reasons. First, in this position your baby doesn't develop sitting balance and good balance reactions. He is going to need these for sport and a healthy back throughout life. Second, he won't be developing endurance and strength in his trunk muscles and is going to tire when he is asked to sit at a desk and learn.

And finally, correct sitting encourages baby to develop a dominant hand: baby chooses one hand to support himself and another hand to reach across his body in pursuit of a toy. It is the beginning of developing handedness: a doing hand and a helping hand. Therapists believe children should have a strong dominant hand by the time they are 30 months old. In support of this, a 2008 study showed that children with poorly established hand dominance were poorer readers.[12]

Dads and dominance

Lots of dads have taken issue with therapists on promoting one hand to be the 'dominant' or 'doing' hand. There seems to be a general belief among men that ambidexterity is more athletic, adventurous, useful and generally cooler than being right or left handed. So why do therapists and teachers disagree?

Consider ruling-up a page. We pick up a pencil and a ruler. We don't need to make a decision about what hand will be used to pick up each. It is an automatic decision. We don't need to think about which side should be ruled. We know it is the left. It is all very quick. Most children in a class don't have to think about this, or try doing it a couple of ways. They simply do it.

But the situation is very different for children without clear hand dominance. Ruling up a page requires choosing which hand will hold the ruler and which will hold the pencil. These children don't just lack a clear feeling of left or right on themselves. They also don't know left or right on other objects. So once they have sorted out which hand they are using for which job, they will be faced with the task of remembering which side of the paper to rule up. And when it comes to reading, these same children will also 'get lost' on the page, and be unsure where to look for the next word. Children without a dominant hand take that bit longer to get everything done.

So what should be automatic and executed without requiring the cortex (the top layer of the brain) to get involved, now requires a conscious decision from them. They are inevitably that bit slower than the other children, and that bit more tired at the end of the day.

Developing a dominant hand also needs hours and hours of two-handed play. This, of course, is the main gift of sitting. A baby can hold a shoe still with one hand and post crumpled paper in with the other. (This was a favourite game at my house.) A baby can hold a box of tissues still with one hand and pull out tissue after tissue with the other. (Another favourite game.) Watch your sitting-up baby and encourage him to use two hands whenever it is required.

The journey to crawling

Crawling is one of those very controversial subjects in early childhood. Occupational therapists, physiotherapists and paediatricians know it is very important. But you will hear occasionally from other professionals another point of view, and, in fact, this is the one that dominates mainstream opinion. Too often parents are given advice like this, which I found on one of the more popular web sites (and paraphrased): 'If your baby crawls backwards, is a bottom shuffler or skips the crawling stage in favour of walking, don't worry. As long as she's getting mobile, no matter how she does it, she's fine.'

With an understanding of how human development actually happens, however, you can see how wrong this reasoning is. Crawling is not only about getting from one place to another. Like every other milestone, the journey to crawling contains others within it:

- refinement of near vision
- replacement of primitive movement patterns with mature reflexes
- growth of the ability to 'cross the midline'
- linking of movement with balance and vision
- the emotional journey of being able to move away and return to Mum as baby wishes.

And, like other milestones, there is a huge range in 'when' crawling is achieved. Whether your child crawls at five months or at 14 months is not the issue: the important thing is that it happens.

From primitive to adult movement patterns

Babies actually do a kind of crawling from very early on. If a newborn baby is placed on her mother's stomach she will 'crawl' using the stepping, rooting and sucking reflexes to find the nipple and attach. For the first 15 minutes or so she will just lie there, but before an hour has passed she has found her way to the nipple all by herself. This is called the 'breast crawl' and assists bonding and breastfeeding. But the crawling that develops between four and a half months to 12 months of age is quite different. It requires the absence of primitive reflexes rather than being dependent on them.

The symmetrical tonic neck reflex has gotten your baby onto her hands and knees. She is up and sitting. She is looking from far to near. But its usefulness is now at an end because she wants to crawl, and it just won't let her. She puts her little head up and her knees bend, she puts her head down and her arms bend. The next step is to integrate the symmetrical tonic neck reflex and usher in a mature reflex: crawling does both these things, apart from being terrifically important all by itself.

So how does baby break free of the symmetrical tonic neck reflex and crawl? She will rock; and rock and rock. The movement begins to look more like the 'seesaw' of the reflex, and ends with baby having her back flat and legs bent and arms straight. That takes a while to happen — baby will begin a rock and suddenly the reflex will be triggered and she will be back flat on her tummy as her arms shoot out straight and her legs bend. You'll notice the little head nodding up and down. The legs will kick. Don't be impatient for crawling to start as it is still a couple of months away when baby is at this stage. All this is very important stuff.

Finally, baby is staying on her hands and knees and the little back is flat. What happens next? She will begin by going backwards a little as she rocks while she is discovering that to go forward she is going to have to move one arm independently of the other and balance on three limbs. Those righting reactions already developed in sitting are about to become useful. But something else is needed as well.

Due to her rolling and clapping and the time spent on her back passing objects from one hand to the other, your baby has already lost the asymmetrical neck reflex (the reflex that makes baby watch her outstretched hand). Why does it need to be gone? Because the human brain waits for the disappearance of this reflex to release yet another mature movement pattern. It's called the amphibian reflex and it allows us to have every limb in a different position, regardless of head position. It also causes us to bend our legs every time our hip bends, so we need it to crawl. You will sometimes see children crawling with their legs kept straight — this is called bear walking and it tells you that a child still has their symmetrical tonic neck reflex.

So baby is crawling on hands and knees. She's free of tonic neck reflexes, both asymmetrical and symmetrical. The amphibian reflex is allowing her to have her limbs where she wants them and for her hip and knee to work together. Now she only has to integrate the tonic labyrinthine reflex in walking and she's through with her primitive reflexes. But the benefits of crawling don't finish there.

My baby isn't crawling

Very frequently the reason why your baby hasn't started crawling is that a primitive reflex is blocking further development. The ones to suspect are the tonic labyrinthine reflex, the asymmetrical tonic neck reflex and the symmetrical tonic neck reflex.

The tonic labyrinthine reflex is, I think, the one causing difficulty for Pearl, my friend Emma's baby girl. This is the 'fish-flip' reflex discussed extensively in previous chapters. If it is still active it won't allow a full expression of the symmetrical tonic neck reflex, which allows hips to bend, an important marker on the path to crawling, and nor will it allow expression of the amphibian reflex. It is the reflex to 'suspect by default' if a baby seems not to be on the pathway to crawling.

These are the games I suggested to Emma:
- *lots of flying through the air like a little aeroplane as this will trigger another transitional reflex which inhibits the TLR. Hold her under her tummy, not her chest, and encourage her to reach forward to grab something*
- *any game where Pearl stretches out like a snake and curls up like a snail might be helpful. See if she can 'fish-flip' along the floor*
- *use music and songs with as much of this as you can. Vestibular or balance difficulties are always helped by music. High sounds are particularly valuable, especially if you can get her to make them. The auditory and vestibular nerve are the basically the same, so when you stimulate one you stimulate the other.*

When this reflex remains active children also show lowered muscle tone. Pearl's physiotherapist has suggested a 'jumper' to increase her muscle strength and endurance, and I think that is a good idea. She has also taught Emma to put Pearl into a 'crouched up crawling position' for her to push up out of, and Pearl likes to do this on Emma's lap rather than the floor.

The asymmetrical tonic neck reflex places baby's hand in just the right position for her gaze. If your baby rolls well and is passing objects from hand to hand with ease, then this is probably not the culprit. If you are not seeing rolling and passing, you might like to play some of these games:
- *encourage baby to pass her own foot from hand to hand*
- *clapping games like Pat-a-cake, Clap around in a circle, Pease*

porridge hot (the rhythm of the song lends itself to a clap with you and then a hands-together clap). Action rhymes in general are excellent for this
- gentle tug-of-war games
- rolling games, such as rolling baby up in a towel and then gently unrolling her.

The symmetrical tonic neck reflex lets baby bend at the hip, sit and be up on all four limbs. If your baby has an active tonic labyrinthine reflex then this reflex won't have emerged properly. It is necessary to get baby into the right position for crawling, but if the reflex remains her movement will be blocked. The 'bear walkers' and 'bottom shufflers' are children who still have this reflex stuck on. If kept past 11 months it has consequences for learning and movement.

If your baby is on all fours but not rocking, encourage the rocking. Help her into a crawling position — onto all fours — and then gently rock her backwards and forwards on her arms and legs, being very careful of her little face. A baby can sometimes shoot forward and bang her nose and chin. I also like to 'crawl' babies along once they are at this stage and send older siblings to crawl along in front of them.

Encourage tummy time and minimise the amount of time in supported sitting in prams or other similar devices. Also, sit baby on your knee, crunch up her hips and knees and encourage her to push up against gravity.

Remember with all these games that the rule is 'little and often'. Play for as long as your baby can tolerate, and it may be as little as five seconds to begin with. You need to both be having fun. Remember, too, that 'when' is not as important as 'if'. If your baby hasn't crawled yet, do not start encouraging walking.

Crossing the midline

It is in crawling that your baby gains most of her prereading visual skills, hooks up movement to balance and vision and gains the ability to 'cross the midline' with hands and eyes. What is 'crossing the midline', you say, and why is it such a big deal?

Imagine your body bisected by a line starting at your head, travelling directly down through your nose and leaving one nostril either side, down through your mouth and on: so your body on each side of the line exactly reflects the other side. Crossing this midline means using one part of your body in the space of the other part of the body. It doesn't sound important, but we could hardly get through everyday life without doing this. We reach across our bodies with our dominant hand to pick up a glass or scratch an elbow. We read across both sides of a page with one eye directing the operation. We write from left to right with just one hand. Crossing the midline with the dominant hand is a critical skill mostly mastered in crawling and sitting, but not in W-sitting.

Once baby develops that 'cross-pattern' crawl, with the opposite arm and leg moving together, she is crossing the midline of her body by using opposite body parts together including the eyes — and, many occupational therapists believe, opposite sides of the brain together. This builds the corpus callosum (the bridge between the two hemispheres), and the latest neuroscience is linking a more developed corpus callosum to better reading skills. (See Appendix III for more details.)

Linking movement to balance and vision

For the first time baby is moving forward under her own steam, her eyes close to the ground. In these months of crawling she will link the feeling of moving (kinaesthesia) to her already linked together senses of balance and vision. The very neat trick our brains have of providing us with a continuous picture of the world despite our movements (one example of a discontinuity is the fact that we repeatedly blink) really takes off now. It is, of course, an illusion, but your baby needs to have it to function in the world along with the rest of us.

Developing visual skills

Hand movements and eye movements go together. As baby crawls along, finding and picking up smaller and smaller objects, her eyes are trained to converge on those smaller and smaller objects. The fluff that baby picks off the carpet is held in a pincer grasp, felt carefully by the sensitive fingertips, examined up close by two bright little eyes and then carefully touched on lips; and then, being so intriguing, put in the mouth for further exploring. (Only stop baby doing this when an item is dangerous because exploring by mouth is as important as exploring by hand in this early period of crawling.)

To 'examine up close' requires considerable eye muscle development. First of all, that your child's eyes are 'yoked together' so that they work together. Next comes the ability to converge. This is the ability to swivel both eyes in to look at a small object up close, and is developed as baby works through the tonic labyrinthine reflex. But having yoked eyes that can smoothly track along or converge upon a single item is just half of your child's visual skills. The other half is the ability to accurately interpret what she sees.

Learning that our eyes can't tell us everything is at the heart of what is called 'visual-perceptual skills'. All that time on the floor crawling is when babies internalise the knowledge that they must bring other sensory memories and past discoveries to bear upon the problem of interpretation.

Imagine you show a one year old a picture of a white floppy object with black marks upon it. This white and black floppy thing is protruding out from behind a clothes basket. At this stage your baby will not be able to tell you what it is. But at just a year older your toddler will find it much easier. She has been systematically matching visual information with tactile information and movement information and so now knows that she's not being shown the whole picture. But where before she was not able to imagine another perspective upon the scene (the one that lets her see behind the clothes basket), her growing cognitive skills suddenly will. Her ever-expanding vocabulary lets her put a name to the match she has made. It is the ear of the black and white puppy she will see on the next page.

This ability to imagine the rest of the puppy to go with the puppy's ear is called visual closure. In upper primary school this same ability will let her look at a word like 'unfinis' and know that it hasn't been fully written. It is a skill that starts when your baby is crawling on the floor. (If a crawling baby is put into a 'walker' — one of those seats on wheels — she will miss out on this visual perceptual development. I strongly recommend against using one.)

Just as motor skills cannot be separated from emotional skills in that first year, visual, movement, balance, hearing and touch skills co-develop also. Trying to 'splinter off' one or two and work on them separately is missing the whole point of this time in your baby's life. It is all happening together. Crawling isn't 'just crawling' but a number of different experiences, all of which your baby needs.

Once baby is crawling, give it a few months before you encourage cruising (walking by holding onto furniture or a hand) and walking. Of course you can't stop a child from walking but you can reward crawling with excitement and pleasure too.

Remember the emotional half of this time, too. For your baby to be a happy little explorer she needs to know you are confident of her safety and ready to welcome her back: the two halves of creating a secure attachment with a mobile child. Being able to crawl is a big moment for you as well as your baby.

Walking

Walking is the physical milestone we care most about as parents. Lots of parents respond to a query about their toddlers with a deprecating but secretly very proud, 'Oh, you know, walking and talking'. But it is the milestone that I have the least to write about. The journey to walking happens after much of the work of integrating primitive reflexes and developing adult reflexes has already occurred. So while it is the milestone parents are the proudest of, it is the least meaningful in reflex integration terms. The journey to walking also takes a baby through integrating the last of the tonic labyrinthine reflex and into the world of toddlerhood.

At birth babies have what is called the 'stepping reflex', and while it looks as if it is there to help baby walk in the distant future, this reflex has an immediate use. We briefly looked at the breast crawl earlier, where, by pushing with his legs and reaching with his arms, a newborn baby can climb up his mother's body to find the breast.[13]

This same reflex is used when babies 'kick' in excitement. It was thought to just 'disappear' by itself, and then reappear when babies learn to walk. In fact, research shows that it merely *seems* to disappear. The truth is that baby's legs get too heavy for the reflex to actually show.[14]

It is now agreed that the stepping reflex is not a primitive reflex based in the brain like the other reflexes, but located in the spine. And it does play a part in helping children with walking. Certainly, something in the spine enables the two legs to 'communicate' with each other; when one is flexing the other is straightening, and that is controlled at the spinal level.[15]

Baby is crawling over to furniture now, pulling himself up and grabbing all the sorts of things that babies are not allowed to grab. Once up he's cruising, putting one foot in front of the other with the stepping reflex assisting the coordination of his legs. It is in this upright posture that he encounters once again the tonic labyrinthine reflex. (Children with either a 'floppy' or a 'stiff' body posture haven't entirely controlled the reflex. See Appendix III for more on this.) Baby will stumble if his head tips forward (his legs will bend) or too far back (his back will arch). He brings all the balancing skills he's learnt in crawling and sitting into play as he cruises: placing legs and hands wide out from his body to increase his base of support. His body quivers as he shifts his weight from leg to leg and back again: his trunk muscles are slowly learning how to compensate for a shifting centre of gravity in the upright position. Bit by bit he removes the control over the distribution of muscle tone from the reflex. And then one day he just walks off into space.

I don't recommend that you use a 'walker' for these reasons. While it gives your child extra support it robs him of the full learning experience. Use of a walker often leads to a child not having such good balance: absolutely the opposite intention of his parents.

The early walker

Parents often discuss the possible significance of the age at which a child walks. While advanced motor skills can correlate with giftedness (but not necessarily so), early walking is actually more a marker of a child having difficulties than a child with gifts.

Occupational therapists are referred a lot of 'early walkers': babies who are walking between eight and 10 months of age. Why? Children with a hyper-response to touch are more motivated than most to crawl and walk. The sensation of having a lot of their body in contact with the floor is experienced as unpleasant by these children. A carpet that seems soft enough to most people would be 'scratchy' for these children. They get up on two legs as fast as they can, usually encouraged by their very proud parents.

But the early walkers who were also early crawlers and rollers will be fine. They have just worked through the motor milestones a little bit faster than most children, which doesn't mean that they are necessarily gifted or not gifted. The important thing is that they have experienced each of the major movement milestones to free themselves of the primitive reflexes and develop adult reflexes. This is what you hope will happen for every child.

Walking gives our baby 'toddler status'. It might happen when your child is eight months old and it might happen when he is 18 months old. The effect is to make him even more mobile. His journeys of discovery — returning to you and launching off once more on his explorations — grow longer and longer. Your baby is growing up.

The parents of the toddler must provide their child with ever more challenging opportunities to grow his skills — and at the same time know that every leap in skill will mean their toddler has accessed a new round of items that can be destroyed, flushed or consumed. The safest place for your toddler is right next to you, which is lucky, as mastering household chores is one of their very first preoccupations. Being given jobs is also a major mood smoother. While it might seem easier to plonk your toddler before a TV set while you whisk around the house, this is actually short-term thinking.

When you finish, the house may be tidy, but your toddler, with no accomplishments behind him, will be far harder to manage. Not to mention the fact that his attention skills will be set back a notch. A toddler who has helped make morning tea, wiped down a cupboard, played with the pegs, sung nursery rhymes with you while putting away clothes (probably unfolding and dragging a jumper to a room) is a happy toddler. Even if the house can never be pristine in the way it was before your child landed, you have achieved an extraordinary amount.

You have kept your child on the skill-building train. You have helped increase his impulse control: 'Just wait until I turn off the mixers, darling, before you put your finger in the mixing bowl.' You have challenged him to 'converge' his eyes on a small mark: 'Can you see that dirty mark? Let's both rub it very hard.' You've provided a just-right challenge to lengthen concentration while building fine motor strength and dexterity: 'Can you make a peg snap like a crocodile? Can you build a chain of crocodiles, eating each other's tails?' By singing and dancing while putting away the washing you've possibly triggered off a new round of balance and movement skills. You've taught the importance of finishing what you started. And those are just a few of the very many things that will have happened in your morning.

You will find information on how active primitive reflexes affect older children in Appendix III. The next part of the book returns to the story of how the self-regulation skills, with movement skills developing well, continue to grow.

Part Four:

How self-regulation skills keep growing

He was learning through experience that feelings can twist and turn and lose their sharp edges. He was learning responsible control as well as expression of his feelings. Through this increasing self-knowledge, he would be free to use his capacities and emotions more constructively.

Virginia M. Axline, *Dibs, In Search Of Self*, 1964. Axline, who developed 'Play Therapy', here exquisitely describes self-regulation years before it was named and became a focus in the rest of child development literature.[1]

Chapter 15

How language and theory of mind grow together

And it seems to me that in order to figure out what a stork would want, we should try to think the way a stork would think.

Meindert DeJong, *The Wheel on the School*, 1961.[2]

The ability to predict what another person knows and to take that knowledge and work out how that person is likely to think about a subject is called theory of mind. It is vital to self-regulation for two reasons. First of all, it is the 'thinking' part of negotiating with other people. Secondly, it is the basis for thinking skills, allowing your child to consider multiple viewpoints and possibilities in terms of actions and ultimately to be able to 'think about thinking'. Of course, thinking is done in language: these two skill-sets co-develop. One day, language coupled with theory of mind will mean your child will be able to ask themselves 'where shall I start this story from' or 'what is the best way to approach my friend about this delicate issue' and thoughtfully weigh up their different options.

A focus for many researchers has been studying at what age children start to show theory of mind. One of the tests used in the research involves two children who are playing. One takes the toy car they are playing with, puts it under the bed and leaves the room. The second child promptly removes it from under the bed and puts it away in the toy box. So where will the first child look for the toy?

Before a child is four years old she will tell you that the first child will look in the toy box. But after four she will tell you that the first child will look under the bed as that child was not in the room when the car went into the toy box.

But parents don't need to resort to these kinds of tests to know where their child is up to in developing theory of mind. All they need is a telephone. Allow your toddler to talk on the telephone to an adult who is not present, and just what she does and doesn't understand about another person's perspective is awfully clear: 'Granny, here's my mud-ball. I made it with Sam.'

The fact that Granny couldn't see his mud-ball was something Rafael couldn't appreciate at just three years old. He could see it, so why couldn't Granny?

But at nearly four this kind of statement is disappearing from his telephone conversations (the mud-balls, however, remain of great interest) with his grandmother. This represents not just a leap in his theory of mind but also in his language. And the two are tied very closely together.[3] The development of language and theory of mind leapfrog each other through these early years of life.

So on the wide foundation of a secure, organised attachment, your toddler has continued to grow her self-regulation skills. From six months of age she has been refining her empathic skills. She can look at your face and detect your emotions and know they are not hers but yours, and she can empathise. She is moving and sensing with more precision all the time. She is able to slow her heart down to concentrate better. And from three years old she has developed all her mature movement patterns: no primitive reflexes are interfering with her desire to switch her attention back and forth. Her impulse control is growing all the time.

And at three years old, with all that in place, the dominance of the early maturing right hemisphere is over. The left hemisphere — the verbal, logical part of the brain — holds sway now. A different kind of skill set will develop: the verbal, logical skills. It is adding these to theory of mind that gives your child both the ability to relate to other people and the ability to 'think about thinking'. So how does it develop?

Baby learns that you and she feel different things

By six months of age babies know that their feelings and your feelings are different, but that feelings can be shared. There is me, and there is you. We connect, but we are not the same. You can help me out when I feel sad so we cannot be the same. You can make me laugh so we are not the same. I can make you laugh and feel joy, so we are not the same. This truth — that we connect but we aren't the same — is the bedrock from which empathy, theory of mind, impulse control and thinking all grow.

Attachment and thinking skills

You can see again the terrific importance of a secure, organised attachment. When a baby is responded to consistently, warmly and sensitively (secure attachment) she learns 'we connect through our feelings but we aren't the same person'. When a baby feels safe (organised attachment) she is able to 'wait a moment' — providing a space in which thinking skills can occur.

Those two capacities are added together and baby can start on the journey of discovering the inner worlds of other people; connecting emotionally, intimately and creatively with others, the source of much of the meaning in life.

But when a baby's feelings trigger the same feelings in the parent (preoccupied/ambivalent attachment), a baby learns 'we connect and we seem to be the same'. This baby becomes a child who will struggle with the boundaries between self and others, and in seeing that there is another point of view. If 'we are the same', how can there be another view?

When a baby's feelings are mostly ignored by the parent (dismissive-avoidant attachment) a baby learns 'we aren't the same and we connect intermittently'. This baby will grow into a child who has difficulty decoding and finding meaning in the emotions of others.

When a baby doesn't feel safe (disorganised attachment) she isn't able to 'wait a moment', so there is no space available for thinking. Baby will grow into a child who 'acts first' (and probably won't be able to 'think later' with ease either).

The next step: you and I have different ideas about things
Once baby has basic empathy she begins exploring another concept: as well as you and I having different feelings, you and I can have different ideas too. You catch your six-month-old baby's eye and point and say, 'Look at the dog'. Baby will sight down your finger and see the dog and may well be excited by looking at the dog, but the experience is more about the dog than the sharing.

By nine months of age baby has begun pointing too. 'I want' is often what a baby means when she first starts pointing. From there it blossoms into 'I want you to look at this too'.[4]

How to grow theory of mind in your older baby

Label your own and your baby's emotions from very early. Link your own feelings with actions verbally. For example, 'I feel so happy you are playing nicely with your sister. It looks like great fun. I'm going to join in.' Or, 'I am feeling tired. Shall we have a rest together and read a story?'

Get into the habit of providing the link between a decision and your reasoning: 'No, you can't go outside without shoes. It would be fun, but it is too cold. Your feet would hurt.'

Avoid as much as you can your child spending time 'looking at a screen'. Baby and toddler DVDs like Baby Einstein and similar products have been shown to markedly hinder language development when watched by children aged between eight and 16 months.[5] If you hinder language development you will also hinder theory of mind.

And at 12 months baby has learned that much of the joy in living comes from sharing our different ideas. 'I saw a dog and showed you. How good it was that we saw that dog together! At first I wondered if it was a dog, because it was only as big as a cat. But you said "dog", so I looked again. And then it woofed and I knew you were right and it was a dog and we both laughed.' There are backward and forward glances, to each other and to whatever is under observation. Baby and parent read each other's expressions in relation to the object with great expertise. (Parents of children of this age sometimes 'hear' or 'dream' complex conversations with their baby, such is the richness of these exchanges.)

As your child moves into her second year of life she has already grasped that:

- There are people. They have feelings.
- I am a person.
- People share ideas and feelings with each other. We do this by showing each other things and comparing reactions.

It is an excellent beginning but there is still some way to go to a sophisticated theory of mind. In the second year of life, with your help, your baby will start to:

- learn to juggle multiple perspectives, which is a skill developed in pretend play
- grow the language skills to work through the different perspectives and share them with you.

While these skills begin in the second year, it is not until the fourth year that you will see them blossom.

Step three: I can imagine how I look to you

A little baby and a younger toddler can't look at their behaviour and see how it appears to you. They are never naughty deliberately. They simply can't evaluate their own actions in terms of how another person will view them.

But from about 18 months of age children do begin to be able to see how they look from your eyes.[6] Researchers are not exactly sure why. Perhaps the ability to 'pretend' that something is something else also lets them pretend for a moment that they are Mum. And, as Mum, they can look at what they are doing and think, 'No, no, stop!' The old-fashioned phrase for this inner voice, and I can't think of a more up-to-date name, is 'conscience'. Nevertheless, at this point they can't stop themselves doing it, they just know that they should.

One of the most endearing things a toddler will do is scold herself for an action even as she performs it. 'No knives,' Sam would mutter while secretively removing three or four from the kitchen drawer. And researchers have reproduced this finding: a child can tell you that she shouldn't do something a long time before she can actually stop herself doing it.

And they are so funny when they are surprised doing something they know they should not. The speed of light evacuation to the other side of the room away from the power cord; the transformation back to ordinary existence of a fork that has been used as a weapon on an older brother — there it lies, on the floor, well away from the toddler's hand. And they are just as funny as they stare straight at you while their hand inches towards a forbidden object.

What this defiance tells you is that they know how their behaviour looks to you. They are simultaneously keeping two different perspectives in their minds: your view ('Knives aren't for playing with') and their view ('I want to play with the knives'). It is a giant leap in mental capacity.

Your toddler is now able to 'walk in someone else's shoes'. While it doesn't initially extend as far as being able to imagine what a person knows at any one moment — Granny can't see my mud-ball because she isn't here — it does mean that your toddler is on the way to being able to imagine her way into many different perspectives.

As your toddler grows her 'working memory' and impulse control so she is able to focus on the relevant parts of a situation, she will get better at knowing just what every different person knows and feels.[7] When this happens — from about three years old — your child will be able to play elaborate 'pretend games'. The importance of these games cannot be overstated.

Playing 'pretend'

One of my first ever appointments as a newly qualified occupational therapist was for a little girl called Renae. I was so newly qualified that I wished to just observe, and the therapist who I was observing was Mum. This gave me a great deal more insight than I usually had into what was happening in the therapist's head.

The child health nurse had asked for Mum's opinion. Was Renae intellectually handicapped? She was 15 months old and hadn't ever said a word.

Watching Mum, I saw her 'ears prick up' about halfway through the session. She and Renae had been playing a game of 'give and take' with a green Lego block. Mum had experimentally 'brummed' it, as though it was a little car. The little girl had taken the Lego block car and then lifted it up. After looking at it for just a moment, she shot a look at Mum and then dragged it down though her soft wispy hair. The block that had been a car had become a comb. It was obviously a highly significant moment in Mum's opinion, but exactly why eluded me.

'She was pretending,' Mum explained afterwards. 'So she might have a speech delay, but there's no intellectual handicap.' It turned out that the little girl had intermittent ear infections which were delaying her speech.

What Renae had communicated to Mum was this: 'I realise what you did was to make new meaning for that block. You pretended it was a car. Well, I can do that too. I'm pretending it is a comb.'

Like other children aged between 13 and 18 months, Renae had made a huge leap in understanding. People don't just react or know. They also *create*. A hairbrush can be a spaceship or it can be a microphone. They know it is a hairbrush, and they can 'hold that thought' and make a new one that can exist alongside.

The little girl had been 'juggling' the different thoughts: she had space inside her mind to have two different understandings of the same object. In fact, she was juggling thoughts with another person. Mum had tossed her the idea of the block as a car, and she had tossed back the idea of the block as a comb.

This is what we do throughout our lives. We throw an idea or a concept out to another person, they put their own spin on it or chuck in another concept in return. Renae was showing us that she too had joined in the game of making meanings and sharing them.

So how does the ability to 'make and share meanings' help children with the problem of knowing what another person knows? It means that they are beginning to see 'thoughts' as separate from people. They are beginning to see 'what Granny knows now' as something separate from 'what Granny knew last time' and from Gran herself, but it is still going to take a lot more practice.

How pretending grows theory of mind

My four-year-old nephew Brennan keeps herds of kittens. They have birthdays, for which there must be presents and parties, and they have wars, for which special kitten battle armour is required. There are near misses and full-blown disasters. There are relationship breakdowns and problematic group dynamics and dynastic squabbles. He makes houses and playgrounds for them. He collects 'olden day stuff' for kitten bowers. He ensures they eat the right things but not too much because 'it makes their skin go runny'. As his mum and dad and big brother play along, just what is he learning?

He is sharpening up all his mental skills. The emotional quality of the game keeps him focusing for longer, building his concentration span. The various conundrums posed by the kittens' squabbles are helping him string together more and more complex 'if-then' sequences. His purposes within the game — to stop the kittens fighting and to keep them safe — are the play versions of goal setting. He is learning that persevering in thinking and talking about his kittens is paying off in terms of more interesting solutions. And as he shares all his different ideas with his mum, his language skills are improving.

Most particularly though, he is practising his theory of mind skills. As he empathises with each different kitten he is gathering skills in taking different perspectives. He works out what each kitten does and doesn't know and then imagines their emotional responses.

'It's Purr's birthday, but the other kittens have forgotten. When he tells them they say it's too late for a party. But some of them are ashamed and so …'

He is 'jumping' from imagined mind to imagined mind, linking events, ideas and emotions. When his mum collaborates with him — 'Perhaps there are some kitten party planners who can help out?' — the game grows both more engaging and more complex. Her interest keeps his attention going longer, but her ideas add further complexity and richness to the game and increase the 'load' on his theory of mind, language and reasoning skills.

One of the great tragedies for children, however, is that our society has forgotten how much imaginative play contributes to the skills that lead to life success. Why? I think it is because imaginative play doesn't have a 'product' that can be used as 'evidence of learning' and time well spent. It cannot be put in a CV or a report. And this preoccupation is having an effect on parents too. We have become so worried about literacy and numeracy that we try to 'ensure learning experiences' within a game such as this. 'One black and three white kittens. One plus three is four kittens altogether!'

For a child caught up in the drama of keeping the kittens from each other's throats, this will be perceived as irrelevant at best, and at worst, an intrusion. At a time where we are increasingly worried about the precursor skills for literacy and numeracy, where every year academia encroaches a little further into the preserves of kindergarten and preschool, where even very little children attend music or drama classes, it's easy to forget that children learn best and most by playing. And the things they are learning are not only going to help with academic performance but also their ability to relate to others, which is arguably far more important.

Many things can eat into this play time. Computer games and television, both of which 'compel attention' in children, for example. Organised activities (such as the classes described above) can be very enjoyable, but, again, too many of them mean that a child doesn't have enough time 'just playing'. Unfortunately, our worry over how our child will perform academically has led to an overriding need in policy makers and parents for 'hard evidence' of learning. Even carers of three year olds are required to provide hard evidence of the learning that has been done in their care: photographs, paintings and so on.

Doing a painting is not the same value learning experience as a really good game (although it is when it's part of the game), and yet, in our incessant need for reassurance, this is what we demand of the carers and teachers of our children. And as more and more children are struggling in our schools, what do we ask? More and more of the teacher's time to be spent not in facilitating learning, but in providing 'evidence of learning'.

One of the best writers on children's play is Vivian Paley. She is an American psychologist and kindergarten teacher who recorded on tape the learning process of her students in play, and then wrote about what she had recorded. All the 'evidence of learning' from her classroom was on these tapes. She spent hours listening to them, pulling out the themes the children explored in their collaborative games. She could hear children improve concentration span and language skills, and she could hear their empathic and social skills grow. She was able to trace over a year a child's development from a teller of simple stories to a master teller of complex novel-length tales.

That development, of course, carries within it many educational outcomes. Stories and play, where children live in their minds, were her teaching modality and her 'outcome statements' all in one.[8, 9]

Our best possible self is a creative one

Pretend play also grows creativity. A child who has learned to leap from perspective to perspective, gathering ideas as she travels, linking problems to solutions and collaborating with others along the journey, will become a creative adult. 'Creative' is a word we too often apply to the arts alone. In fact, there is not a field of human endeavour that does not depend on creativity. Human survival requires it.

We need to let our children play. We need to see it as our role to make play possible for them. Instead of pushing them into formal activities early or 'tranquillising' them with TV or computers, we need to give them time and space and the support of our own playfulness.

And we need to examine just why we require 'hard evidence' of learning. Too often the underlying rationale for 'evidence of learning' is that by 'proving outcomes' we justify the money we spend on paying for carers. This is all about the needs of the adults rather than the needs of the children.

Even if it takes society a while longer yet to work this all out, we parents, at least, can properly value imaginative play. We can judge for ourselves how much our child is learning in childcare, kindergarten or preschool just by listening. If your child says, 'We played a really good game today', you know that it's been a valuable day. And when she is at home with us we can enjoy listening. In this way we can hear our three years olds with their beginning stories told solo — 'Rabbit danced to the music. "Oooh! Nice music," said Rabbit. But then Rafi turned the music off' — grow into collaborative storytellers of complex, richly themed story-games at four:

Raf: 'We are all hiding. We don't know it's only you.'

Sam: 'I come in, and I can't see you or the rabbits.'

Raf: 'So you think I have broken my promise and taken them.'

Sam: 'I go sadly away …'

Raf: 'But I call out and say, "We are here."'

Sam: 'But I am too far away already. I can't hear you.'

Raf: 'So I … I …'

Sam: 'You send the rabbits after me!'

Raf: 'Yes. I say, "Rabbits, rabbits, go get him. Go as fast as you can."'

Raf: 'And they find me.'

Sam: 'Hooray!'

These long, creative story collaborations tell you that your child is able to see a person, an idea and a thought as separate from each other. This is how adults think too.

If we want our child to eventually be able to ask herself, 'What is the best way to begin to approach this problem?', whether it be a mathematical problem or an interpersonal problem, we need to make it possible for her to spend hours simply playing pretend games in the early years. And we need to play with her.

Communicating better and better

As your baby grows into toddlerhood and out the other side, his language skills show exponential growth. From six months onwards you will notice that when your baby encounters something new he will immediately look to you. He is looking to see how you feel about this person or this thing or this smell or this game: 'Is it safe? Is it okay for me?' He sees his answers in your face.

When your baby has begun to do this you will change the way you communicate with him. Rather than providing 'lots of language data' like the long, chatty sentences of the early months, you switch to giving him punchy 'dot points' about the things you are both looking at. You are now providing 'words for things'.

Between six and 12 months you will find that you are pointing to things to share them with your baby. You point, and he will look. And you will tell him what it is you are showing him. A white bird. The blue sky. A fallen tree.

At 12 months of age everything changes. Now he points and you look. With a younger baby it can be a challenge to follow his lead, but that is the case no longer. Twelve month olds are very clear communicators. The focus for parents now is on supporting baby in his interests. If he is fascinated by a pot lid, don't attempt to redirect his attention. Talk about the pot lid. Play alongside with pot lid. Together explore the possibilities of pot lids, like hiding things underneath it, rolling it along the floor, spinning it like a top. (One of the 'red flags' for therapists watching parents play with their children is when parents try to 'wrest back the reins' by redirecting their children's attention continually and interfering with the direction of their play.[6] Parents are support staff. The children are in charge.)

A new set of games appears in your play repertoire. Often these are only new games for your family or your baby, because they are games that have been played for generations. 'Peek–a–boo', 'There were three in the bed and the little one said roll over' and 'Chasey'. Just like routines, the patterns that these games follow give baby something to peg language to. And they also allow more complex variations on 'same and different'. 'Last time we played chase Daddy around the house he came out from behind that door … Is he there? No. Is he on the other side of the bed? No. Oh! He was in the cupboard! Let's run away!'

Hopefully you have been reading to baby long before this, but if not, books will feed your baby's appetite for looking and listening together better than anything else.

A good book: your helpmeet and friend

Books often serve as a great scaffold for tired parents to help them keep talking to baby in those early months. So even if your one-month-old's eyes only fleetingly touch upon the page, he's deriving benefit from simply listening to the pattern of your speech. An easy to hold book of nursery rhymes helps you keep on singing.

One of the very best ways to deal with a toddler jealous of baby is to make baby's feeding time also story time. Until your baby becomes interested in looking at pictures, which often starts happening at about four months old, the stories chosen by older children are perfect. There are many authors who seem to have a tired mother in mind every bit as much as they have an eager toddler or preschooler.

These books are not just a joy to read — letting your mind rest and your heart take over — but carry with them the author's faith that you are parenting to the best of your ability. For example, nearly all books by Mem Fox or Roald Dahl tell the story of the carer as well as the child. In the midst of a hard day they are like a perfectly judged hug or an invigorating pat upon the back from a much older and wiser person. Sharing a book becomes an island in time and space to which you can both go when it all starts to be too much.

There is no research to support this speculation, but it's hard not to wonder if some books help parents build a secure attachment. I am sure Mem Fox crafts her books with this in mind. Certainly there's research showing that securely attached mother–child pairs get more out of book reading and tend to do it more often. This is simply because sharing a book in a sensitive and responsive way is a pathway to better understanding your child — mothers learn far more about their children's capabilities and interests and are able to better match and grow them.[10]

For simply building your baby's language skills, the sharing of books is one of the best things you can do. His vocabulary blossoms as you, inspired by reminders that there are tigers and they do have stripes, provide glimpses of a much wider world. Can television do this? No. Babies only learn to talk from being talked to. Conversations overhead, television, radio and so on, are merely so much noise to the child under two. Time spent in front of a screen robs baby of time learning.

When to see a speech pathologist

The right time to go to see any health professional as a parent is when you are concerned. That's not just a 'touchy feely' statement. Across Australia a new way for child health nurses to screen infants and children for developmental issues is being rolled out. Like most acceptable screens it has a 70 to 80 per cent sensitivity rating, but it is much simpler than older screening tools. How does it work? Rather than a set of tests being carried out, it simply works from parent's concerns about their child. In summary, 'concern' is a very valid reason for seeking a speech pathology referral or any other referral, whatever the age of your baby. We will discuss some of the things to watch out for.

Babbling
Between about six and 11 months babies will begin to babble. Those are the delightful, one syllable pattern songs, 'ba ba ba'. If you don't hear sounds like these, you need to consider going to see a speech

pathologist. Children with speech disorders rarely babble as babies. Tim didn't babble. On the advice of my sister-in-law, a speech pathologist, I babbled to him. I made up songs full of babbled patterns and soon Tim was singing along. 'Ba-ba-ba, Barbara-ann' or the 'La la la, laa la lalala' song from the Muppets. Was it a marker for a speech disorder? It was. Tim developed a stutter at about two.

Expressions of concern from other adults

And speaking of Tim's stutter, I couldn't hear it myself, and neither could Mum. We were both too close. If someone suggests that your child has a stutter, or is difficult to understand, pay good attention. Parents are much better at understanding their children, and they are also famous for being oblivious to speech difficulties. Children who have stutters, or any other speech difficulty, are better off being seen sooner rather than later. Waiting lists for speech pathologists can be long, so having your child's name on the list as soon as possible is important.

Number of words

By 18 months you would expect your child to regularly use some words. Before your child turns two you would expect him to be using 50 or 60 words. At two years of age you should hear two word 'telegram' sentences: 'Ladybird puddle'. At three you would expect three word sentences, at four years of age, four to five word sentences.

Comprehension

At about six months baby has learned his name[11] and also knows when you are happy and when you are cross with him. Before 12 months you'll realise he knows the words for all sorts of things, and will be happy to play the 'where's …?' pointing game. Many babies love to play this with a table full of family members. Between one and two years of age your child will start to point to things in books. Between two and three it's possible to give baby a two-stage command and have it followed: 'Please could you pick that block up, and put it in the basket over there?'

Intelligibility

At around 18 months you should be able to understand about a quarter of what your child says. From around two you should understand about half to three-quarters of what he's saying. And at approximately three years that amount rises to 75 to 100 per cent of all of what's said. When your child is around four years of age, his speech should be 100 per cent intelligible to both you and others.

Why worry?

Speech development is a concern for its own sake and for theory of mind, but it is also a concern for another reason. Children who have problems with learning to talk are at risk of also having difficulty learning to read.

Just why children have reading difficulties or dyslexia is hotly debated. A few researchers believe there is no such thing as dyslexia, just poor methods of teaching reading.[12] But most researchers don't. There seems little doubt that the immediate cause of difficulties in most cases (but not all) is a child's difficulty in hearing all the sounds in a word (phonological awareness).[11] And this is something that shows up early. But why does a child have difficulty hearing all speech sounds? That's at the core of the discussion. Some researchers suggest a common neurological cause for both the phonological difficulties and the motor problems often seen together in the child struggling to read.[13]

Our own clinical experience, in addition to other research, strongly supports this theory.[14] Very rarely does a child in difficulty just need an occupational therapist or a speech pathologist. He usually needs to see both. The best results come when the child's brain is stimulated from a number of directions.

Poor phonological awareness is something that is revealed by early speech and language problems. It's a heads up to parents that their child may have difficulty reading later. Early speech pathology will minimise the likelihood considerably.

You might be wondering whether Tim's lack of babbling and the stutter were predictive of difficulties with reading. In his case they were *not. At age 11 he reads well, however spelling remains an issue for him. So his lack of babbling was probably connected to his difficulties with hearing all speech sounds, which later showed up as spelling difficulties.*

The worst that can happen if you read to your baby from his first weeks of life is that people will laugh at you. The best is the development of a 'book habit' in your child. This will stand you in excellent stead during the long hard days of parenting to come, particularly if you are going to be at home alone with your children.

My sister Megan just rang to say that Leo (nearly six months old) wasn't really into books just yet despite her reading to him at night. And I realised that I hadn't conveyed properly that to hook babies into books (particularly when there isn't an older sibling there to show them that books are great) you need to use books much the way you'd use a toy. For example, if reading Eric Carle's *The Very Hungry Caterpillar*, stick your finger through the holes the caterpillar has eaten and wiggle them at your baby. (This is terrifically funny.) All good baby books have both visual and tactile qualities — shiny mirrors, fluffy ducks, scratchy snakes and so on. Some books have buttons to press to make an intriguing noise. You need to investigate them with your baby. If they can't yet reach out to touch the 'touchy-feely' object on the page, lift it up so they can mouth it, or rub it on their forehead or cheek.

It is worth taking this time to market books to your baby because in the coming months of parenting there will inevitably be days when you long for a break. What can you do when there is no-one to give you that time alone? You won't be able to recoup your forces with a long hot bath away from the world. But if your child has developed a 'book habit', you can withdraw from the world together. With a pile of books, a 'nest' of pillows and blankets, a plate piled high with chopped-up fruit and a hot chocolate or lemonade each and the phone lifted from its hook, you can build a memory that will give both you and your toddler joy and strength for some weeks to come.

Communication and theory of mind

So at around the same time that pretend play starts, so too does the flowering of communication skills. It's important to look at both what your child can understand and what he can communicate.

Children learn that just as a block can symbolise a car, a word symbolises an action or a thing or a feeling. People can be talked about in their absence. Something can be requested by name as easily as by pointing. Children can understand a great deal more than they can say, and what they can communicate to you in language and gesture is just the tip of the iceberg.

This flowering of understanding and using symbols to communicate matches with your toddler's growing ability to 'pretend'. Together they mean that he can see there is a distance between the world right in front of him and the one in his head. He can share the world in his head with someone else, knowing that there is an inevitable gap between one person's perspective and another's, and work hard to bridge it.

And at three years of age, when the logical and verbally adept left brain comes online, he will begin the journey of adding reasoning skills to his theory of mind. So at four years of age, in the case of Rafael's telephone conversation about the mud-balls with his Granny, his thinking will go like this:

- This is a particularly good mud-ball. The grass is helping it hold together better than usual.
- I think Granny would be excited by it as well. I'm going to tell her about it and see if she is.
- I will have to describe it to her when she is on the phone to me, as she can't see it for herself.
- I hope her reaction is better than Mum's — often it is about things like mud-balls.
- I will then put the mud-ball in the shower where Mum won't see it and where it can stay damp and held together.
- If Mum actually finds it then I will have to explain why I put it there and perhaps she will understand. And she might not find it either.

From now on every discussion you have with your child is a chance to further deepen theory of mind. The strategies of Haim Ginott (see Chapter 4) are your best guide.

When you concentrate on 'empathising first', your child sharpens up his ability to connect to his own feelings and link feelings, thoughts and actions. And that becomes his guide to the hearts and minds of others. The questions to ask are, 'How do you think they are feeling?', 'What are the different results that course of action might lead to?' and 'What else might you have done?' Don't take over his problem solving or thinking, just guide him through it by asking the questions.

In this way you can make sure that every interaction with you, whether it's talking, problem solving, resolving conflict, imagining or building, will grow your child's theory of mind skills further. In just two years, your four year old will need those skills for school and not just for learning, but for coping with the interpersonal quagmire of the classroom.

Chapter 16

Impulse control — giving your child the power to choose

Between stimulus and response is our greatest power
— the freedom to choose.

Stephen R. Covey, *The Seven Habits of Highly Effective People*, 1989.[15]

If your child can put a moment between an impulse — to hit back, to cry, to blame, to laugh — and putting the impulse into action, they have time to choose from among a range of actions and select the best one. It will be an advantage to them for the rest of their life. Impulse control is simply the ability to 'stop' or to 'wait a moment', but it is not so simple when you pull it apart. To stop doing something a child needs:

- the ability to put a 'thinking space' between an impulse and an action
- to know that she needs to stop, and this requires that she is able to both listen to an inner voice (conscience) and accurately interpret cues from her environment (perceptual sensitivity) and from other people (empathy and theory of mind)
- to be motivated to stop, which requires the ability to reason ahead and know that she won't enjoy the consequences of 'not stopping'. And it will be a history of consistent responses from you that has taught her that
- to have the ability to switch her attention to the cues that are telling her to stop and to concentrate long enough on those cues to pick up the message.

So how can you help your child with all of that?

The importance of being consistent

The circuits for impulse control are located in the right hemisphere of the brain, which is growing and dominant until your baby is three years old. So you start with a focus on building the best quality relationship possible with your child.[16] A child's impulse control is positively correlated with a secure, organised attachment with her parents.[17] In terms of impulse control there is one feature of that secure, organised attachment which counts in particular: consistency. And it does this in two different ways.

Firstly, it is the consistency of 'always responding' to your baby. Your baby knows you will come, and so she learns to wait. This is what creates the 'thinking space' between impulse and action. One day that thinking space will fit a thought like, 'I'd better stop doing that because I might hurt my brother.'

Secondly, it is applying a consistent response to her behaviour later. If sometimes she is in trouble for hitting her sibling but not other times, then she isn't going to develop particularly strong motivation to stop. Responding consistently, however, does not mean responding *harshly* or in a way that removes the responsibility for her own impulse control from your child.

With the child who is very impulsive it is very easy to revert to using the commands, 'Stop! Don't! Right now! Do as I tell you.' These sorts of tactics are part of the repertoire of the harsh parent. While tempting to use, they actually minimise your child's opportunities to develop her own skills in impulse control. You are suppressing her inappropriate behaviours for her, and so she can't learn to do it herself. Every time we do this as parents we are preventing our child from learning.

Parenting and temperament are working together here towards a poor outcome. The less controlled the child, the more controlling the parent becomes — and the more controlling the parent, the less opportunities the child has to learn control. So the responsibility for impulse control must be given to the child. How do you do this? Ginott's approach to parenting, discussed in Chapter 4, is an excellent road to take.

This same very controlling behaviour in a parent can create a different problem in the less impulsive child. There is the risk that a child's impulse control will not be a flexible, adaptable skill but simply

How good is your child's impulse cr

A child with good impulse control is able to:

- *sit still (but not before four)*
- *wait her turn (at around two and a half)*
- *stop when asked to (from two and a half)*
- *resist temptation (but not before three).*

If a child struggles with waiting, staying still, resisting temptation, planning ahead and following instructions then she has low impulse control. Obviously, this is a call you make over weeks rather than days. And you must consider just what impulses she might have to suppress, because some children have a more impulsive temperament. That type of temperament coupled with a birthday party, for example, will mean that a child 'blows the lid' of her impulse control. Common sense also tells us that such basic factors as good health, good nutrition and adequate sleep are important here too.

a blanket inhibition of all impulses. This is impulse control taken too far, leading to a child who expresses and does little but thinks a great deal. This leads to depression and anxiety in the long term.

Being consistent is a big part of good parenting but it is very hard to be consistent consistently. It is hard work even without an external opposing force, and children are a significant opposing force from about 18 months old. They prowl the boundaries you've set, methodically testing for a weakness in the current of your will. The velociraptors that tested the fences in *Jurassic Park* have nothing on a child. Why do children do this? I think they do it to reassure themselves that the boundaries that keep them safe are strong ones. When the current of our will appears to have weakened — when we are tired or busy or distracted, particularly by the telephone — our children will then renew their efforts to test the fences. What I've discovered during 12 and a half years of parenting is that the more frequently your fences 'give', the more your children will test them. Testing behaviour tends to disappear the more consistent you are. It took me some years to work this out, however. So even though the

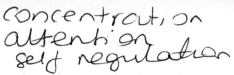
concentration on attention self regulation

effort to be consistent is very tiring, inconsistency is ultimately more tiring still.

I think it is this bit of parenting that puts it over the line for 'the hardest job in the world'. To have the energy and endurance that being consistent demands, parents need to have 'fuel in their own tank'. This is a drum I've banged in the early chapters. Good quality childcare and income splitting and supportive workplaces — all of these would help parents meet this bit of the parenting job description.

Apart from consistency, what else helps in the development of impulse control? Parents improve impulse control by improving the other self-regulation tools — empathy and theory of mind (already discussed), perceptual sensitivity (a big subject covered in the following chapter) and the ability to switch attention between cues and to concentrate long enough on those cues to pick up the message.

Growing attention and concentration

Attention is the ability to focus on one thing to the exclusion of others. It has a huge role in learning as it lets us dismiss irrelevant information and focus on what really counts. A child with good attention skills is able to wield his senses like a high-powered spotlight, keeping them trained on the relevant detail and excavating for deeper insights all the time. Concentration is all about the length of time the spotlight can be flicked from detail to detail. Attention is the intensity or the level of focus, while concentration is the endurance or length of a play episode.

Most parents want their children to be able to play by themselves for a while. A child who demands to be constantly entertained and played with is exhausting to parent. For our sanity we need them to have the capacity to amuse themselves. Fortunately, this is something that we can teach.

The most important thing to remember is to play with your baby for some of the time. Don't leave the job of entertaining him up to a toddler or to the TV. The longest play sessions babies have are with their parents and it is these play sessions that stretch their ability to sustain and focus attention.[18] By 'stretching' them with these sessions, you are lengthening the time they can play by themselves.

The kind of games you play also contributes strongly to your child's attention skills. You need to create a balance of play by including some very exciting games where your child's attention is compelled, but also some of the very simple games which require your child to pay attention: the low intensity pleasures (see page 80, Part Two). Check whether you are seeing your child doing such things as completing puzzles, playing with dolls and having time in the sandpit with water and toys.

I cannot recommend these low intensity pleasures too highly. Although it wasn't a connection I made until recently, over and over again I've seen low intensity activities lead to a child with better self-regulation. For example, a highly emotional child who just months after developing a passion for Lego or Mobilo was far better at keeping a lid on his emotions; a highly active toddler (and being highly active at this age is a risk factor for attention problems in preschool) who had many stories read to him a day and went on to perform very well in kindergarten; a little girl who was lagging behind her age peers with fine motor skills and who completed a low intensity therapy program with not just her fine motor skills but her attention skills greatly improved.

And it fits with the research into the way environment impacts upon temperament. Dr Theodore Wachs conducts research in just this area. He is clearly a man with a sense of humour, although not the kind particularly appreciated by mothers of young children. One of his measurement tools is called the Chaos Questionnaire, which further breaks down into the Confusion, Hubbub and Order Scale.[19] He also measures the rooms-to-person ratio. His findings? One was that more tractable toddlers come from more ordered homes with a higher room-to-person ratio. He relates this to the fact that less caregiving occurs in busy, disordered settings, which is a very reasonable conclusion. However, it also seems likely that it is much harder for children to engage independently in low intensity activities in such a setting, and that this has long term consequences in terms of self-regulation.[20] Fascinatingly, he also found that boys suffer more negative consequences from living in such busy homes than do little girls.

So how do parents build the capacity to enjoy low intensity activities in their children? It is partly done by managing the environment. A quieter home with less stuff, more order and less

no TV /computers

emotional confusion means that children can have their attention caught and kept by the low intensity occupations.

Avoid heavily structuring your child's day. Such things as time spent sitting in a sandpit letting the sand drip through fingers or lost in a picture book might look like time wasted, but in fact it is extremely valuable. Your child will be building attention, concentration and perceptual skills in this time. Equally, time spent playing computer games and watching television should be minimal. Even though they are not intense physically, neither entertainment television nor computer games ask the child to focus. Instead, they compel focus through highly intense pictures and sounds, as parents need to do to engage a very young baby (or a child with an intellectual disability), but normally less and less as a child grows up. Children cannot develop good attention and concentration while watching a screen, and time which could be spent developing these skills is lost.

So get rid of the television or keep it turned off most of the time (or perhaps, as my cousin Penny has done, hide it in a cupboard and only bring it out for special occasions). A 2008 study of very young children showed that their occasional glances at the TV, which seem so harmless, actually reduced not just the length of a play episode but the amount of focus they brought to their play.[21]

Like behaviour, movement and everything else, attention and concentration have developmental stages. In this case, they correlate quite closely with a child's age. By recognising the different stages you can better know how to intervene to help your child onto the next stage.

Moving your child up to the next stage

Your baby will get bored quite quickly, and a bored baby is not a baby who is trying to focus his attention. Limit the number of toys available at any one time as this will help your baby pick out one thing from his environment and focus upon it. Also, give him the chance to explore something new regularly, or, at the very least, rotate the toys you have. (Lots of practice focusing will also make your baby tired and he'll sleep better after an interesting day.)

Your *one year old* should be able to concentrate for at least three minutes in a moderately distracting setting. But from time to time his attention will be 'caught and dragged' when he'd really rather have kept on with what he was doing. Apart from when he is doing something he really shouldn't, don't interrupt him when he is absorbed in play by himself. Independent play is the beginnings of the ability to work independently.

At *two years old* children are less distractible and can keep playing for longer, but their attention still has a brittle quality. His attention is held rigidly by what he is doing, but once his focused state is broken he is unlikely to return to what he was doing. Two year olds have difficulty coping with any interference in their play. The older sibling who attempts to join in may be greeted with tears or a turned back or (worst of all) biting due to frustration over the loss of a happy play session. If a two year old is playing happily alongside you, talk about what you're doing without interfering with his play: for example, 'I'm just pushing my truck down the road.'

If your two year old is happy to have you discuss what you are doing, expand the discussion out and talk about what he's doing too. Gradually modify his play by making your play a little ahead of his play instead of alongside: for example, drag your train in front of his, or bounce your doll up the pathway to the house ahead of her doll. From this he will gradually learn to accept new ideas into his games without losing his attention on his own game. The ability to widen focus without losing attention is a critical one in learning throughout life: we all need to know how to accept new ideas.

At *three years old* children are able to switch between looking and listening and are able to listen to you and then return to their play. Expect them to come more slowly out of their games and to need a clear cue to stop play and start listening. In kindergartens you will hear teachers say, 'Have you got your listening ears on?' or, 'Whole body listening please, class' before delivering the information. So at three you should definitely anticipate that your child will need extra help to switch between looking and listening.

The next stage, at *four years old*, is when the child is controlling the switch between looking and listening for himself. To help your three year old achieve this you need to prompt him to listen, and then, afterwards, prompt him to return to his game. When you are playing with him, build on his ideas to make the game more elaborate. Not in an intrusive way, but it is during this three- to four-year-old time period that children begin to really love collaborative play. 'And then we put a whole lot of bushes into the garden.'

'Yes! Then they have flowers.'

'And they need to be watered with flower water to really blossom.'

'And we make special flower water by mashing up old flowers.'

From *four years to five years* games grow in length and complexity. They can have episodes, with children returning to further elaborate or add more details to a storyline. This is enabled by the ability to sustain attention despite distractions. While your child might still need a little help to know that it's time to listen, it is now destructive to his attention skills to demand that your five year old show he is listening by looking at you. Why? Because at school he will need to be able to deal with the teacher saying something like, 'It's five minutes to recess. You need to finish colouring in the picture before then and pack up.' Stopping work to listen is going to disadvantage him in the classroom.

If your five year old looks up (as he will do if it's a long message) that's fine, but it's not something that he needs to do to prove he's listening. At five you are hoping to see a child who is beginning to be able to look at one thing and listen to another.

At *six to seven* this ability needs to be well enough developed so that he can listen to a long message while looking at something else. When a child can follow a complex set of directions without looking up, his attention and concentration skills have developed sufficiently for him to be able to cope with formal schooling. One other way of recognising school readiness is to listen to 'pretend' play themes. If children are collaborating to make up societies or worlds, sustaining themes and storylines over long periods of time and are able to stay focused on their game despite distractions, then their attention skills are ready for the demands of school.

Impulse control added to attention

Being in a classroom is a big strain on children's attention skills. The average classroom features lots of visual stimulation, a bombardment of sound and the unpredictable behaviour of classmates. The need to block out other competing information becomes far more pronounced. At this point impulse control skills, the ability to stop ourselves doing something, need to be added to attention for children to cope. They need to be able to stop themselves listening to a friend and not the teacher. They need to look at a book and not out the window. And that impulse plus attention combination is also vital for formal learning.

For a child trying to learn to read it is strong attention that lets him dismiss the irrelevant information and focus on what really counts. He might see a 'c' at the beginning of a word and the urge to say 'cat' might occur, but strong impulse control lets him continue attending to the whole word, which turns out to be 'cow'. The two self-regulation skills work together. Learning is really 'creating useful memories': where attention and impulse control work together to create a memory. As children get older and their attention and impulse control improves, they become better at creating these useful memories.[22]

So what can you do to practise this in the short years before school? You are probably doing most of it already. With a one year old, games like 'Where's Mummy?' are excellent. He must choose to *not* point at any of the distracting objects but at the right person or thing. For older children, these games do the same thing:

- Pointing to pictures in books. The Usborne puzzle books, *Where's Wally?* and Australia's own Graeme Base picture books are great for this. This helps your child practise the skill of 'not looking' at those things designed to distract him from the real target.
- Sleeping lions. This remarkably silly game works better with a group: all the children have to lie down on their backs with their eyes closed and not cover their faces with their hands. Then you say something funny and they mustn't laugh. They mustn't quiver or squirm! Some choice phrases are, 'pig's bottom' and 'little baggy elephant bums' and 'exploding bu — I mean bombs'.
- Playing card and board games. Learning to wait for your turn is excellent practice in impulse control.

And there is one more thing: impulse control is something that you teach by having good impulse control yourself. And this can be so hard. Again, parents need support so they are not too tired or too busy or too stressed to be able to be in command of themselves.

Chapter 17

Growing perceptual sensitivity

*… there was so much to see, and hear, and touch —
walks to take, hills to climb, caterpillars to watch …
the special smell of each day …*

Norton Juster, *The Phantom Tollbooth*, 1961.[23]

Our inherent sensory preferences and sensitivities shape the people we become: our likes, abilities and vocations. The child with a genetic propensity for good coordination has a lot of room on her body map: she will be capable of far more refined movement as she is able to better organise information coming in through her touch and body senses. This is the baby who is sitting up and accurately matching pot lids to pots at five months of age. Another baby may be humming in tune at eight months: he is better able to register and organise auditory information than most children.

In fact, most of us don't think of perceptual sensitivity so much as skills but as character traits because they have so much influence on how our child behaves. A child who is super-sensitive to touch is not going to be as outgoing as other children. She will be more easily upset. This looks like 'difficult behaviour', and yet any of us who experienced touch as taxing, invasive bombardment would behave the same way.

There are so many cross-linkages between perceptual sensitivity and the other self-regulation skills. Perceptual sensitivity is strongly linked to attention: we pay attention through our senses. Our senses are the spotlight we use to illuminate the world, and attention directs that spotlight. Perceptual sensitivity is also required for empathy, impulse control and theory of mind, because without it we do not detect the vital clues coming in from other people and the environment.

In the western world we tend to know most about the external senses: vision, touch, hearing, smell and taste. In our culture, making sure our babies have a range of different experiences in each sensory modality is something parents do well because it is part of our preoccupation with stimulating our babies. We tend to know less about the internal senses, the ones that detect head position, body position and movement. And yet these 'secret senses' play such a big part in a child's learning.

Attachment and perceptual sensitivity

To grow the senses your baby needs movement. As your baby explores space, movement and time her already interconnected 'sensory processing' brain areas become a rich tapestry of pathways. She needs to devote as much time as possible to this, exploring for more data and sorting through what she's learned. What allows a baby such a free rein and grants such confidence? A secure attachment.

In the beginning our babies are drawn into the world through their contact with us: the pleasure of loving touch, the enticement of our smiles and voices and smell, the stimulation of being rocked and held. We are their world to begin with, and the more predictably responsive we are, the faster our babies learn.

So a secure attachment is a big player in creating strong perceptual skills. Insecure attachments create children who are more focused on what Mum is doing; even the avoidant child, though apparently 'off exploring' is doing so in order to keep Mum close. The child's attention is not on the wider world, but on staying safe. Learning occurs when a child is truly paying attention: the insecure child is not. A less well-developed sensory system will result.

With the world of Mum under her belt, the securely attached baby ventures out into the wider world. She knows that she is watched, that she is delighted in, that she will be rescued when it is required. This utter confidence that she will be kept safe allows her to enjoy the multi-

sensory buzz of moving, seeing, hearing, balancing, touching all at the one time and under her own steam. Your baby learns to organise, synthesise, store and select from this massive volume of data to create a 'continuous' picture of the world. Eventually, her strong perceptual skills will bring her a great deal of joy: she will dissolve into a blue sky, surrender to music and feel herself accelerate away from the starting line.

I have just read all this to Mum. To my astonishment she responded by roaring with laughter. Eventually she stopped laughing and explained that my words had triggered her memory of how she and Dad had tried to teach me about the danger of falling off something. The house was full of such traps: verandas, high steps and so on. So they would place me up high on the mantelpiece or on the cupboard or on the forbidden top step and watch me anxiously for signs that my depth perception and sense of danger was developing. As soon as I looked like falling they would catch me.

So did I learn that high was dangerous? I didn't. The entire time that I was up high I was being delighted in, kept safe, and rescued as required. What I learnt was that high was fun. By the time my siblings arrived my parents had learned to teach 'danger' simply with a warning gaze, a shake of the head and saying, 'No, dangerous'.

The secret senses

As I write I frequently reach out to a mug. It's an automatic motion. My hand 'knows' where the mug sits due to the information coming in from my peripheral vision. My expectation of the mug's weight is already influencing the amount of muscle power I am recruiting to lift it. My hand is setting itself to wrap around the mug based on the 'memory' of its size. My fingers will slip around the outside and grip. I can bring it to my mouth without looking: tipping and opening my mouth will coincide without me needing to think about it.

So what makes this possible? It is my 'inside senses' at work. I have a sense of head position, called the vestibular sense, which tells my hand where to bring that cup. My kinaesthetic (body movement) sense is feeding back about any changes I make in my position. And, holding this all together is my sense of where I am in space, my proprioceptive sense. This is what is telling me where my mouth is in my head, where my hand is in relation to the cup and so on. I don't need to look — I can just 'feel'. With all those secret senses working in harmony with 'touch' and with each other, I can close my eyes and still know where every bit of me is. This is so basic to our lives that we don't think about it.

When those senses are well developed our child will be able to write letters without looking because her hand will 'know' the shape of an 'A'. I am often referred children who don't have the sensory development to do this: they watch every letter as it is shaped by their pencil. They can't get to the 'automatic' stage because they have to look to know what they are doing. They can't just 'feel it'. They can't store the 'memory of that feeling' either. They are stuck.

What do therapists do when they meet a child like this? They go back to scratch, putting in the early sensory games that this child obviously needs more of to grow this particular sense. And we recommend that it is you who plays those games with her. Your child learns that way. Having fun with someone you love leads to the release of oxytocin, not just the love but the learning hormone, and rapid brain (neural) growth is the result.

Every child is different. Some children need more time to develop a particular sense. Some children are hypersensitive. But when parents play as much as they can of these games in early childhood, this rich, detailed sensorium can grow 'the first time round'. You will find many early games described in the rest of this chapter, and more in Appendix IV.

Growing the balance sense

In fact, we are born with just one sensory system 'ready to go' and it is this one: the vestibular or balance sense. The neurons that connect to the tiny little hair cells deep in the ear which detect position changes are hard-wired and working well before birth.

You might be thinking, 'What about the auditory sense? Isn't that also fully matured?' They are very close to the same thing. The senses of hearing and balance share the ear. Physicists see both sound and movement as 'vibration energy', albeit vibration at different speeds. And this is something we all know innately. The near-exploding boom box that we can both feel and hear is the perfect example.

Fascinatingly, your baby doesn't move around in utero just 'because', but in response to different sounds.[24] So hearing and balance and movement are tied together from the very first.

On page 131 I wrote, 'Beyond survival, though, the reflexes also link movement and sensation tightly together, paving the way for perceptual sensitivity and precise movement later.' The reflexes are already linked to the 'ready to go' balance system, and their action tunes all the other senses to balance first.

Both my sisters are heavily pregnant at the moment. And because I always ask, they tell me just what their babies are doing. I like to hear that my nephews are kicking them in the ribs, because that means that baby is 'head down'. This is a sign that baby is responding properly to gravity. I also like to hear that the babies are whizz–popping around because I know this means they are getting an unerring feel for upside down, right way up and 'over to the side'. The babies who don't settle head down in the womb or don't move a great deal are at a disadvantage. Their sense of balance, to which all other senses are tuned, is not tuned correctly itself. Everything else will therefore be 'out of whack' (a lovely technical phrase!).

And it continues to be whole body movement that grows the balance sense. When you hold your baby close and roll over and over, tumbling the baby like a lioness does her cubs, you are growing the balance sense. When you rock your baby while gazing into her eyes you are helping her link balance and vision.

The kinds of activities which build the balance sense are:

- Rolling games like 'There were four in the bed and the little one said, roll over, roll over'. Help your baby or child roll, and start with quarter rolls and then back again. Encourage spinning games when your child is three and older.
- Hanging upside down games. When your baby has good head control, sit her on your lap, then lean back a little and bring her up again. For an older child encourage her to swing sitting up on a bar, and then slowly encourage her to hang upside down with her eyes closed.
- Holding your baby close, dance in a rocking motion to music with a steady beat. Rock an older child over a gym ball, with her in charge of the rocking.

- Singing to your baby and your toddler. What stimulates the ear will also stimulate the vestibular nerve. So sing, sing, sing!
- Rockers, seesaws, gym balls, scooter boards, barrels and giant saucers are all excellent for older children, indeed they are far better than the kind of toys and playground equipment that doesn't move. What you are looking for is equipment that re-creates the early experience of being rocked and carried.

Growing the 'body map' and body movement senses

The receptors for position and movement are deep within the body, in the joints and muscles. They are activated by being stretched or squashed by muscle movement and pressure from outside — by weight, in other words. Children need to push, to pull apart, to lift, to squeeze between, to slide under, to tug, to jump, to climb, to hang: all the activities that require strength and the cooperation of big muscle groups.

There is far less of these types of experiences in children's lives now. Toys are mostly made of light-weight plastic. The backyard trampoline has been replaced with indoor toys. Parents and teachers need to deliberately return heavy work or heavy play activities to children's lives.

Here are some ideas to help grow the movement senses:
- Rock your baby from side to side, or compress her shoulder joints gently when she is rocking backwards and forwards in preparation to crawling.
- Let your child fill up her backpack with rocks and wear it. Don't say, 'Isn't that too heavy?' She might be seeking that very feeling.
- Wrap up your child tightly in a sheet or blanket and then play that she is a caterpillar hatching from a cocoon, or a dragon hatching from an egg made of pillows and doonas.
- Make objects your child likes to shift heavier: for example, tape phone books under chairs.
- Play 'wheelbarrows' and wheel your child along.
- Look for what she seeks and help her find it in safe ways. If she is rocketing off you or the walls she is seeking touch information to help her navigate. Play blindfold games so she can really fine-tune that sense.

The clumsiness that goes with growth spurts is often a result of a child not having yet linked her new body precisely to the map in the brain. If your child becomes very clumsy and even a bit emotionally uncertain after a growth spurt, you might like to consider helping her improve her body schema by adding in some touch feedback. Push firmly and heavily down on her shoulders and head and do a heavy compressive massage along her arms and hands.

The known senses

Although I'm discussing the senses individually, the important thing is that they work together to tell a coherent story. Consider the 'Where's your nose, where's my nose' game that babies love so much. Baby is learning how far to reach to grab her nose and your nose without injuring herself or you. She is matching up visual information with the internal knowledge of where she is in space and time (her balance) and movement information and touch information and verbal information too. Each piece of information is being used to confirm the other pieces.

We find great joy in 'playing' with our senses throughout our lives — eating weird cuisine, spinning round and round, studying the illusion of depth in a hologram — and each of these experiences re-alerts us to the world. The ghostly touch in an empty room; the smell that seems to come from nowhere; the good taste of blue ice-cream coupled with its repulsive appearance; the sound of a train travelling past us in the cinema although there's not a train in sight. All those illusions strike at the heart of what we learned in the first months of life: that information from one sense is always supported by information through another.

Vision

We only have to open our eyes and the world streams in. However, we are not just 'receivers' but interpreters of information. It is very easy to overload our babies and toddlers in our very visually stimulating world. When things are kept simpler then their interpretive skills are given a head start. So keep the environment as visually simple as you can. Think about keeping the number of toys available for play down to minimum (the one toy for each child rule is very useful here). When you do this your children will be able to better attend to just one toy, building both attention and visual skills. These are some ideas for early games:

- When you notice that your baby has a particular toy she loves, play 'Where has it gone, here it is' games.
- All games where your baby gets to 'track' a moving object are great. Encourage her to watch it move around the room. Roll balls and have your crawler chase them.
- Lie your baby on her back and have her swipe at or try to catch a suspended object, or even your hand. This can get very giggly, which is an excellent thing.
- Toys that operate by blowing and bubbles are great for helping children focus close up.[25]
- Combine balance and visual stimulation by playing catching and throwing while a child is swinging, or grab playfully at baby's feet while someone else moves them.
- Books that have pop-outs, or make noises, or have different materials to touch encourage looking and touching and listening together, which supports the development of visual attention.

At the end of their second year of life, toddlers learn to position themselves near bookshelves or a favourite toy and wait for an unwary adult to walk past. They place one hand upon your leg and the other on the pile of books, and you have been caught in the toddler trap.

This pile of books is significant. Children are beginning to compare a bear in one book with a bear in another, and this is something to encourage. Your child is able to learn that a picture of an apple isn't the same as another picture of an apple, but that both, regardless of differences, are apples. This is the same as knowing that the letter 'A' in one book is the same as the 'a' in another.

Slowly children become more and more able to tell the differences between shapes that are quite similar. An 'a' and 'p' are not so very different, but nowhere near as different as a horse and a giraffe are from each other. With lots of looking at things and lots and lots of talking about same and different, children get better and better at seeing differences. Discussing just how the horse and giraffe are different from each other is, in fact, how children are eventually able to tell you that an 'a' doesn't have a tail but a 'p' does, than an 'a' looks to the start of a sentence and a 'p' to the end of the sentence and so on.

This is what your child is looking for when she traps you near the book pile or her favourite toy. This is what she is looking for when she asks so obscurely, 'Why is it a truck?' She doesn't want to hear, 'That's just what it's called', she wants to hear that it's because it's bigger than a car but smaller than a bus. That it carries all sorts of things, but that cars carry people and so do buses. And so on. Visual perceptual skills are not developed just by looking; they are developed by looking and talking and doing all at once.

Make sure that you include in the book pile some rhyming books and alphabet books. Dr Seuss's *ABC*, Lynley Dodd's *Hairy Maclary* books, illustrated books of poetry full of C. J. Dennis and Robert Louis Stevenson, zoo animal alphabet books, Aussie icon alphabet books, rhyming alphabet books: as much rhyme and alphabet as you can lay your hands on. It is in this time period when children will want the same books read over and over that you can most easily build an appreciation of rhyme and alphabet. Make sure that as you read you don't just point to the pictures, but also spend some time running your fingers along the text.

The current research is heading more and more to the view that reading is not actually helped directly by rhyme.[26] Rhyme is something that children absolutely love, however, and if they love the rhymes, they will be more likely to love books. It does seem that lots of practice hearing the different sounds of the alphabet does help in learning to read.[27]

Not only that, but when reading alphabet books we tend to point to a letter, which is bolded and highlighted and much larger on the page, and say the sound it makes. We are explicitly teaching children that the sound goes with the shape. It is not terribly different from pointing to a cat and saying 'miaow'. When you are reading, make sure that you don't say 'ay' for the letter A but the main sound the letter produces, the short 'a' sound in cat. And so on. Knowing the sounds a letter makes is more helpful than knowing its name in learning to read.[4, 11, 28]

Smell

Our smell sense is working well from early in life — and while some senses can be missing in some people, just about everyone is born with a sense of smell. Babies know the smell of their mother's breast milk because of its close match to the smell of her placental fluid.[29] Because of the way the brain develops 'up', a good sense of smell helps grow a good touch sense. So a good sense of smell is more important than you'd think.

And anyone who has ever had an aromatherapy session knows that smell can improve mood, attention, planning and alertness.[30, 31] And that using essential oils can be very helpful with a cranky, tired toddler. In general, though, I suggest that you talk about and share your responses to smell with your child, from the stinky nappy to the smell of furniture polish.

Touch

The touch sense is what gives precision to fine-motor movements and boundaries to our 'body map'. In fact, there are different sorts of touch. 'Light' touch is what teaches precision while 'heavy' touch engages the body position and movement senses.

Infant massage is a celebration of the touch sense, but the most important part of infant massage, according to practitioners, is 'asking the baby's permission'. It is not about the right techniques but responding with sensitivity to your baby. Nothing changes as our child grows up. In introducing any kind of new touch experience, such as a new food, playdough, slime, sand or foam, show your baby that you expect it to be fun, but look for any signs that she doesn't like it. Never push them to continue with an activity that is clearly making them uncomfortable.

Talk about same and different in terms of how much something weighs or how something feels. Same and different are vital concepts. From same and different your child will build 'more and less', 'bigger and littler', 'darker and lighter', all the way up to 'p not b'. If this knowledge is purely delivered through the visual sense it is not as powerful. Linking what is seen with what is felt and what is heard is the way to go.

Hearing

Just as we keep the environment visually simple to help our babies learn to interpret what they seeing, we also need to keep the aural landscape simple. To hear the difference between 't' and 'k' babies need to be able to focus on our voice. Try to keep other sounds to a minimum when your baby is awake and playing: this means to turn off the television and radio for as much of the time as possible.

Once baby is crawling and grasping and banging, remember that she needs to hear the sounds she is making. Let her be in charge of the noise in the house, let her bang away on the pots and pans, make scraping sounds with a shovel, hammer or jump on bubble wrap. Sing songs with her where she gets to 'turn the music up or down'.

Talk about sounds with her as they happen: birdsong, vehicle noises. Play games where you try and pinpoint just where the noise has come from. Then see if you can work out together what made the noise. Finally, play games to do with the sequence in which noises happen. This is following the normal developmental sequence: Where is it? What is it? What's the order in which it happened?

From about two years you can start to play the sound remembering games:

- Singing nursery rhymes with one line missing and ask your child to spot what was missing. Further refinements in this game include missing just one word or, eventually, just a sound.
- Make 'mistakes' when reading her well-known books. Start by missing out words at the end of rhyming sentences, because they are the easiest to spot. (Lynley Dodd's and Dr Seuss's books work very well for this.)

When children turn three their language skills are such that most of them can hear phonemes (the individual sounds that make up w-or-d-s) quite well. You can slowly say to them 'c' (pause) 'a' (pause) 't', and they can blend those together and say 'cat'.[11]

One of the best pre-reading games you can play with your kindergartener or pre-primary child is to ask them to do this. You give them the sounds separated by a brief pause: 'i'… 'n'. What word does that make? When your child can blend two sounds together then you can move up to three and then four. (Other good games for auditory skills can be found in Appendix V.)

A large number of the pieces for reading come together in this preschool period. Does this mean your child is ready to learn to read? Probably not. This is covered in more detail in Part Five.

In all of these interactions, remember that babies and toddlers are not passive recipients of our efforts. From very early they are shaping us into the teachers and carers they need us to be. Recently Mum saw a five-month-old baby girl. Her mother explained that the baby would not hold her bottle for herself although all her friend's babies were able to manage holding a bottle. So Mum explored every single reason a baby might not want to hold something.

Was the baby uncomfortable with tactile stimuli? No. The baby enjoyed touching and mouthing all kinds of objects. Was the position in the pram somehow uncomfortable for the baby — was the little neck 'out'? No. The baby tolerated all sorts of different positions without difficulty. Was there a problem with grip? No. And so it went on. Eventually Mum tumbled to it. The baby had discovered that if she refused to hold the bottle, her mother would pick her up and cuddle her during the feed. She wanted those cuddles.

At five months old this little girl was 'advance planning' to get what she needed. That is what our children do, and from very early on. When children love a game they reward you with their delight. That tells you that this is a game they need to play again and again.

Also remember to follow your child's lead. Never impose upon her. Never push past her comfort zone. Stop straightaway if she isn't enjoying the game for whatever reason. When a parent demands that a child keeps playing despite her distress they are not just damaging the relationship but reinforcing a 'yucky feeling' going with a particular sensation. If you are not both having fun, then stop.

In Appendix IV you will find information about what can go wrong with sensory development and how to help a child with these kinds of difficulties.

Chapter 18

Self-regulation and mood

Because he wasn't feeling happy,
Wombat became hard to get on with.

Ruth Park, *The Muddle-Headed Wombat at School*, 1966.[32]

In the first three years of life it is the frustration–effort–success cycle
of developing movement skills that most shapes our children's
behaviour. From then onwards it is the development of self-regulation
skills.

How children move through these behavioural stages, including
how hard they hit the bumps, depends greatly on the nature of the
child. When a particular age and a trait collide the result can be some
extreme behaviour or moods; the already imaginative child at the
highly imaginative ages of four and five can almost never be believed.
For example, Sam at five years old never went to collect the eggs
from the chooks without seeing *several* foxes departing from the hen
house. The introvert will be more introverted at seven and nine than
will the extrovert. The high-energy child will be a blur of motion at
the age of eight. And so on. So some children will seem to 'float
around the course', changing only a little as the years go by, whereas
other children appear to be having an experience akin to white-
water rafting.

Temperament and behaviour

You might be wondering if there are some 'emotional' temperament
traits that impact on self-regulation and behaviour. It is actually not
clear. Researchers are still wondering, as are parents, whether a child
is 'easy' because of temperament or because of parenting.

The model of temperament — with its emphasis on the self-regulation skills — that I've used was developed by researcher Dr Mary Rothbart. Like so many people, her interest in temperament was sparked by how very different her two children were. As well as the traits I've called 'self-regulation skills' (she calls them 'effortful control'), she has two other sets of traits.[33, 34]

The first she calls extroversion/surgency, which is a combination of 'go-getterness' and 'outgoingness'. The second she has labelled 'negative affectivity', which is the tendency to feel the sadder emotions. Both traits impact on a child's self-regulation, and they, in turn, impact back upon them. For example, when his perceptual skills are too sensitive then a child is going to be more easily upset. When a child has less sensitive perceptual skills he is going to find it harder to learn, so he may be an 'easy' baby but start to struggle at school at about year four. That difficulty with school may then lead to the child having more of the sadder emotions.

In this example, you can see how normalising one of the self-regulation skills is going to alter a child's behaviour. Equally, if it is a really 'good week' for some reason, a sensorily sensitive child is not going to get upset as easily. I guess the message is that everything is interacting with everything else, and parenting goes straight into that mix.

In fact, what the temperament research is suggesting is that you and your baby are both engaged in the work of creating the other person. The kind of parent you are is in some ways a creation of the kind of baby you have. The calmer baby creates a calmer parent. Equally, the kind of parent you are shapes baby's temperament: brain structure, neurochemistry, hormones, even the switching on of particular genes. And then the changes to the baby's temperament go on to affect how you parent him.[19] Researchers have begun to track how parents' own temperament impacts upon their children, and how, in turn, children's temperament impacts upon their parents' personalities. Extroverted parents help children develop 'effortful control'; neurotic or more worried parents have children who express more negative emotions. Highly active children actually make parents less worried. These transactions — baby changing parent and then parent changing baby — never end.[35]

What I take from the research, and what I have seen as a parent too, is that children change. A tearful and fearful toddler can become a serene teenager. A very, very extroverted preschooler who misses the subtleties of mood in others can become an empathic adult.

Some traits are stickier than others, however. Highly active children are likely to remain so and to become extroverts. The shy child who has the more easily activated amygdala has that throughout life, but he can learn to hide it when required, too.

So, to answer the question about parenting and temperament, which one is it that creates a child's behaviour? It is both. They are interacting with each other, and with your child's inner development and the demands of the environment. We usually ask ourselves this type of question when we are faced with a behaviour we don't like. I believe blaming the child's temperament for a particular behaviour or expression of mood is very frequently, although not always, a cop-out. In thinking about any change in our child we need to ask ourselves many different questions:

- Has something changed in his world?
- Am I rewarding this behaviour somehow?
- Am I not connecting closely enough with him? Will more time with me stop the behaviour?
- Is he having enough sleep?
- Is he eating the wrong food? Is he getting enough food?
- Is he getting ill?
- Is my child struggling with a mismatch between his self-regulation or other skills and what is being required of him? Is too much being asked of him?
- Is he bored or under-challenged or under-occupied? Is not enough being asked of him?
- Has he hit a tricky behavioural stage that matches an existing temperamental trait?

In the following pages you will find the Gesell Institute's different stages in the years three to seven, which might help you answer the last question. Remember, this is just a general guide because each child is different.[36]

Three to four
The storm of development calms briefly at three. As the left brain takes over from the right, you will notice that your child's speech

suddenly improves. He can say almost anything he wants. He can even say 'yes', which seems to be nigh impossible at two.

With his better understanding of why you feel the way you do, he very much enjoys the feeling of 'having done the right thing'.

On the movement front, he has now developed the last of the 'mature reflexes' that support good movement skills, so the stage is set for the building of ever more refined skills. Everything is in balance.

Three and a half, though, is where it all breaks down. In seeking to master new goals, newer kinds of relationships (this is the age when play becomes more cooperative), your child can place such emotional pressure on himself that even his motor skills founder slightly. If he has not fully resolved primitive movement patterns, this is the time they may begin to show up as tripping, fear of heights and falling. He may complain that his ears and eyes don't work. And this physical insecurity spills over into relationships. Three and a half year olds are often very jealous, needing a great deal of reassurance that they are valued as much as another sibling, or even another friend. What is happening in the minds of others is now a preoccupation (and, of course, one that remains with us for most of our lives).

Four to five

Four is best described as 'an out of bounds age'. Whereas at three and a half your child had difficulty managing his moods, at four it comes a lot easier. Normally this is a good thing for parents but not this time! The four year old is confident and independent. In fact, he is so confident and independent that he confidently breaks every prohibition. His new theory of mind skills have taught him that Mum and Dad aren't omniscient, and so he knows that technically it is possible for him to get away with all sorts of things. Naturally, he's going to try a few of them.

But four makes way for five, which is one of the periods of greatest equilibrium, and four and a half is the time of transition. Emerging fine motor control is matched by emerging emotional control. The time of 'talking to learn' has well and truly arrived, and four and a half year olds are hungry for details, perhaps to help them learn the line between reality and imaginings, or perhaps to boost the details in their recounts of imaginary events.

Five to six

Children are often at their sweetest at five, although unfortunately this is the time when they enter their first year of 'proper school' and they spend much of the year exhausted. Despite this, they want to be good, and they have all the skills they need to be good — so they are happy with themselves and their parents are also happy. All the years of tender caring you have spent are suddenly reciprocated in great bursts of consideration and affection.

And at five and a half, as he once more sets his sights on new fields to conquer, and inevitably discovers that the skills required aren't present, his serenity and docility disappear.

Six to seven

Six sees a return to defiance. It is an age of expansion, where every new experience is desirable and decision making becomes as vexed as it was at two and a half. Peer relationships become very difficult, particularly when all the children in a group are aged six. They all have to win. They all have to be right. This is probably not the age to try and introduce board games, so introduce them earlier or later. Like other ages where skills don't match ambitions, distress is only a heartbeat away. The six year old can switch from happy enthusiasm to tearful despair in an instant.

From six and a half these behaviours appear less and less often. The more thoughtful age of seven is approaching. Developmentally, it is at about seven years of age that most children can reasonably be asked to cope with formal schooling. Unfortunately, however, our children are being required to cope with these demands well before this age.

In Part Five we will focus on the skills that underpin school success in such things as making friends and reading. Many of the skills have developed well before now but this is the time to make sure they are all 'lined-up' so that your child can cope with school.

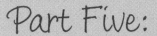

Part Five:

Ready for school

Children will not enter school ready to learn unless families, schools and communities provide the environments and experiences that support the physical, social, emotional, language, literacy, and cognitive development of infants, toddlers and pre-school children.

From the US National School Readiness Indicators Initiative, cited in 'School Readiness', Australian Research Alliance for Children and Youth, 2007.[1]

Chapter 19

When should formal learning start?

It is important to remember that much school difficulty can be prevented entirely by not starting the child in too soon in school.

Frances Lillian Ilg and Louise Bates Ames,
The Gessell Institute's *Child Behavior*, 1961.[2]

In Australia children officially start formal education somewhere between five and six years of age. Many children do cope with formal learning at that age, but some children (approximately one quarter in Australia at the moment), most of them boys, learn instead that they aren't good at learning.

Formal learning requires the melding of so many different elements of skill and self.[3] It is something that is forgotten in our drive to prove educational outcomes and to alleviate our anxiety about our child's ability to succeed. Anxiety has won out, at the cost of not just our children's confidence but of their ultimate learning outcomes.

We are asking more and more of our children in terms of 'learning outcomes' and giving them less and less time to get ready for the demands of formal learning. There is another way, and it is demonstrably more successful than our own.

If our goal is indeed a better childhood and better eventual skills for our children then we need to look at what actually works. This does mean that we need to look at countries other than the United

Kingdom and America because neither the UK or America is performing particularly well in terms of educational outcomes among the wealthier, Western countries. The Nordic nations are the best performers, and it is worth examining why,

Currently in Australia, schools are beginning the huge project of formal learning, particularly learning to read, earlier in children's lives. But what about turning that idea on its head and promoting that we begin formal learning a great deal later?

The best way to examine this idea is to compare the educational outcomes of two countries with very different educational systems. In 2003, the UK Office for Education Standards, a government department that reports straight to Parliament, compared Finnish and English methods and outcomes. The report focused on six year olds. These children were in their first year of compulsory education in the United Kingdom. In Finland they were attending a kind of preschool which is not compulsory. Bear in mind as you read that Australia's education system has a great deal in common with the one in the United Kingdom.

> In the English classrooms children spent the overall majority of their time with reading, writing and text-based activities … in Finland the situation is almost reversed. There, the curriculum for six year olds centres on children's social, physical, interpersonal and moral development, while literacy and numeracy are viewed as essential yet take their place alongside other early learning goals.
>
> … the level of challenge was higher in England in terms of the demands on children's skills and knowledge in written language … Almost none of the work in Finland required children to write.

So what is the result of the two different approaches?

> At the beginning of primary school in the equivalent of the English Year 2, Finnish children seem to start behind the English children in reading and writing, but at 15 years of age the Finnish students have overtaken them.[4]

What is going on? The English children are clearly made to work earlier and harder at learning to read, writing and mathematics than the Finnish children. Despite this, somewhere between eight and 15 years of age the Finnish children overtake them across the board. If you are wondering, the Finnish children have better educational outcomes than Australian children too, although we are not far below them on the table in the report.[5] But their children are required to do less school and still have better outcomes. How much nicer is that system from a child's perspective!

Is the difference only one of language (because Finnish is much easier than English)? Or the fact that the Finnish children have more fish to eat? Is it because as a society they don't have great gaps between the haves and have-nots? Or perhaps it is because their culture positively exalts books? Or is it because a teacher is a high status job? Or because teachers are almost completely autonomous, and have no need to spend hours justifying their salary? All these factors play a part, but I believe that the difference also exists because the Finnish children are not made to start formal school until they are ready.

Waiting until children are ready to start formal school before requiring them to participate is not a new concept. It is something that child development experts from many fields have recommended for many years. Here is occupational therapist Barbara Knickerbocker, writing about American students in 1980: 'There is also a group of children whom I have labelled pseudo learning disordered whose learning problems I feel stem directly from the adverse effects of the accelerated rate of learning promoted in this country.'[6]

Finnish teachers are focusing on helping children develop self-regulation, language and physical skills before asking a child to learn to read. They are setting children up to succeed before commencing formal schooling. And they give them plenty of time to do it. In Australia we are beginning to teach children letters and numbers in kindergarten and handwriting and basic maths in preschool. In Finland they don't begin formally teaching reading until children have turned seven. Outside my four year old nephew Brennan's kindergarten is a list of achievements that he should have mastered before he goes to pre-primary. The list equates to what children were required to have at the end of pre-primary 20 years ago. We have fast-forwarded Australian children by a year and somehow believe there will be no consequences for their learning!

Finnish children begin formal learning up to three years later than Australian students. And as English is considered a much harder language, perhaps we should be leaving it later still.

This is a national issue. But there are things parents can do to help their children prepare for school. Remember that it is the security of your relationship with them that predicts their eventual success in life better than anything else — certainly far more than early reading or writing or maths skills — and care for that ahead of all else.

In this and the following chapters you will find the skills a child needs in place before beginning formal learning. Make sure she has these in place before you expect her to be able to learn. Too early a start can mean that a child loses confidence in her ability to learn. The best definition I've seen for a child who struggles to learn goes something like this: a child for whom the inner voice of judgment is so loud that she cannot learn in the present moment.[7] And, of course, it is in the 'present moment' that we do learn.

We would not consider requiring of a six-month-old baby that she waves at us, and berating her for failure when she does not. We know that this would be destructive. And yet, we are doing something very similar when we are requiring and testing for evidence of formal learning in children who are not ready. It is destructive. We teach children to judge themselves so harshly that we also compromise their future ability to learn.

If your child finds school too hard at first, express your faith that she will learn in the end. Tell her not to worry. Remember that such things as repeated testing or 'asking to demonstrate' will not build her confidence but rather convince her of your anxiety. These are all things I have learned through painful experience. Ultimately, your child will catch your confidence in her abilities.

Before reading

There are a great many skills that need to be in place before a child can learn to read. Reading is not, of course, the same as 'learning' to read. So your child needs to know how to focus his effort despite difficulties or interruptions before he makes the attempt to learn such

An important difference between boys and girls

If you have a look at any 'special education' class you will notice that it mostly contains little boys. The general thinking has been that boys find it harder to learn. But, in fact, the difference is not one of intelligence but one of processing speed.

From the age of about six until early adulthood, most girls find it much easier to rapidly process information. The typical school worksheet, which requires completion within a tight timeframe, is much harder for boys than girls for this reason. Both reading and maths have processing speed as a major predictor for success.[8]

Indeed, if you read a list of what characterises 'dyslexia', it does seem strongly connected to processing speed. When children, despite perfectly adequate intelligence, struggle with such things as rapidly naming letters, rapidly decoding words, rapidly writing words, rapidly shifting their attention, quickly suppressing irrelevant information and speedily finding the important information, we call them dyslexic. It is for this reason that more than one person has suggested that dyslexia merely describes a child (boy or girl) who matures later.[9] There are gifted children who display all of these difficulties also.[10]

Having appeared at six years of age, the difference disappears again in young adulthood, but unfortunately, all too often boys have concluded that they are simply 'dumb'. They can see the work isn't hard, but they simply can't do it as fast as the girls sitting near them.

In requiring our teachers to more clearly provide evidence of their efforts, we are also requiring more and more 'writing' by children. For many children (not just girls) this does not present a difficulty. But for boys, whose strengths are in verbal abilities and in general knowledge, this means less and less time is spent in their areas of strength. Is our society's obsession with having evidence of exactly how a teacher spends their time further 'feminising' our education system at the cost of our sons' educations?[8]

a complex system (see Chapter 22). On top of this he also needs to be motivated and to have the following abilities and qualities in place:

- Does he like books?
- Does he love stories?
- Has he consistently said to you he wants to learn to read?
- Can he easily blend together 'c (pause) a (pause) t' to make 'cat'?
- Can he easily match letters with letter sounds?
- Has he integrated his primitive reflexes, particularly his asymmetrical tonic neck reflex (ATNR) (see Chapter 13)?
- Does he have 'good enough' mood management skills to be able to keep trying in the face of the inevitable frustration that learning to read brings (Chapter 16)?
- Can he shift his attention at will?
- Is his impulse control and attention sufficient so that he doesn't impulsively respond to a 'c' and say 'cow', but stops and thinks?
- Does he have a dominant hand?
- Does he have a dominant eye?
- Can his eyes track along a straight line without a 'jerk' in the middle?
- Do his eyes converge — both eyes point at the same close object?
- Can he tell you what sound a word starts with?
- Can he tell you what sound is in the middle and on the end of a word?
- Does he have a good memory for what he has seen?
- Is he good at noticing subtle differences in pictures?

We would expect a child to develop these skills somewhere between two and eight years of age. Not every single one of them is required, however. Motivation, of course, most definitely is. Having most of these skills, across a range of areas (visual, auditory, motivation) will be enough to indicate your child is ready to learn to read. It is when there is a cluster of undeveloped areas, either taking out one entire learning modality (for example, auditory) or important parts of each learning modality, that makes a child not yet ready.

Wanting to read

The very first requirement for reading is a love of stories and of books and the pronounced desire to be able to read for himself. How does this happen? In short, your child learns to love books and stories because you love sharing books and stories with them. (Paul Jennings' book *The Reading Bug* tells the story of how this happens in far greater detail and I could not recommend this book more highly.)

Well-developed eye movements

Your child needs both eyes moving together, with one in charge. This dominant eye leads the 'sweep and flick', where the eyes travel from left to right and then jump down to the beginning of the next line. When can you expect this to develop? It develops somewhere between two and seven years, but 90 per cent of children have developed an eye dominance at six years of age. (Cross-dominance, where the dominant hand and eye are on opposite sides of the body, has been shown not to be a risk for difficulties in learning to read.)[11]

Does your child have a dominant eye? This is something you can check for yourself with a kaleidoscope or a pretend-telescope. A younger child will often centre the telescope between his two eyes or hold it a little way from his face and use both eyes. If you hold out your arm to one side, and he swaps the telescope over on his face the better to see, you also know that he doesn't have eye dominance yet. It is when your child consistently uses the same eye for looking through things that he has developed a dominant eye. When he is looking through and has shut the opposite eye, he is further along the continuum still.

Is your child able to converge his eyes? In checking this, don't expect him to be able to follow your finger in to his nose. Just see if both eyes can follow a finger in and out as it stops about 10 centimetres from his nose. Try his left eye and his right eye separately. Can your child smoothly track his eyes in pursuit of an object? If you see a 'jump' or a 'jerk' in those pursuits, your child is going to lose his place far more easily on the page. Your child's eyes need to be able to cross his 'midline' just as his hands do.

Helping your child strengthen their hand dominance

If you are not sure which hand is your child's dominant hand, these questions may help:

- *Which hand does he like to clean his teeth with?*
- *Which thumb is wider?*
- *When he is doing any bilateral task, is there one hand that is doing most of the manipulation and fine work?*
- *Ask your child which hand is the best one for tricky jobs.*

This may take some time.

With that hand identified, do encourage your child to make one hand the doer and the other the helper. Prompt him regularly and reward him with praise when he corrects this behaviour himself. If you really can't find a dominant hand and your child is over three years old, consider visiting an occupational therapist.

Understanding just what it is that you are seeing

Next on the list comes the ability to accurately interpret what is seen. If your child has difficulties with eye movements, visual perception will naturally be delayed also. These are the visual perceptual skills discussed in Chapter 17 and, as we saw, they require loads and loads of talking to develop in the first place. Is your child able to quickly point to same and different? Does he enjoy the puzzle books where he has to solve a problem from visual cues? The maze books, the *Where's Wally?* books, the same and different puzzles? All of these are great practice for the job of telling letters and numbers apart. They also give your child heaps of practice in 'sustaining visual attention', which is required for learning to read. With good visual attention and the ability to clearly identify and name differences, his visual memory skills will take off.

Does your child possess a good memory for what he's seen? Can your child contribute to a discussion of what was seen on a recent walk or car trip easily and accurately? Can he remember the order in which you purchased your grocery items? Is he able to remember where he has left something? A good visual memory is just so important, otherwise your child will keep forgetting the words he has so painfully tried to learn. Learning to remember 'big' things is where you need to start. Words are slippery customers, and the usual suspects are all similar enough to be brothers: then, the, that, them or who, what, when or go, do, to.

Is your child able to easily rotate jigsaw puzzle pieces to match into place rather than struggling to see 'how they go'? This is a marker for how well a child understands position in space. A 'b' and 'd' are the same shape that has been flipped over. To be able to deal with them a child needs a strong sense of his own position in space and to be able to read a shape's 'direction' in those terms.

If you read through this chapter and notice a few things on the list your child does not have, remember that visual acuity can be an issue too. Sometimes the problem is not 'interpreting' but plain old 'seeing'. This can be very difficult to identify as a parent. My vision was very poor. Leaves, for example, were things that I found under trees. It wasn't until my glasses arrived that I realised they actually grew on the trees first. And Mum didn't spot the problem, it was the music teacher who did. Very often it is not parents, even dedicated parents with relevant qualifications, who notice problems with hearing and seeing and speaking but someone else, so make sure you are listening!

Understanding what is heard

The letters 'b' and 'd' are not just difficult visually, they also sound alike. Tim was reading and writing well by seven and a half except that he used 'b' and 'd' almost at random while spelling. Reversal is normal until around age eight, so I didn't worry. But at nine he was still using them interchangeably. In fact, he couldn't hear the difference.

This was something Mum and I discovered on a lengthy car trip. For the rest of that trip Tim practiced hearing the difference. And he worked something out. When you say 'b' you make a firm line with your lips, like the straight line with which a 'b' commences. 'D', on the other hand, requires a slightly open mouth, the rounded shape with which a 'd' commences. The problem just faded away after that. If you are teaching a child to read and they are struggling with 'b', 'd', 'p' and 'q', a finger gently pressed to their lips for 'b' and 'p' works very well as a cue.

Hearing the difference between the teen number and the 'ten' number is similarly difficult. Thirteen does sound a lot like thirty. This is just one reason why talking and listening are terrifically important parts of preparing children for reading.

How do you know if your child's auditory skills are sufficient for the job of reading? To begin with, you need to expect them to be weaker than visual skills. A Finnish study showed that children's auditory skills mature considerably later than their visual skills.[12] It also showed that boys' auditory skills matured later than girls' too. It's also important to know that most experts say that the immediate cause of difficulties in learning to read is a lack of awareness of the sounds of speech.[13] And this is a big deal!

There is a clear order in which children learn to detect letter sounds in words, like 'c-a-t'. First of all they learn to hear syllables. A syllable is the 'beats' in a word, and you can easily hear them if you put your hand under your chin and speak. For every syllable your chin will drop.

The next step is hearing the first sound in a word (onset) and then the vowel and consonants afterwards (rhyme). For example, for the word 'stop', the 'st' is the onset and the 'op' is the rhyme. Last of all comes the awareness of the 'phonemes': 's-t-o-p'. The sounds are being broken down into smaller and smaller parts.

Children aren't 'suddenly' behind when they reach school age. There are some clear markers in early life for reading difficulties later. If your child did not babble, or had a tendency to muddle the syllables in multi-syllabic words (for example, saying 'vig-en-ar' for 'vinegar'), or had lots of ear infections early, or had any language or speech difficulty, these are all big markers of auditory problems. If any of these describe your child, go to a speech pathologist and ask for an assessment of all prereading skills before allowing him to start trying to read.

Time and music
One of the earliest writers on children who had difficulty learning to read was Newell Kephart.[14] He emphasised that these children had

difficulty not just with processing auditory information but also with processing sounds (and other sensations) in relation to time. Which sound came first? Which sound was closest? Which sound was loudest? What rhythm do the sounds come in? What he taught therapists to appreciate was that time allows humans to put experiences in order. The child who has difficulty with time is the child who has difficulty linking sounds together correctly. If you can't place sounds in time, you might not hear 'c-a-t', but 'c ... t' or 'a-c-t'. He strongly recommended that therapists play beat games to build in this missing skill.

One of the latest focuses in the research findings on dyslexia is exactly this. Most concepts of dyslexia now include 'impaired timing skills' as fundamental to the problem.[15] (And also, researchers have just begun to suggest that people with ADHD also have disordered time perception.[16]) While researchers are still sorting this out, the good news is that Kephart's ideas have helped parents and therapists create some very effective sound games to help children who are struggling to read or, indeed, to prepare children for learning to read. And, of course, learning music teaches this to children better than anything else. It was something we once appreciated in Australia.

Only a few decades ago kindergarten and pre-primary teachers were often music specialists, and a little child's day was full of music-making — and literacy rates were far higher than they are today. When the kindergarten teacher found a child who had difficulty hearing and tapping out a rhythm, she would spend more time helping that child 'find the beat'. While this seemed unconnected to the later task of reading, the new research is showing just how essential it was.

Also, an interesting correlation was found between spelling ability and the skill of tapping out the rhythm of a song, which both involve the skill of syllable segmentation. These results support suggestions that timing is a difficulty area for dyslexic children, and suggest that rhythm skills and rapid skills may need particular attention in any form of musical training with dyslexics.[17]

This could easily have been written by Kephart in 1971, but it actually comes from an article published in the journal *Dyslexia* in 2003.

Just like the many therapists who have written for years on the importance of music for reading, the authors suggest that singing, too, might be helpful for children learning to read. They draw attention to the fact that when we sing, syllables are elongated and emphasised, helping children hear each sound more clearly. And yet, tragically, we have largely lost our music specialists from early education. Perhaps the growth in 'sound therapy', a well-proven adjunct to treating children with learning difficulties, has only developed in the absence of these music specialists from our schools?

Chapter 20

Starting on formal learning

But a time will come, O Babe of Tegumai, when we shall make letters — all twenty-six of 'em — and when we shall be able to read as well as to write, and then we shall always say exactly what we mean without any mistakes.

Rudyard Kipling, *Just So Stories for Little Children*, 1950.[18]

Once your child is at school — and, you believe, mostly ready for formal learning — you are then faced with some of the most prolonged and complicated debates in education. What is the best way for a child to learn to read? To spell? To write? To do maths? In the rest of the chapter you will find some answers to these still hotly debated questions, as well as ideas for how to support your child's learning.

A best way of learning to read?

So how should children be taught to read? Should the focus be wholly and solely on phonics, or on 'look and say' whole word methods, or a mix of the two? This isn't just 'school business' as parents do a great deal of the teaching in their own homes. I don't feel brave enough to make a call on this one. Children do need to be able to decode words, and phonics are very useful for that. But children also need to care about what they are reading, and phonics are very dry all by themselves.

The approach I'd recommend for parents is to find a book that your child will just love in addition to the school readers. Book selection is absolutely key here. It says to the child, 'I know who you

are' and also, 'I know you are going to get this'. Read him a chapter at a time, and then pick a short passage you both particularly liked, and read it a couple of times to him. Then ask him to read it with you. He can then read it aloud to you or quietly to himself.

Home readers can bring out the sharks

One of the awful things that can happen to a child's reading is the response of parents to 'home readers'. Suddenly reading together stops being about having fun and becomes, 'What will the teacher be thinking of me and my parenting if my child can't read this tomorrow morning?'

The entry of that imaginary third and potentially critical person upon the scene is very destructive. With them looking intrusively over your shoulder you stop supporting your child's fledgling attempts to read and begin speaking in a 'teacher voice'. You stop saying, 'Oh darling, that was brilliant!' and, 'I didn't think you were going to get that one, but you did!' and start saying things like, 'You've got to sound it out again because that was wrong', and, 'Are you even trying?'

Often there is shark music playing (see Chapter 4). You might need to listen for it attentively in that whole learning to read period. Your anxiety can greatly slow down your child's reading once it has started, and you will be left with a residue of regret that you let an imaginary negative other person into the arena that once belonged to just you and your child. Ghosts! Shark music! They must be banished over and over.

The school readers are hard to make fun at the best of times. Systematically teach the hard words before even starting the story. Talk about what the book is likely to be about. Remember to giggle over the fact that there are few surprises in school readers. Most importantly, never ever let your child feel he has failed — and, indeed, never let him fail. If teaching a few words doesn't work, read the whole book to him. Then read it with him a couple of times. Then let him read it with you. Let your child be in charge of how much help you give. One strategy I've recently developed is to say 'I'm going to say the words

> anyway, if you want to you can beat me to it'. I leave enough time for a child to say the word, but not so much time that the meaning of the sentence will be lost.
>
> Children need to be supported to take risks. When you hear such things as 'I could have done that Mum, you didn't need to tell me' you know that your safety net is a bit too constrictive. When you hear 'it's too hard' then you know that you need to strengthen that safety net more: an easier reader, more teaching time beforehand, more fun, less judgement.
>
> Grow in your mind a picture of a successful reader and let your child catch that picture from you, rather than the picture of your fears that he will never learn.

But perhaps your child is missing a few of the items on that list? Please don't start to worry that he is falling behind. Remember that language skills and knowledge are also developed by talking and listening. Make this your focus in addition to helping him develop the different qualities and abilities required for reading discussed in the previous chapter. Read aloud and then ask him to tell the story back to you, provide audio books and ask what the story was about, talk to him, listen to him.[19] All of this will push along his vocabulary and understanding of how stories work. Remember that Finnish teachers mostly require oral work from their students for many years, yet at fifteen they are outperforming Australian children who have been required to do written work for a great deal longer.

In addition to reading, maths, writing and spelling are also important. If children possess the precursory skills for reading then they are mostly ready for the rest of formal schooling. There are a few caveats to this statement, however, and you will find that information in the rest of this chapter. (If you are looking for more ideas to help a struggling reader, you will find them in Appendix V.)

Mathematics

According to a recent review of the skills required for arithmetic, there is only a little crossover with skills required for reading. The main one is the ability to hear differences in sounds. This allows children to easily recognise number names and begin to learn what 'ten' of something looks like compared to 'twenty' of something.[9]

In this same research the finding was that the very biggest contributor to maths skills is something called 'digit magnitude judgments'. For example, is a three bigger than a seven? Is a four bigger than a three? The suggestion was that children develop an innate understanding of numbers in relation to each other.

The tests used in this study actually used the names of numbers, rather than real world objects. In doing so they explicitly linked language with numbers. But what happens if you take language out of the equation? Can children develop number concepts if they don't have the words for them? It seems as if they can. According to the authors of a 2008 study, 'Here, using classical methods of developmental psychology, we show that children who are monolingual speakers of two Australian languages with very restricted number vocabularies possess the same numerical concepts as a comparable group of English-speaking indigenous Australian children'.[20]

What this means is that children do not learn about numbers just from words. This is actually an important understanding for parents to have. Children learn about numbers by playing with groups of objects. From crawling and picking up pieces of fluff they learn that three pieces of fluff on the floor are more than two or one piece. In fact, when my mother (who at sixty five years old is one of the most experienced Occupational Therapists I know) is asked to help a student with maths difficulties she teaches them to play a game called 'stones'.

This game does not require numerals at all, just the opportunity to sit on the floor and mess around with a pile of stones. Little bears or counters or blocks could equally be used, but my Mum likes to use stones best of all.

They are rough, so they are satisfying to touch. They are quite heavy, so they engage the proprioceptive (knowing what a body part is doing without needing to watch it) sense. They don't roll away. They are all slightly different from one another, so they are a bit more visually interesting. And they make a sound as they drop.

What does she do with the stones? She encourages children to play with them. Is eight still eight when they are in a line? What about if they are in a little stack? Is this still eight? Is eight sticks the same as eight stones? Is eight 'taps on the ground' the same as eight stones? What happens if you make them into two piles? What happens if you make them into four piles? What happens if you find a matching stone for every stone you already have? If you take two away, how many do you have? And if you put them back together, and take away six, how many do you have? If you add one more, how many are there? If you take one away, how many are there?

In this game, which has surely been played by children for thousands of years, lie all the number concepts needed for the first few years of school. There is constancy — because eight is always eight — and magnitude: nine is always bigger than eight and seven is always smaller. There is 'reversability': the way that subtraction and addition match each other ($2 + 6 = 8$ and $8 - 6 = 2$) and the way multiplication and division match each other. It's all in there. The best way for you to see whether or not your child is ready for the formal requirements of mathematics is to sit down and 'play stones'.

Spelling

Reading and spelling have a great deal in common: words, sounds, letters, meanings. But there's one critical difference. Spelling a word requires you to have more information stored in your memory than reading that word. To read a word your child must 'pull out' from her memory the sounds that match the letter shapes and say it. To spell a word your child must hear a number of different sounds within the word and then match them to the correct letters and then write them down.[21]

The critical precursor skills for spelling are:
- the ability to identify syllables in words
- being able to hear the different sounds in a syllable
- strong memory skills: visual, auditory and proprioceptive
- strong proprioceptive skills (knowing what a body part is doing without needing to watch it) so that writing a particular word can become as automatic as writing a letter shape — so it just 'flows off the pencil'.

Spelling and reading are both language based skills, but use different parts of the skills base. For example, being able to hear and clap out syllables is vital for spelling, although it isn't important in reading. Once a child is reading they don't need to worry greatly about hearing the separate sounds in a word — but they do for spelling.

How to teach spelling is an even more vexed topic than how to teach reading. There is the look, say, cover, write, check method, which, if used by itself, seems remarkably like the 'whole word' method for teaching reading. It asks children to learn a whole word. This method certainly works well for children with a very good visual memory. Then there are the methods that focus on analysing matching sounds to letters and these definitely work better for children without that extremely good visual memory.

This problem is one that the education researchers are likely to be working on for a long time to come. Different schools use different methods, and parents can spend quite a lot of time comparing and matching the different methods. One research report surprisingly suggests that dyslexic children need to find the method that works best for them for learning difficult words. Perhaps this is wise advice for all children in learning spelling: to simply work from their strengths?[22]

After reading that report I thought long and hard about my older children's various strengths and difficulties and instituted a 'problem-solving' approach. They are now able to hear all the sounds in a word, and know the different ways a sound could be spelled (and sometimes there are many!) Choosing which spelling to apply was the next step for them. My (and their teacher's) approach involves pulling their decoding skills and spelling rules together to work out how to approach spelling a particular word. For example, the 't' sound can be 'ed' in many words. 'Equipped' sounds like 'equipt', and that is what the boys wrote. So we are teaching them to always ask themselves, 'Is there a base word here?' They are learning not to rely solely on the rules, but on a thoughtful application of those rules.

Writing

Writing really comes in two pieces. First of all comes the ability to actually form letters and words. With that in place, writing is then the ability to put our thoughts in written form.

To be able to write, children need to understand the way their culture sees the world. In some Islamic cultures paintings are all abstract. There aren't paintings of people, horses and dogs. When someone who grows up in that culture is shown a picture, say, of a horse, they may well not recognise those curves and straight lines and filled in forms as representing a horse. When we look at Indigenous art we might see emu tracks but an Indigenous observer might see the emu. Conversely, the same observer might not see an emu in a painting where we would. One example of this is that children learning to draw and paint frequently begin by drawing their people and animals upside down. They haven't learnt the convention that feet are always pictured as down and heads are up in art.

Australian children need to learn that letters join together to make words, and that they run from left to right across the page. They need to know this before they attempt to write. Books are obviously essential in teaching this but more powerful still is writing at a child's request.[23] Anywhere between two and three years children will begin to have little stories that they would like you to write down. (If you do this you will also have the keepsake of a window into your child's mind from an earlier age to treasure.)

Pushing children to begin physically writing early is counterproductive. Every parent has noticed that their child's writing of her name looks far more babyish than her other writing attempts. This happens because our brain is quick to 'automate' letter shapes. Children learn to write their name first of all. Once this has become automatic it resists alteration. Children become 'stuck' with this immature writing of their name until they become conscious enough of it to deliberately rewrite the program.

It is better to wait until their fine motor skills are precise enough to make learning to write something they do once, rather than many times. There is a huge variation in how fast children obtain both of these skill sets. The children with well-developed proprioceptive skills (who know just where every body part is and what it is doing without looking) will find this easier.

Holding a skinny stick and precisely controlling it to make a set of prescribed forms on a slippery piece of paper requires highly developed fine motor skills. Children need to build up to it. Games such as threading beads, painting, modelling with playdough, cooking, sewing: anything at all where your child is enjoying using her hands is very helpful.

Parents need to be very sensitive in our approach to early attempts at writing. Literacy teacher Judith Duff specialises in preventing 'reluctant writing' in classrooms. She says, 'Too often teachers and parents will rewrite the child's words underneath the child's writing: "This is a picture of Mummy and me cooking." What I ask the teacher to do is write: "Thank you very much for this picture which shows you and Mummy cooking."' The same teaching occurs but without the message that the child's own writing isn't good enough.[24]

It is not reasonable to expect children to coordinate writing with creative composition until writing is automatic. And yet this is the approach we take. The risk with doing this is that children will not develop good thinking skills as they get used to writing a 'stock answer' neatly. The other risk is that they will hate writing as the gap between what they can write and what they can think leads to harsh self-judgment. It is hard to imagine an equivalent situation for adults, but perhaps being taught how to play chess one year and then being asked to take on the grand master in a well-publicised match the next would come close.

Finding words to suit the writer's purpose is quite a different skill from the physical production of writing letters on a page. Expect that you may need to scribe for your child even into the teenage years if he is to learn to capture his thoughts upon the page. Let him experience the satisfaction of seeing his ideas plain upon the page occasionally. This makes a big contribution to eventual 'true' writing success. Mum scribed for me until I was ten or eleven. Not all the time, but often enough for me to catch the writing bug.

In Appendix VI you will find ideas for helping the child who has difficulty in any of these areas. The learning of academic skills is just one part of attending school, however. The rest of this section of the book is devoted to how to help your child develop the other skills that make a difference at school.

Chapter 21

Coping with the social side of school

But then he froze, for he had had an idea and it was a
particularly amazing one.
'No! Hang on!' he cried. 'Let's share.'

Margaret Mahy, *A Villain's Night Out*, 1999.[25]

Whether or not a child enjoys school has a great deal to do with whether or not she has friends. Friendship is a very big deal. The lonely child is also the depressed child. There is even an argument that the child without friends learns less as learning is so often done in groups.[26] Being able to make friends isn't just a big deal at school either. The ability to interact well with others is the biggest predictor of mental health and life success through the life spectrum.

Teaching your child how to be a friend

So what are the skills for having and making friends? Researchers developed the following list after talking to parents, teachers and children and having them all vote on what was most important:

- friendly — smiles and says hello
- trustworthy
- empathic — recognises when someone is sad and tries to help
- fair — takes turns, doesn't always try to be the boss, can compromise
- respectful of others and their property
- doesn't verbally hurt others

- loyal and reliable
- praises and compliments others appropriately
- funny
- positive and happy
- likes to spend time with you.[27]

You can see straightaway that the self-mastery skills are very important. The very impulsive child is at a clear disadvantage when it comes to such things as taking turns. Another standout theme is, of course, theory of mind. The better your child can imagine another child's perspective, the easier most items on this list will become for her.

The shy child

There is an exception, however. Shy children battle to smile and say hello, to have the confidence to take their turn, to pay compliments and praise another child. This puts them at a clear disadvantage when it comes to making friends. Shy or inhibited children are shy because their amygdala has a hyperactive response to stress. Social situations are stressful, and these children experience a feeling of painful conspicuousness as their amygdala floods them with stress hormones.

They want terrifically to join in, but at the same time their over-the-top hormonal response tells them they will lose the ability to manage their behaviour if they do so. Social isolation, even self-imposed social isolation, can lead to difficulties down the track. Shyness can lead to victimisation and a further loss of confidence in social skills.

But the shy child does not have to stay 'shy'. Research shows that it is the interaction between temperament and parenting style that lays out the path a shy child will take. Some shy children remain shy, and by teenage years this can immure them in isolation and victimhood, agonising for the parents to watch but far more agonising for the person themselves. Other shy children 'grow out' of their shyness and are indistinguishable from others by middle childhood. And there's a range of pathways in between.

> *What kind of parenting is associated with overcoming shyness? The kind of parenting associated with secure attachment: sensitive, positive and consistent. In addition, research suggests that shy children need to be provided with firm guidelines about what to do. Never chastise your shy child in front of others for not saying hello, because this is frequently counterproductive: it further destabilises the child's already overloaded stress system. Before any meeting, however, make sure your child knows that you expect her to say hello.*
>
> *Another big 'do not' is being derisive or making jokes about her shyness or trying to shame her out of it. This actually leads to further social withdrawal. Trying to control your child in a social setting by intervening on her behalf with playmates, or speaking for her and so on, has the same effect.*
>
> *The way forward is to be positive and encouraging. Your attitude needs to reduce the level of stress she has in relating to social occasions. Over and over again the message you are sending her is, 'You can do it'. The more you do this, the less shy your shy child will become.*[28]

It is during the pretend play at four and five that children practice making and cementing friendships. In all those games the fodder is their own lives — children take a word or a concept and 'play it out'. A great deal of what they reflect on is their relationships with us and our relationships with our friends and family, so the quality of their attachment to you and your relationships, both marital and family, are powerful predictors of a child's ability to make friends.[29]

If you are somebody who is a good friend to other people — in particular your partner — you will have ample opportunity to teach your child just how theory of mind leads to empathetic action. Your child sees you placing yourself 'behind the eyes and in the life' of your partner or your friend, and taking action to help. She will take this skill straight to the playground.

Sadly, the converse is true too. People with poor theory of mind cannot teach it to their children. If you repeatedly become 'stuck' in arguments, unable to give an inch, this is what you teach your children. If you must be in charge, this too is what your children bring to a game.

DUCK !!!

Always having to be in charge or having everything their way or getting upset and staying upset make children undesirable play partners. Play, like life, is about flow, compromise and accepting change.

Teacher Meg Roche, who travels Australia teaching schools and families about resilience in children, says that this ability to move on and establish a compromise is of vital importance. She tells children that they can either be a duck or a sponge. The sponge soaks in the misery until it starts to dribble out. The duck, in contrast, just lets it slide off its feathers and paddles off to do something else. These two symbols are very effective in reminding children that they have a range of options for responding. Again, seeing the ability to pick and choose among behavioural options is one of the gifts of theory of mind, and giving children clear symbols for different choices allows them to more easily juggle and choose.

Using books to further grow theory of mind

We enjoy stories because we have theory of mind. The characters in stories are animated not just by the author but by the reader stepping inside and inhabiting the character. Our mirror neurons (described in Chapter 7) are active even in reading — deeply immersed in a book's characters we embarrass ourselves in front of the one we love, stare into the before-dawn abyss, make the mistake of our lives and abide by the consequences. Without theory of mind, stories would have no meaning. Not just that, but our ability to juggle thoughts lets us hold together multiple plot lines, or join together all the separate pieces of a whodunit.[30]

Our 'mirror neurons' are activated when we read, just as they are when we watch a movie. The activation of mirror neurons means that intimate contact with a book works much as intimate contact with another mind does. It is transforming. Sometimes we can feel it happening as we read, but mostly we do not. Safely tucked inside different characters we are able to see problems surface and be worked through. As we have lived within the skins of the characters, we can come out the other side of the book a slightly different person.

This is what makes stories powerful. Some books we remove from our children saying, 'Not that one, not yet'. We find ourselves saying, 'How about this one?' There is, in fact, a brand of psychotherapy called 'bibliotherapy', which is about applying different books to wounds or needs in the client. For example, for the child struggling with the death of a friend there is Goodnight Mr Tom *or* Bridge to Terabithia. *Parents, the experts on their children, can do this far better.*

We find a book about a little bear or a princess who doesn't want to use the potty for our toilet-training toddlers. We read the Narnia books to our spiritually questing seven year olds. For our nine year olds, not quite sure of themselves, we find books on those other, just slightly older identity seekers: J. K. Rowling and Eva Ibbotson have written wonderful books which show children finding their way. In each case, your child's theory of mind skills are both reinforced and expanded as she reads. And from having rehearsed life from inside another's skin the characters will bring richer understandings to her own life.

Children don't just gain this benefit from their own reading, of course. When you read to them this happens too. Keep on reading to them even after they are reading to their interest level — this way you can ensure they benefit from books they might not read on their own.

So our children need to know just what qualities characterise a good friend, and they need us to model those skills and require those behaviours from them in dealing with their siblings. This is something we can teach them within everyday life.

Teaching your child to 'play fair'

'Fair' is something children can begin to understand when they have developed theory of mind, but it still has to be taught. A child who breaks the rules isn't playing fairly and will promptly be excluded from games by other children.

So how do you teach fairness? You ask your child questions and involve her in family decision-making. Whose turn is it to decide what game we play? The choice of game tends to dictate winners and losers (for example, older children win word games), so an awareness not just about what is fair at that time for all members in the group but also across time is built in. What food shall we eat? How do we work out where we go for holidays? Discuss decisions in terms of what is fair, and teach children how to weigh up a scenario from a number of different perspectives.

Household chores also teach fairness. The way in which you distribute jobs will prepare your child for when they are organising a game among a group of children. There is a gorgeous early reading book about two sisters who travel the country putting on plays. One sister is writing a play called 'The Princess and the Troll'. The trouble comes when it is casting time because both sisters wish to be the princess. In the end, they write a new play called 'The Two Princesses'. No-one wants to be the troll all the time. No-one wants to have to clean the bathroom or wipe down the benches or put away the washing all the time. Fair allocation of tasks teaches your child how to be fair in play with her peers.

I tend to think in terms of work teams. These days it works best if I team up with Rafael as I'm still teaching him how to work: about the fact that scrubbing the floor requires you to push hard, to look at what you are doing and that yes, you will feel tired when you finish. Tim and Sam can be left to work together on something. The ages of your children and how many you have dictate how you achieve fairness and also the teaching of work skills.

With all your concern to be fair you will never compete with your children's avid interest in the subject. Children are the secret police of fairness. The child who is given extra privileges or extra attention by a teacher or a parent will often be punished later. And, of course, some children actually need more scaffolding, more support, more of everything. You need to teach children that fairness means giving each child what they need rather than everyone getting just the same thing. For the siblings of a child with a learning difficulty or an illness, this can be a hard concept to get across. You need to acknowledge the issue with your children, and even within a class.

Another one of the fairness issues is seeking exclusivity in friendships. Being exclusive is not a fair request to make of another child, and it needs to be taught from that point of view. What happens, you can ask your child, if she is not there one day? Who will her friend play with? And from your child's point of view, such exclusivity puts her at much greater risk of heartbreak if the friend moves away. It is more often little girls who seek such relationships, as they feel happy with just one or two friends. For little boys, who feel more comfortable being part of a larger networked group, this is going to cause trouble. The other boys may well resent a friend who doesn't allow them to have other friends.

The line between 'funny' and 'hurtful' is only a thin one

Parents play a big role too in teaching children some of the other unwritten rules of friendship. While being funny is a desirable quality in a friend, saying hurtful things loses friends. Sometimes children may not realise that the things they are saying are actually offensive to other children. Name calling is never acceptable, even if it is meant as a joke. Put downs, which can be used in jest by parents who enjoy bantering with each other, are also negatively perceived by children. Be careful exactly what you model to your children, and make sure that you don't laugh at something that has the potential to hurt another child.

Model in your own conversations this concern for the feelings of others above the need for wit. Make clear to your child the difference between friendly teasing and teasing that is designed to hurt. A child desperate for attention from other children is at great risk of using tactics such as teasing in order to be perceived as funny and a desirable playmate. Sadly, this frequently backfires, leaving the child more alone than before.

Not being picked for teams?

It is worth parents knowing what the 'in game' is among their children's peers. Perhaps it is marbles, perhaps it is skipping but whatever it is, being able to play moderately well is a passport for social inclusion. Ask your children if they would like to practise at home, and be available as a play partner (not coach!) for them. Do not offer constructive criticism, just let them lead the play.

> *If they are having difficulty keeping up with peers in playing these games, do check through the troubleshooting section (see Appendix III) to make sure their primitive reflexes have been integrated and their adult reflexes are in place. Such games require precision, and this requires a body under full control.*
>
> *While your child is still building up her skills to the group standard, she can offer to take on other roles. She can offer to score, umpire, manage the sports kit and so on. Often children who watch, and are assisted through the thinking process by their parents, can also come up with strategy ideas for teams.*

Helping your child learn how to cope with 'being different'

Children's creativity and individual passions are the best drivers of all aspects of their lives. Helping them preserve this, the core of their true self, is also part of a parent's role. Unfortunately, the social environment can be a barrier to keeping a child's sense of self intact. What you want your child to have, at least some of the time, are relationships that grow that blossoming sense of self.

Good social skills are more than just survival strategy. Theory of mind is more than just the ability to think from a number of perspectives. Together they are your child's way in to connecting emotionally, creatively and intimately with other people, which lies at the heart of our satisfaction in life.

For some children the hardest part of going to school is the other children. This can be nearly as hard for the parents to hear as it is for the child to endure. Somewhere I read the story of a little girl asking her mother a riddle about school.

'What do you look for every day, and sometimes you think you've found it, but the next day you have to start looking all over again?'

It is not a funny riddle. Eventually the little girl tells her mother the answer.

'Every day you look for someone who likes you and sometimes you think you have found a friend, but the next day you have to start again.'

Doesn't your heart just sink? Friendship is based on similarity: birds of a feather flock together. If your child is gifted, learning disabled, both learning disabled and gifted, culturally or ethnically different and so on, making friends is going to be harder. Being a 'rare bird' is not an advantage in childhood, no matter how useful it becomes in later life. For 'different' children the groups of the schoolyard are often just something to be survived. Some children cannot be their true self at school.

In this situation you can say to your child that a good starting point is to try to find something to like about everyone, and try to 'reflect' that back. The more closely we mirror another person, the more they tend to like us. Sometimes, though, mirroring another person requires us to be untrue to who we are in our hearts. At this point, you could say to your child, there's really no choice to be made. You are you. There are children who you like, and who like you: there just might not be any around right now. Encourage your child to simply 'get by', not fighting, not being the victim or the bully. In adult life there are always times when we can't be with our friends, and those skills will be valuable then.

In these circumstances a child will need to accept that she cannot be her 'true self' at school. Help her see that this may be the case for some of her classmates as well. Ask your child to observe what strategies seem to work well for other 'different children', and what strategies work poorly. One observation is that making yourself as small a target as possible is a safe way to go. This is not the same as trying to be the same as the other kids, but to intentionally reveal less of yourself. But this is no way to enjoy life.

While perhaps your child can be her true self at home, she also needs to be that person with other children if at all possible. Real acceptance (and as she grows older, intimacy) is something every child needs to feel some of the time from other children. Parents need to gear their response to demonstrating to their child that her 'true self' is worthy of being valued.

A special effort should be made to find friends for your child out of school: similar children with whom your child can build a lasting friendship. In addition, provide your child with chances to experiment with her identity. School groups restrict a child by their expectations. The occasional party with children she doesn't know well; the out-of-school church group, finding a friend at the beach on holidays: all such events help your child develop a sense of having a complex self with a number of aspects.

Bullying

In Australia, a 1999 study of 25,399 children found that 25 per cent of them were bullied on a weekly basis.[31] So if it happens to your child it does not, sadly, qualify as unusual.

Bullying is being approached in a number of ways by researchers. They are examining societal factors, family factors and child factors. Unfortunately there is a disconnection between the research and the mainstream books that are published on the subject. One researcher writes that of three books recently released on bullying the messages within each one are wrong.[32] While the researchers have not yet completed their work, this is a synthesis of the findings that might be useful to parents.

Our society is only just beginning to clearly see the damage done by children to children by bullying. In an article addressing our lack of discernment the authors begin this way:

> Joyce, busy at her desk, didn't see it coming. The assailant ran through the door, clobbered her on the head, and ran off. Joyce fell to the floor screaming.
>
> a. (Joyce is 25) Her co-worker reached for the phone and dialed 911.
>
> b. (Joyce is 5) The kindergarten teacher, Mrs. Coyle, looked up and asked, 'What's going on here?'[33]

They almost need say no more. As you read these words you realise that, implicit in our responses to child-to-child violence, is a society-wide belief that violence by children to children is not as serious as violence among adults. We look with our eyes at the threat to the child, and not with *their* eyes. They are all just children, we think. We need to look again and use our developed theory of mind to stand in our children's shoes. As adults most of us don't believe that being assaulted is a 'learning experience'. Nor do we believe that workplace bullying is character building.

With this double vision we then need to set about dealing with the problem. The perpetrators are just children, so we cannot assign

positive self talk

to them the level of 'knowingness' we assign to adults. But we equally must not minimise the damage done to their victims. Being bullied, mentally as well as physically as a child, whether by siblings or by other children, puts children on the path for academic and mental health problems later on. Why academic problems? As we discussed in Chapter 4, children must feel safe to learn. Fascinatingly, bullies are also more likely to feel unsafe. Whether your child is a victim, a bully/victim or a bully, his prospects of success in life are greatly damaged by these early experiences.[34]

The research distinguishes between the bullying that is physical, relational or verbal and behavioural. Physical bullying involves physical intimidation or injury. Relational bullying, now far better recognised than it was, involves rumour-spreading, social exclusion, unpleasant letters and name-calling. As this type of bullying is often done behind a child's back it is extraordinarily difficult for them to counter. Behavioural bullying is when a child does something mean, such as stealing a lunch or scribbling on a book. One child seeks to 'build his ego' by making the other child perceive himself to be less acceptable and either physically or psychologically weaker. In all types of bullying there is a sense of the behaviour being systematic and designed to hurt.

So why are some children bullied? Why do other children veer backwards and forwards between bullying and being victimised? And why do children bully?

The children who are bullied are those who are more sensitive to negativity in the environment, and reveal that sensitivity to others in terms of irritability and impulsive and aggressive behaviour. They are often described as introverted and with lower self-esteem. Both things go hand in hand with sensitivity. This is something we remember from our own childhoods: 'The more you react, the more they will pick on you.'

The research defines two sorts of aggression: reactive aggression and proactive aggression. Children who are easily upset, get angry quickly and are generally emotionally up and down are displaying reactive aggression. They are frequently victimised, usually by the child who is 'proactively' aggressive. Some children with a reactive aggressive profile are not just victims but bullies: their esteem is lowered by being bullied and they then 'rebuild' by attacking another child. They are called bully/victims in the research.[35]

The 'pure' bully is a very different kind of child. They are often children who are insecurely attached to their parents, so aggression becomes a pathway through which they have their needs met at home, and that continues away from home. They are described as proactively aggressive, and are more often extroverted children. They are usually bullying by the time they enter kindergarten, and at this point they have a poorer theory of mind than their peers. By bullying, however, they actually learn about people: who can be bullied and who cannot. They then develop a strong theory of mind, which, by middle primary, allows them to accurately identify just which children will succumb to their tactics. At this point their ego-building behaviours become targeted to those children who will most easily succumb.[36]

What does the research suggest you can do to prevent your child becoming involved as either bully or victim?

Good sibling relationships are highly protective

Creating a secure attachment for your child is first on the list. If your child has siblings, next comes ensuring that you have an equally warm relationship with all of them and there are no favourites. This sets your child up for a strong friendship with his siblings, and good sibling relationships are highly protective.

When children have positive experiences of sibling relationships they also expect to have just such experiences with their friends. They are then far more likely to both be 'prosocial' and to attract such friends, even if they fit the sensitive introverted profile of the child who is more often bullied. The prosocial child is a child with strong theory of mind, and who uses this understanding to nut out solutions to social problems. They often become 'defenders' — the natural counter to bullies — from kindergarten onwards.[37]

Friends, even those who are not prosocial, are highly protective. There is some research to suggest that those tragic events that happen from time to time, such as when a child is pushed by his peer group into taking a risk that proves to be fatal, or into hurting another child, rarely happen when children have a good friend present. The damaging potential of a group is greatly reduced when a child has a true friend among those present.[38]

Next comes setting clear rules for behaviour among your children. Clearly define for them just what bullying is. Monitor their behaviour

Helping your children be friends with each other

The sibling relationship is one of the longest lasting we have. It is common for siblings, having lived quite separate lives until then, to move to live near each other for their last years. Helping your children become a 'sibling support group' is one of the great gifts a parent can give. So how do you do it?

Look after your relationship with your partner. Research shows that if the marital relationship is strained, so is the relationship between siblings. Even with a warm marital relationship, however, favouritism by parents damages sibling relationships. In contrast, when parents have an equally warm relationship with all their children, those children will all relate positively. And this counts in the outside world. A study of Mexican families showed that the children with the least behaviour problems had the warmest relationship with their siblings.[39]

But there are some families where, despite a strong marital relationship and no favouritism, siblings don't relate warmly and lovingly to each other. What is happening here? This has more to do with family norms. Perhaps believing that siblings are natural rivals, parents don't have a family rule that you must treat your siblings lovingly and fairly.

Ginott's rule of 'allowing all emotions, but not all behaviours' works well here. A child is allowed to feel very angry with a sibling but he must not express that anger in a way that hurts the relationship. Getting angry is permissible, but hitting, name-calling, bullying, playing favourites among siblings and humiliation is not.

As well as verbalising this rule you support it in practice by:
- rewarding children for playing and behaving lovingly with each other. Take photos, organise treats, sit down and play too. Do everything to convey how much you love to see them dealing warmly with each other
- refusing to take a side in an argument. Children often stage arguments to receive attention from parents. If you refuse to reward

fighting behaviour by taking sides but institute the rule that they must go outside if they are going to behave that way, you will see a decline in fights

- *having the same rules for each child. If you have different rules for different children then you are not treating them as individuals but playing favourites.*

I once paid a home visit to a mother of two sons in a small country town. Dad was on a tough fly-in fly-out schedule. The two boys were very different. Both had learning difficulties, but one was far more confident and proactively aggressive. The other son, their teacher had told me, was frequently victimised by other children at school, including his older brother.

'I know you should treat your children as individuals,' the mother began, and I obediently nodded. 'So I have different rules for the boys.'

The younger boy was able to sleep in Mum's bed in Dad's absence but the older boy was not. The older boy had to do the chores as he needed to learn responsibility but the younger boy was 'naturally responsible'. The younger boy's confidence was low, and she encouraged him to assert himself at home against his brother. And so it went on.

Unable to convince the mother that treating your children as individuals did not mean having entirely different rules for each child, I sought my mother's advice. With her help I developed a home program for the younger boy that revolved around chores, and for the older boy, lots of reading with his Mum, and we added in whole-family games as well. As you can see, we were trying to ensure that each child had the chance to take responsibility, be nurtured and enjoy whole-family time.

Treating your children as individuals means accepting that they will feel differently about different things, and need more or less help on different occasions than their siblings. But the rules need to be the same for every child, otherwise you are playing favourites. Favouritism, by way of damaging your children's relationships with each other, has a habit of spreading to their experiences at school. A number of studies *have shown that half of all children who bully and are bullied at school were also bullied at home by their siblings.* [40, 41]

The research on birth order can also show parents how their behaviour impacts on sibling relationships. One finding is that the middle child may be less close to his parents, particularly to his mother, when a mother is older at the time of the child's birth. The risk is that such a mother is more likely to invest most of her time and energy in her very last baby. The last baby often gets favoured treatment because it is 'the last one'. Watching out for this is one of the messages from the research. The other message seems to be to cherish your middle children. Remember that they don't ever have that special one-on-one time which is the prerogative of the youngest and oldest children. [42]

How does the birth order research fit with the rest of this book? If we return to Chapter 1, where we looked at baby growing his idea of himself in response to your idea of him, we see how much a child's need to 'de-identify' or 'find a niche' may well begin in a parent's mind. When our second baby arrives we look for differences from the first. We begin trying to establish a niche for the new baby right away — a new place in our minds and hearts. But perhaps the message from the birth order research is to stay open-minded about who this person is going to be. Be aware of any ideas you may bring from your family of origin (such as, 'If the first is easy, the second won't be') and make sure that they don't contaminate the niche you are growing for your new baby.

with an eye to exclusion, saying nasty things, name-calling, hitting and so on, with both siblings and with peers. Children are far less likely to bully when this kind of monitoring and rule setting is in place at home. If there have been previous incidences of such behaviour among your children, know that you are not going to be able to just leave them unsupervised to play for a while.

Watch and listen. If you do see some bullying, pull the child aside immediately and label the behaviour for him. Then talk him through it. Help him stand in his sibling's or friend's shoes and reflect upon how it feels to be bullied. Questions like, 'How would you feel?' are the ones to ask. See if you can help him identify why he felt the need to bully. Very often it is dissatisfaction with self that leads to the desire to 'build some ego' at the other child's expense. Teach him it is never acceptable to 'lay violent hands' on either the body or the personality of another. Explain that he does not just damage the other person alone. Bullying seems to work as a strategy up until high school. 'All signs,' writes one researcher, 'now point to a difficult adulthood for bullies.'[33]

Dealing with the school

Help the school your child attends to see bullying as something that will work against academic achievement. There is certainly adequate research to support this statement. Report any bullying you see and encourage other parents to do the same. Encourage your school to introduce an anti-bullying scheme that has been evaluated rather than one that hasn't. Some programs can actually make the problem worse. Any tolerance of bullying simply sends the message that it's okay.

Always keep a close eye on your children for signs that they are being bullied. Warning signs include an increasing reluctance to go to school, added to changes in behaviour such as nightmares, poor sleep, irritability, bullying siblings, nervousness, tearfulness and increasing introversion.

And what do you do if your child is being bullied? There will be a pathway at the school your child attends for you to work through. If this pathway does not lead to a prompt change for your child, consider removing him from the school. He will not be learning there. In fact, he will simply be being damaged by the experience, both academically and emotionally. Just write it all out in a frank and polite way for the school, and take action.

Chapter 22

The other skills for school success

When I come home I shall have new things to tell you ...

Friedrich Froebel, *Mother Play*, 1895.[43]

Succeeding at school requires more than social and learning skills. Very prosaically, children need to be able to care for themselves, including being able to cope with toileting by themselves. Having good work skills is also essential, and, just like toilet training, this is something children need to learn at home first. Getting ready for school also means getting ready for a change in how you relate to your child. Your child still needs you as his safe haven but that safety is something you provide in a different way. When your child comes home they will have new things to tell you: it is by listening and talking that you provide them with that safe haven.

Toilet training

Children need to be toilet trained to cope with school. This is perhaps one of the only statements about toilet training that everyone would agree with. There is a great deal of information in the community about toilet training and much of it is contradictory.

My sister Stephanie thinks children sit along two continuums when it comes to toilet training. The first one is to do with sensory perception: there are the children who are distressed by that wet or pooey feeling, and there are the children who don't notice it. The second is to do with the degree to which they are eager to please: that is, there are the children who can be quickly convinced by their parents of a particular viewpoint — in this case, that being trained is important, while there are the children who take some convincing on any issue. These children have an independence of thought, which, in this instance, leads them to think that you, the parent, have a problem with something that is very natural.

Why am I quoting from Steph? Because my children trained almost independently due to their dislike of having a dirty nappy. But Steph's boys Declan and Brennan coupled not noticing dirty nappies with the habit of great independence of thought. When it came to toilet training there was no doubt that they believed it was their parents who had the problem. Making them care was extremely difficult because for them, any interruption to their game was a far worse experience than wet pants. Toilet training is all about motivation, and Declan and Brennan's starting position was, 'So what?'

When a child isn't trained you get a lot of unsolicited advice. So Stephanie has talked a lot more about toilet training than I have. She's an excellent resource on the subject, partly due to all those parents who have told her just what worked for them and suggested she try that too.

Motivation

Steph believes the million-dollar question is, 'What will motivate your child?' If you are lucky, it is going to be the horrid feeling of dirty pants. Mind you, a child who is hyper-responsive to touch sensation may also have difficulties with fine motor activities, so while it may be useful on the toilet training front, it is not an unalloyed advantage. Likewise, your child might be solely motivated by the pleasure of your approval. But it may well need something added to it, such as the ability to stay in an older sibling's schoolroom or perhaps monkey-patterned underpants or even chocolate.

For the child who isn't intrinsically motivated by the desire to have a clean, dry bottom, the motivation is going to have to be something substantial. Mum's undivided attention while she changes your nappy is a big thing to give up. Additionally, if Mum is very busy and a poo in the nappy invariably gets attention, then a child is very unlikely to be motivated to train.

Toilet training needs, then, to be something your child knows is prestigious: big kid stuff that gets him big kid privileges. So it is a good idea to think ahead here and keep some privileges aside for this time. Being trained needs to lead to something else that is desired. It needs to be something that matters to your child. As part of the overall 'Now you're a big boy' spin-doctoring it is a good touch to actually let your child use the adult toilet (perhaps with a child-sized seat insert so they can't fall in) rather than a potty.

Of course, I am anticipating here. Before motivation comes into play you need to be sure your child actually knows what is being required.

Linking sensation with consequences

One of the reasons for very promptly changing nappies in infancy is that it trains in a sensitive response to a dirty nappy. Cloth nappies, too, promote early training by needing more frequent changing, so I recommend using the modern cloth nappies with their latest fabrics and fasteners.

Your child's first step is connecting 'going' with the feeling of 'needing to go' that happens directly beforehand. In fact, from the first months of life your baby can begin connecting the feeling of needing to go and then 'dirty nappy' and then clean nappy and how nice that feels. But the penny really drops when he can see it as well as feel it. Multi-sensory learning is the most powerful type of learning. When the weather is warm enough, let him be nude — not just when you are beginning toilet training, but well before.

Watch your child attentively for signs that he's making those connections and talk to him about the fact that he's noticing. Remember, what he can say is just the tip of the iceberg. A toddler may only use two words at a time but he can understand a great deal more. The next step is teaching him just what you want him to do.

Knowing what to do up on the chair with the hole in the middle

Many years ago Mum had a young mother bring her four-year-old son in for an appointment for 'general concerns'. He was a dear little boy and seemed to be doing very well. The mother was vague about what she felt the problem was so Mum patiently checked each skill domain. And then, halfway through one set of observations Mum noticed the little boy was wearing a nappy. And yes, this was the unspecified concern. The little boy wasn't toilet trained and he was due to attend kindergarten shortly.

A further appointment was made at the little boy's home to discuss why this perfectly normal child was not using the toilet. After asking lots of questions Mum discovered that neither the boy's mother nor father had ever used the toilet in front of their son. The door was kept firmly shut at all times. The little boy hadn't known just what he was supposed to do up on the chair with the hole in the middle.

So drop any inhibitions you may have on the subject and let your child see you going to the toilet. Theory of mind will help your child put himself on the toilet seat in his imagination and help him see that there is an alternative to the nappy.

Start when you are sure your child is ready

How do you know when your child is ready to train? It is when he demonstrates that he has made all the connections and he has a good motivation to learn.

Make sure that you have a good clear run of time in which to cope with the extra washing. Don't stop–start on toilet training: this sends the message to your child that it's not really an important skill after all. Get rid of all the nappies except for those used at night. Send a really clear message to your child: if he wets his pants, he wets his pants.

Responding to accidents

The first thing to remember is that children under the age of 11 cannot actually learn from negatives. This might sound like a statement on parenting theory but it is in fact a finding in brain research.[44] So saying such things as, 'Don't do it in your nappy or on the floor or around behind the couch', isn't going to help him learn. Instead, say what you want to see happen: 'Poos go in the toilet.'

You can use a star chart to note down each success. I suspect they work not directly by motivating a child but by helping us to remember to praise each success. It is your praise that really counts.

Teaching your children how to work

You may have noted my mention of teaching Rafael how to work in an earlier chapter. 'Work skills' are one of the first things that Mum

puts into any occupational therapy program, wheth.
for individual children. In fact, although I've incorpora
programs for years at her request, I've only just really un.
how important they are. Children need to learn to work, nc
some Calvinistic work ethic reason but because learning how ι.
work harnesses together the self-mastery skills like nothing else.

How? Take learning to scrub the floor, which is what I was
teaching Rafael yesterday. In learning how to scrub a floor Rafael,
who is nearly four, was also:

- sharpening up his perceptual sensitivity — finding white paint
  spots to scrub off cream tiles and manipulating a thick bristled
  brush and knife
- shifting attention — from the job, to my feedback about tools
  ('Try a butter knife on that spot') and back to the job
- increasing his concentration length despite the inherent lack
  of interest in the task — praise for 'sticking at it' was needed
  here
- judging his own performance — a theory of mind skill
- being motivated by his empathy as he heard just how much it
  meant to me to have him helping.

One researcher refers to the self-mastery skills as the Swiss army
knife of temperament, a tool so powerful that all situations benefit
from its use. Your child's participation in any work activity or
household chores, gardening or volunteering is going to strengthen
her ability to meet her goals in any other type of endeavour.

But that is not the only gift that accrues from these various prosaic
activities. Work skills:

- teach children what trying is and how it feels
- contribute to mental health
- build self-esteem
- give children skills to succeed in a workplace years down the
  track
- help a child feel safe.

Learning to try
The aspect of work that harnesses the different self-mastery skills is
the focusing of effort. And this, in itself, is terrifically important.

Children have to learn to work and to know that it is necessary. Rafael had to 'try' to succeed in removing the dirt and paint. He couldn't just gently swish the bristly brush over the tiles. He had to scrub.

The thing about physical work is that effort is visible: they can see it and you can see it. It is something concrete, so it makes understanding the concept of trying far easier to grasp at a much younger age.

Knowing how to focus your efforts is required to meet challenges. What seems to be less well grasped is that children must be challenged if they are to learn how to do this and to further sharpen their existing ability to try. A job that is 'too hard' or 'too easy' doesn't allow this learning.

If our children know how to try, how to pull every bit of themselves into a task and only stop when something has been achieved, they are far more likely to be successful. Why do some children with learning difficulties go on to considerable success in life? Children who find learning difficult have to put more effort in than their peers. Some of those children do learn to put that effort in. They have learned to try, and gotten into the habit of trying hard most of the time, far earlier than other children. It is very hard at the time but those children do then go on to succeed.

If you are told that your learning disabled child will never catch up with her peers, ask the teller, 'By when?' It is my experience that they might not have caught their peers by 10 or 15 years of age but, with strong support from their parents, the gap starts to close at 20.

Conversely, the gifted child is at a disadvantage when all the work is 'too easy'. And the best programs for gifted children don't simply expose them to harder material but require them to harness their self-mastery skills in a work task. My friend Debbie provides this for my sons: Tim and Sam have spent the last two weeks (also known as the school holidays) working solidly on a plasticine animation. As well as all their self-mastery skills, they are using science, art, mathematics, language, computing and design skills. What is keeping them so engaged?

Flow: a 'must-have' for mental health

Every now and then Tim and Sam are having an experience that is truly addictive: 'flow' or 'being in the zone'. The magic moments when you are fully engaged by a task that is 'just right' for your skills; where time seems irrelevant, where you pay attention to the right things at the right moment. You have a sense of stepping out of your own way to simply perform.

This is a state we usually associate with highly creative endeavours or with athletic performance. But it is not necessarily produced by running or composing a symphony. It can just as easily happen when you are polishing the furniture. The child who has learnt how to try is the same child who can find tremendous joy and meaning in doing.

Once experienced, we return to the activity in which flow was experienced over and over again. There is some speculation that regular 'flow' experiences proof children against the need for artificial stimulation such as mild-altering drugs and high-risk behaviour but, even without that benefit, flow enhances life greatly.[45]

The term 'flow' was coined by Mihaly Csikszentmihalyi after observing the extraordinary immersion of artists in their work. He then observed that same heightened immersion not just in artists but in hobbyists and doctors, and concluded that it was part of being human. In one of his many experiments in flow he first asked participants to identify their flow activities, such as sailing, gardening, cooking. Then he asked them to not do those activities for a month. What happened to the participants? They became depressed and their relationships suffered. His conclusion was that participating in flow activities is vital for mental health. Not only does it guarantee joy during the experience, it also leaves a residue of meaningfulness that permeates the individual's sense of wellbeing for days.

Helping with the house and station work has taught my children to focus their efforts. The 'just right' challenge that Debbie has presented them with is letting them experience flow and hooking them further into the benefits of trying hard. And, of course, they know that at the end of it they will have something to show for all their work. This too is a powerful inducement.

Reward for effort

Housework, although only briefly alas, does show a result for effort made. One of the important things to remember is not to redo something a child has done. Work alongside them and coach them through doing as good a job as they can but don't sabotage their esteem by fixing up their work afterwards.

I find Ginott's advice on praise very useful in this context too. Having briefly left the room to answer the phone I found Rafael still scrubbing hard at the floor. I didn't say, 'You are a wonderful little boy' but 'I feel so thrilled that I went away and came back to find you still working'. I also showed Rafael's patch of floor to both his grandad and dad and told them he'd kept working in my absence. Rafael was able to infer from this praise and the notice taken of his physical achievement just what a great person he is. The deductions that you make yourself always have the greatest credibility.

Back to attachment

Asking children to help around the house makes some parents uncomfortable, particularly parents who were asked to do too much in their own childhood. In that case, the tasks were not fairly delegated because the result was that they didn't have a childhood. (This is something that is associated with an insecure attachment.) The last thing these parents wish to do is ask too much of their own children so, sometimes, they swing too far the other way. Children aren't asked to contribute at all, and this has its own consequences.

Quite apart from all the missed benefits of learning how to work, having roles, routines and responsibilities makes children feel safer. Feeling safe is an enormous contributor to the quality of attachment. Like so much in parenting, knowing just how much to ask of children in terms of work skills is a balancing act that you improve upon over time.

I think of self-esteem as the rewarding feeling we have about our own efforts. Self-esteem is something that we build, not something that we are born with. By giving our child opportunities to focus their efforts in a task or for a purpose, they have the chance to build their esteem. While *only* doing housework isn't good for anyone's self-esteem, contributing to the creation of family life as part of a team certainly is.

From home to workplace

These same team skills are also required in the workplace. The ability to work cooperatively, to appreciate that everyone has a role in a successful outcome, to tolerate and respect your co-workers, all can be learned doing family chores. And that's just the teamwork component of work skills. The ability to communicate, to problem-solve, to sequence and organise, to show initiative, to manage your own behaviour, to quickly learn a new task, to focus effort — all these abilities are required in the workplace. Indeed, they are of equal importance to literacy and numeracy in terms of employability.

Keeping the connection

Finally, your school child needs to know that you are still there, supporting them, even if you are not physically present. Once your babies and toddlers needed you to hold them physically but now they need you to 'hold them' as they explore the world of other people. You can support from the sidelines only. I think this is much harder parenting than the early physical kind. So how is it done?

We do it by listening and by telling stories. [46, 47] We tell stories to our children both directly and indirectly. In Part One we looked at the ways stories are learned indirectly — for example, by always being responded to, securely attached children build a story of the world as responsive to their needs and people as trustworthy. But parents of older children also do this by 'talking'. One set of researchers found that mothers tell their children about 6.3 stories an hour! [48]

Most of our stories are to do with something that has just happened to our child. Perhaps a classmate who was a friend yesterday isn't a friend today. So you listen, and draw your child out with questions about how he feels. 'And you're feeling pretty upset because you really wanted to play with James today.' When your child is calm enough, the storytelling can start.

'Well, I happen to know that James did the same thing to Christopher last term. Chris was at his house and they were getting on like a house on fire. And then James and his Mum had a bit of an argument in front of Chris and his Mum, and James ended up having a temper tantrum — yes, just like they did with us. And then James didn't want to talk to Chris anymore after that. What do you think James might be feeling? Yes, I think he's embarrassed, and he doesn't want to remember how he behaved. I think he might be having difficulty knowing how to get over what happened. What could you do? Oh, so you teased him about it today …' And so on.

The story in this case is not just about your child but James as well; about walking in a friend's shoes and imagining how a friendship might be repaired. But you might equally have told a story about a fraying and then mended relationship from your own childhood. Or even found a book or made up your own story about such an event.

This is a story where a one-off solution is possible, but often such problems require your child to develop a strategy. Let's say that James often plays games of exclusion–inclusion (sometimes a child is allowed to participate in a game at lunchtime, sometimes they are not), that he's a clever child with high self-esteem who enjoys bullying others. You will need to use stories to help your child 'categorise' James and the experience, and then to practise, in story, anticipating and managing his emotions on such occasions. And next to trial various long term strategies, such as to never play with James no matter how nice he is that day, or to keep playing with James but know that he could change at any time, or to set out to make better friends with other children and support anyone who James picks on. The logical sequence of the story is the way humans work out all the different consequences that might stem from an action. 'But what if?' is the question that storytellers ask themselves all the time.[47]

A securely attached parent and child pair are able to do this much more successfully (although it remains very hard work) than the insecurely attached parent and child.[49] Why? This is a new area of research so for the time being these are just my thoughts on the subject.[46, 50]

First, mother and child tend to be more emotionally matched in general so that the stories told are well matched to the child moment-to-moment, making it easier for the child to learn from each story. Second, as the parent who can create a secure attachment is the parent who has come to terms with her life — that is, there aren't any areas that are off-limits emotionally — it is easier for her to find a story to tell, and tell it coherently, so that it is really useful for her listening child.

Finally, some research seems to be indicating that the 'all emotions are okay' quality to secure attachment is vital because it is the stories about handling negative emotions that are particularly important in the development of social and emotional wellbeing.[50, 51] When we look through the various lists of skills required for social and emotional wellbeing generated by experts such as psychologist Dr Michael Bernard (who works with schools) or Daniel Goleman (who popularised the notion of emotional intelligence), many are to do with dealing with negative emotions.[52]

Dr Bernard states that for a child to be able to get along with others he must accept that everyone acts unfairly towards others some of the time, think before responding when he is treated badly, play by the rules and be socially responsible.[52] This is a tough skill-set to master.

In reporting on his recently completed study of the social and emotional wellbeing of more than 10,000 Australian children and teenagers, Dr Bernard highlighted the research delineating the single most important contribution a parent could make to their child's social and emotional wellbeing: 'parents needed to talk to their children about emotions and talk about coping with stress'.

Parenting the older child is all about talking. I once asked my friends Emma and Rossco, who manage the tricky task of parenting teenagers well, for their advice on the subject. Emma said, 'Talk, talk, talk. Talk!' Of course, she had put in the groundwork first. Telling stories, asking questions and listening had been family habits long before their children were teenagers.

You will find as your child grows older and his theory of mind and empathic skills grow stronger, that these conversational exchanges grow richer. The gift of a child of our own is the gift of deep personal knowledge of another person from the very beginnings of his life. Each conversation lets us see more and more of the person our child wishes to become: his best possible self. It is the reason that being a parent is the biggest privilege life offers.

Ultimately, these conversations bring you as much joy as did the little hand in yours not so very long ago.

Behavioural stages from eight to ten

Once again, these stages only approximately relate to age. I include them because I've found them useful tools, in particular to remind me that all things pass. You will note the preoccupation with language and ideas of each of these ages. Children now have theory of mind well grasped and are using it as a tool to think and relate.

Eight: Talking takes over

At eight years children grow in all directions. They explore new interests, find new passions, drop them in favour of yet more fascinating enterprises: they devour life whole, racing out to meet the world. In fact, voracity and speed become their defining characteristics. They talk so fast that they are often incomprehensible, even to their parents. Walking disappears.

One area of particular expansion is in relationships. They begin to see themselves as equal partners in relationships, and begin to consciously give back. They relish intimacy and shared jokes, and are especially looking to be close to their parents. At all ages children need to be 'delighted in', but this need is very close to the surface at this age.

Nine: Thinking about feelings

The Gessell Institute researchers describe nine as being more like five and seven. This is an inward and more melancholy age. For many children, nine is the age at which the 'inner critic', which goes on to haunt us life long unless we take action, is switched on.

Often children spend this year perfecting all the skills they attempted in a slapdash way at eight. They spend time thinking: they worry about the state of the world (as they did at seven) and they worry about their own imperfections. It's a more 'feeling' and less adventurous time. They rebel against their parents, sometimes openly but quite often with more 'passive aggressive' behaviours: rather than refuse to do an unwelcome task they will complain about sore eyes, hands and tummies. In contrast to eight, a time of great closeness to parents, nine year olds can sometimes prefer to be with their friends.

Ten: Briefly back in balance (10)

This is one of the 'golden ages' for parents. Ten is an age at which children are more likely to obey their parents, to approve of their parents and to feel happy with themselves and their place in the world. Enjoy it, say the researchers in a most poignant aside, because you will never again enjoy this same level of approval from your children. This kind of equilibrium — of confident mood — doesn't reappear until your children are 16, when it is unlikely to be paired with unqualified approval of parents.[53]

Appendices

Introduction

My friend Cindy says that if she found this book in a bookshop or library this is the section she'd be turning to first: 'Forget everything else, I want *answers*!' She also says that I need to tell you straightaway that this isn't the only part of the book that gives those answers. This part of the book is particularly for parents of school-aged children who are having difficulties. You might like to keep on reading through the appendices sequentially. Of, if your child has a particular learning issue you might like to turn straight to Appendices V and VI.

So far we've gone forward 'through time' to tell the story of how children develop. But when a child has difficulty we can hit rewind and go back to see where that difficulty has begun. That's what this part of the book is all about.

There are many reasons why a child might have a problem. Let's take 'attention' as an example here. There are a great many reasons why a child might have or develop difficulties in attending intensely enough to engage with learning material. For example, a recent event may have distressed her. It could be a relationship problem with the teacher. She might not be having enough sleep. She might have developed a cluster of food intolerances. She might have a sensory issue that so dominates her attention she can't focus on anything else. She might be bored. Her visual perceptual skills might suddenly have fallen beneath the requirements of school. Going further back in time, she might have unintegrated primitive reflexes. Going further back still, she might not have fully developed her right brain due to the absence of a secure, organised attachment. And despite listing all these possibilities I have probably left something out!

It is by asking and answering questions that parents and therapists work together to discover the reasons why a child has a problem. In these appendices you will find the questions Mum and I ask on the way to pinpointing why a child is having difficulties — matched up with the strategies we employ to help missing skills develop.

Troubleshooting development

If you are concerned about your child, the first places to begin looking are prosaic: sleep and food.

Sleep

Three years ago I briefly had a teacher staying with us and teaching the children while I researched one of the very early versions of this book. After a month Lesley came to me and said that Tim's mathematics was going backwards: he was unable to do some things that he'd mastered before she arrived. When I went to talk to Tim I found Lesley was right: in fact, he couldn't do maths mastered two years earlier! Being prone to catastrophising, I immediately thought of brain tumours.

Fortunately the *Weekend Australian Magazine* had run a story about the consequences of sleep deficit in children the previous weekend. All I needed to do was join the dots: Lesley had taken over the schoolroom when daylight saving had begun. What the article said — and I've not been able to track down the original research — was that a half-hour less sleep a night equates to a two year drop in performance.

I blacked out the windows in Tim's bedroom and after a very long night's sleep he was able to do maths again. So now when I see a child I tell this story and ask:

- Does she have sleeping difficulties?
- How much sleep does she get a night?
- Is she tired during the day at all?

Sleep problems cause children to struggle to think and to learn, and are also strongly connected to behavioural problems, particularly with impulse control and attention.[1, 2] Sleep problems are also connected to weight gain. Studies aren't consistent, however, showing different effects for different age groups.

For six and seven year olds, lack of sleep means behavioural problems and weight gain.[3] Children sleeping less than 10 to 11 hours at night are those at risk of becoming overweight or obese.[4] One study recommends that parents pay particular attention to their child's sleeping patterns and take preventative action as early as possible if they have a child who doesn't sleep enough. If your child is overweight, clearly one of the first places to intervene is ensuring that she has enough sleep.

Consider what sleep aids your child uses. Does she play music, or have a television or computer in her room? The research is showing that children who use 'media' as an aid to sleep are far less likely to get enough sleep.[5] Remove all such temptations from her room! Instead, consider putting a pile of books by the bed and a bedside lamp.

If your child isn't sleeping properly and is struggling with learning, make sorting out sleep patterns a very high priority. You might find that it is all you need to do.

Food and the environment

It would be so much easier to bring up our children if we could keep them in a safe little bubble. There seems to be little concern in the wider economic and political community for children's needs. An important part of the parental role has always been protecting our children: we now must extend that into protecting them from the wrong food and an increasingly polluted environment.

Does the right food make a difference to learning and behaviour? Is the right food for one child the right food for every child? These are the kinds of questions that most people with children who have learning difficulties work through. And the answer is yes to the first question and no to the second.

In fact, every parent can learn from the specialists who case-manage children with more severe behavioural and learning difficulties. Where do these specialists begin when faced with a child from a very normal family who can't learn, can't behave and is terribly miserable too? They start by looking at the things that influence a child's biochemistry: environmental factors and diet. Food additives,

vitamin and mineral deficiencies, essential fatty acids and ami.
deficiencies are all carefully explored. The first intervention is
frequently a dietary one.[6]

The safest food for humans is food we prepare ourselves from
scratch. The packets full of food additives, the ready-to-go meals, the
fried trans-fatty acid fast foods have all been shown to be dangerous
to human health. The difficulty is that preparing food from scratch
takes time. When the media bitterly attacks the mothers of toddlers
for failing to feed them properly, they fail to mention just how time
poor many of us are. It is not so very different to the criticisms of
mothers who do not breastfeed.[7]

Parents' anxiety about children's eating also spills over into
mealtime. In the face of growing obesity and of decreased time for
cooking, when we do make a meal we want children to eat it.
However, one of Ginott's recommendations was that parents never
make an issue of food — again, a very prescient statement as research
is now showing links between fathers' (not mothers'!) parenting style
and obesity.[8] The parenting style that Ginott advocated is the one
that is associated with the least obesity in children. It is particularly
difficult to remember not to insist that children finish everything
when we are looking at plate of fish (omega threes!) and vegetables
(beta-carotene!). Of course, when they do eat there is that delightful
feeling of having properly nourished our children. When they don't
eat the let down is considerable.

I am not going to quote the current food guidelines for children.
Like just about all of modern life they have become confused by
interventions from commercial interests. (In fact, research is showing
that food advertising on television all by itself is a factor in the obesity
and overweight epidemic. Experts are calling for policies limiting
children's exposure to food advertising.) By a process of observing
your children from the moment they first have solids you will work
out what food best suits them. If a sudden temper tantrum follows an
ice-cream on more than one occasion, you might suspect that sugar
or milk and your child don't mix. Being sensitive to your child is the
constant across all domains of parenting.

Again, just like insufficient sleep, sorting out issues with food or
an unhealthy environment might be all you need to do to help your
child.

If sleep and food are not the answer, or only part of the answer, then we have to go further back in time. Occupational therapists have a 'bottom up' approach and start by fixing the lowest levels of development. Attachment is the very first level of development so this is the place to start. A program that addresses the next layers, the primitive reflexes and sensation issues, however, can also be part of building attachment. It is important to remember that there is a clear developmental sequence laid out. There is little point working on scissor skills or visual perception, for example, if a child still has active primitive reflexes.

And, of course, with the co-development of so much in early life, there is very rarely a 'single answer'. Usually it is a number of factors conspiring together to create the problem.

For example, a baby might not crawl because she doesn't like the sensation of the floor on her legs, because she has a problem with 'touch' sensation. Because she doesn't crawl she's left with an active primitive reflex. Equally, a little boy may have never been offered tummy time. While his sensory system is fine, he hasn't had the opportunity to develop crawling. Both children will now have problems with attention and fine motor skills, but the little girl also reacts badly to smells and touch.

We are made up of hundreds upon hundreds of feedback loops. There are the negative feedback loops, which are all about keeping us comfortable. For example, we get hot, we sweat (or glow or perspire) and then we cool down. And then there are the positive feedback loops: when you begin labour the contractions cause a release of oxytocin. The oxytocin causes more contractions, which cause more oxytocin to be released. Negative feedback loops keep things the same: positive feedback loops make changes happen. A 'vicious circle' is when a positive feedback loop goes wrong.

Sensory problems and reflex integration problems and attachment problems and attention problems (and other kinds of problems too) often join together in just such a vicious circle. And, in order to work out where to intervene first, it is important to work out where the breakdown actually happened. No-one can do this better than a parent.

Much of the rest of the appendices are given over to questions to help you track down where a problem lies and suggestions for strategies, games and activities to help your child. Grab a pencil and paper, and once you hit a 'problem area', note it down. Then write down each game listed. You can read through the entire section or simply stop at the end of the appendix in which you first thought, 'That's it, that's where the problem is'. Or you could read through and write down every single relevant game or activity or strategy.

When you finish reading the appendices you will have a big list of ideas. You might be thinking, 'Where do I start? What about the very similar activities?'

So where do you start? You start with the lowest level of development. If the issue is attachment based, that's where you start. You ignore everything else until you feel you are on top of that. Next comes reflex integration. Again, ignore everything else until you are on top of those issues. You will begin to notice similarities in recommended activities — that tells you that you have indeed hit a 'hot spot' — just pick one to do.

From there, you begin to look at perceptual sensitivity, eye movements and fine motor skills. It is the same developmental progression described in the rest of the book.

When you've decided on the activities that are going to help your child, organise yourself a clear space of time — 21 consecutive days — in which to build the habit of spending time with your child doing these things. However, and this is a very big 'however', remember to work from your child's strengths and never push her into an activity or sensation that she feels unable to do or tolerate. It has just the same effect on her brain as on the brain of a baby left to cry: all that terrible distress can be seen at the neurological level as a flood of the catecholamines that burn out neurological connections.

Interestingly, at a recent workshop on building resilience for parents I heard the same message.[9] Imagine a child who fits the stereotype of low resilience. She's easily upset. She finds it hard to risk her shaky self-esteem by 'trying' at a difficult task. How do you help? Imagine this little person is great with Lego but not at sport. She finds it hard to make friends and her literacy is also poor. How do you best help her become more resilient and able to return from a failure with the ability to try again? Do you try and 'work on her weaknesses' by increase her sporting opportunities and so on?

You don't. You strengthen the strengths. You spend more time playing with Lego with her. In doing so you also build the relationship between you deeper, which then goes on to grow her sense of self. With that increased sense of self she will then be able to take risks and begin to try — with trying she will begin to show small successes and these will ultimately build her self-esteem and her ability to cope with failure.

When do I need to get help from someone else?

Follow your instincts. For us, these are the indicators that an outside person is definitely required:

- You feel your relationship is suffering.
- You feel that your child's learning is suffering.
- There are many environments in which she feels uncomfortable.
- There are many occasions on which she is not prepared to try.
- She is dominated by negative moods.

Choose a person to help based on the quality of the relationship you feel you and your child can have with them. It might be an occupational therapist or a speech pathologist or a physiotherapist or a psychologist. Ask that person to refer out to get in the other expertise you and your child require.

Troubleshooting attachment

The messages of Part One were:

- a secure, organised attachment leads to a strong right brain
- changing a negative attachment pattern is something that you can do at any time.

While reading Part One you might have wondered what characterises a child with an undeveloped right brain. In fact, the profile is a familiar one — it looks a lot like attention deficit disorder. Attachment and neuropsychiatric researchers do link hyperactive behaviours with insecure and disorganised attachment. They describe it as a 'right brain dysfunction'.

This is not to say that all children with hyperactivity have a disordered attachment. But for some children it is the case. A child who's had a lot less time experiencing that heart-to-heart, body-to-body, brain-to-brain communication with his mum and dad shows it in mostly behavioural ways:

- He struggles to build relationships with others, both with adults and with peers.
- He has low empathy.
- He is very distractible.
- If bright this child will still show reasonable verbal and logic skills, but without the emotional richness and meaning you'd expect to accompany them.
- He is more likely to fall into a bully or victim role.
- He will have a pronounced tendency for all-or-nothing thinking, leading straight to poor impulse control.
- You might see a 'typical mood' which dominates his behavour. This mood is the one created by the parenting style used at home. So he may be mostly angry. Or he may be superficially

bright and placating and very competent. Or he may be very distant.

- In terms of schoolwork you notice spatial difficulties that affect handwriting and maths.
- When you ask for stories about 'connecting' to a reading text, this is the child who struggles to come up with rich, detailed examples as his autobiographical memory skills are very undeveloped.

The first port of call for helping a child like this one is going to be a long term relationship to enable him to grow his right brain. If you are reading this as a parent, read on for some ideas to help you with changing the prevailing attachment pattern. If you are reading this as a teacher, and Mum and Dad's lives and your own are too complex to allow this to happen, consider asking your school to employ a 'visiting grandparent' for this child.

In addition to building the relationship, what else can you do to help this child whose self-regulation skills are so lacking?

- I would begin with removing, or at least severely curtailing the use of, televisions. Certainly remove them from his bedroom. You want your child to be in the shared family space, talking to you.
- Greatly limit the use of the computer. It is a hard thing to accept but children now introduce each other to pornography. If this is not something you want to happen you need to take steps to prevent it: move all computers in your home into 'public' areas. Where accessing pornography in the past required a trip to a shop, it now simply requires an internet link. Horror, violence and pornography both 'trigger' a response from the amygdala (a startle response in fact) and, the brain being the responsive organ it is, that part will grow correspondingly.[10] That research becomes particularly relevant when we tie it to the study showing that more aggressive teenagers have a larger amygdala.[11] If we are letting children 'grow' this part of their brain, then the result is going to be a less mature mind, where the higher 'self-regulation' circuits cannot exert a great deal of influence over behaviour.

- Deliberately set out to engage and grow your child's empath pattern-detecting 'right brain': music, theatre, art, pets, emotionally rich narrative, touch, cooking ... all the richly multi-sensory experiences that life offers.
- Board games, card games and just 'talking talking talking' around a shared meal will contribute to the self-regulation skills.
- Add in movement to lift mood. Both simple exercise — bushwalking, playing in the garden and patterned movement such as dance, gym and circus. These patterned movements can also re-expose children to early missed movement patterns which help rebuild the brain.

Building a relationship by changing your own attachment pattern

If you are reading this as a parent, remember that the right brain grows in response to events throughout the whole of life. You can learn to tell your story coherently and meaningfully and become free from the past, thereby breaking the pattern for future generations. It is never too late to start on the project of changing your brain. Here are some of the principles that have worked for other people:

- Forgive! See your own parents as inheritors of intergenerational patterns too. If you can step back to see it all from that intergenerational perspective it becomes a lot easier to
  — jump off the tracks laid down behind and ahead of you in your parenting
  — also (keeping the train metaphor going) to 'decouple' the heavy load of anger from the past that you are pulling
  — and finally to look at your own engine room and examine what is driving you to behave in a way you don't want in the present. If you can see things from the symbolic perspective you might be able to usefully study your own behaviour rather than being distressed and overwhelmed by it. For example, 'I was hearing shark music. I wonder why?' rather than, 'I did it again and I swore I wouldn't. I'm no good in this mothering role.'
- While you are working through all this heavy emotional stuff, don't talk about it to the people involved. Those 'confrontations'

don't do any good. Instead, they are likely to keep you mired in past patterns.

- In Chapter 4 we discussed the work of Haim Ginott. Don't just follow his suggestions for your child, but 'parent yourself' with them as well.
- In Chapter 8 there is a discussion of the role of the heart in both empathy and thinking. Again, don't just apply these insights to your baby but to 'parenting yourself' as well.

Over the next few pages you will find a list of statements that would fit into a particular attachment pattern. You might like to see if you identify personally with any set of statements. You might also like to type 'attachment style questionnaire' into a search engine and see what you find. You might find this helpful in seeing intergenerational patterns as separate from the individuals caught up in them, and from there find it easier to forgive.

Organised or disorganised: do you and/or your child feel safe?

A disorganised parent might say something along the lines of:

- You couldn't ever get it right with him. You never knew what would send Dad off and once he'd lost it, you had to look out. Even on his good days we were scared of him, and I reckon he liked it that way.
- Mum was just as bad in her own way. I could never work out what I had to do to keep her happy. God knows I tried. She'd just stop doing anything altogether for us sometimes. We were kids and it was her job to look after us, but she didn't. She thought we were little adults, able to fend for ourselves.
- I spent my time trying to keep her happy, telling her stories to cheer her up and trying to help her keep herself together by doing everything for her. Really, it was like I was the mother.
- I feel like I was born sick of my mother. I know I was really unpleasant to her, bullying her just to try and get some order into our lives.
- Sometimes my impatience with her spilled out into violence. She was just maddening.

- My childhood left me pretty scared of other people — you never know what they might do. What's to stop it being you that someone takes their emotions out on?
- I just hate it when someone gets angry or cries. The boundaries between me and other people are thin and I find myself feeling their emotions are in me.
- You don't want to push me or I just blow up.
- I was like a companion to my mother — she needed me to keep her company because she didn't have any other major person in her life. It was like we were the same age.
- Mum did her best, but we knew that everything wasn't rosy in the world outside. There were bombs, there was the enemy, and if you went too far away you might never come home.

And they might say of their own children:
- I know they aren't good management techniques, but if your kids are scared of you they will do what you want. And, yes, I know that it can't be good for them, but if you tell them that you'll leave if they don't behave or that you'll give them to someone else — well, they behave then too.
- My little boy is just wonderful to me. Everyone tells me how mature he is and how amazing it is the way he looks after me. And he is amazing. If I feel down he cheers me up; if I can't think what to do, he tells me. You'd never believe he was only four.
- My little boy is just horrible. He hits me, he screams at me, he won't listen to me when I ask him to do anything. He says nasty things too.
- If my toddler goes away from me to do something, I feel like he is saying he doesn't need me. That gives me the worst feeling.
- My kids will just go to anyone. They'll smile and be as loving as if they've known that person forever instead of just five minutes.

If a number of these statements resonated with you, you might like to go back and read Chapter 2.

Secure?

A parent able to create a secure attachment might say of themselves:

- My parents are/were supportive and loving and I know they did their best for me.
- My parents found it hard to support me and to express their love; all the same, I know they were doing their best.
- My childhood contained loss, adversity and pain.
- My childhood has left me with wonderful memories.
- I'm not angry with my parents.
- I don't speak of my parents in derogatory terms.
- I've come to terms with my childhood, even the things that were very difficult to cope with at the time.
- There are very few 'unhealed wounds' left in my relationship with my parents.
- I believe the relationships you have in early life are important.
- I'm able to remain close to a person over long periods of time without making them uncomfortable.
- I find that when life is difficult it helps to have someone supporting me and that when life is good, it's better if there is someone to share it with.
- I believe that if my partner is unhappy it is part of my role to support him through those times.
- I trust my partner.
- I feel comfortable displaying all my emotions in front of my partner, and I'm equally comfortable with all of his emotions.
- I'm comfortable with physical affection from family members.
- I assume the best of people rather than the worst.
- I'm mostly able to regulate my moods so they don't interfere with my relationships or my goals for myself.

And they would say of their children:

- When they are hurt, they come straight to me or my partner for comforting, and they usually calm down quickly once they've had a big cuddle.
- I don't require my children to always be upbeat and positive. It's okay if they are feeling negative.
- Sad, needy and angry feelings in my children don't trigger those same feelings in me.

- My children trust me.
- If I've been away for a short time, my children are always delighted to see me.
- My children and I are comfortable touching each other affectionately.
- My children aren't affectionate towards people they don't know very well.
- My children always know that I'm watching, and it makes them feel safer and more confident.
- They call out, 'Mum, look at this', very often and I always look — if I can't look immediately I explain why, and look as soon as it is possible.
- There's lots of laughing with each other in our house.
- I believe that no-one is more important in a child's life than his parents.
- My children and I are able to make up quickly after a disagreement.
- My children mostly get on with each other and with the other children they know.
- One of my attitudes is that all emotions are okay but not all behaviours are.
- My children understand social rules and mostly obey them.
- I'm emotionally available to my children at all times: I'm never too sad or too frightened or too angry for a child in need.
- My children are empathic and understand how their actions affect others.
- There are no favourites in my family.

If you drew a blank on 'disorganised' and these statements regarding secure attchment resonated strongly with you, your children would be classified as 'organised, secure', which is linked to the best set of outcomes. If the preceeding set of statements also resonated strongly, then your children would fit into 'disorganised, secure'. Finding a safer environment or dealing with whatever it is that frightens you would help your children to better outcomes.

It can be helpful to keep reading to see if any of the other attachment patterns also appear sometimes in your parenting. Most of us have a mix of styles.

The first type of insecure: dismissive?

Dismissive parents might say of themselves:

- I can't remember much about my childhood.
- I do sometimes find myself denigrating my parents in terms of their importance to me.
- You choose how important other people are to you.
- I find it hard to be close to someone for any length of time.
- I'm generally a positive person, but I'm fairly prone to anxiety.
- My emotions don't get in the way of the things I want to do.
- I tend to keep quite a lot private, even in a close relationship.
- I can be a bit compulsive in the workplace because I'm a high achiever.
- I like to pick and choose when I receive or give physical affection.
- I don't like to depend on my partner.
- People trying to get too close make me nervous.
- I believe that if someone is upset, they should be left alone.
- I find it annoying when someone wants to talk to me about 'my feelings'.

And they would say of their children:

- When my children are hurt they prefer to be left on their own to work through it by themselves.
- I really don't like whingeing, needy kids. I've trained mine to stay positive.
- It really makes me feel uncomfortable watching people picking up and cuddling their children over the smallest of falls. Those kids are going to get a rude shock out in the real world.
- I have taught my children not to be too trusting because life is unpredictable.
- My children and I don't engage in much physical affection.
- My children know how to keep a safe distance from other people.
- My children are more independent than other children the same age.
- They stay close to me but they don't ask for my attention all the time.

- If I come back from having been away, my children often don't even look up from what they are doing.
- I have very clear memories of what happened when I tried to comfort my kids when they were toddlers and it was one of those social occasions when people expected it. They actually leaned out of my arms to get away from me.
- We all tend to be very positive in our house. Things are okay.
- My children understand that I just can't stop when it suits them to deal with their issues.
- I don't believe having a favourite child need damage the other children.
- My focus with my children is helping them learn what they need to get on in life.

If these statements resonated with you more strongly you would be said to be 'dismissive' and your children 'avoidant'. (See Chapter 3.)

The second type of insecure: preoccupied?

'Preoccupied' parents might say of themselves:
- My parents probably shouldn't have ever had children, although I suppose they did their best.
- I find myself thinking from time to time, in fact quite often, that I wouldn't like them much if they weren't actually my parents.
- My childhood contained loss, adversity and pain and those wounds still bleed from time to time — often when Mum and Dad do something without thinking about how it actually makes me feel.
- I'm still angry with my parents.
- Issues from my childhood are still very much in play in my life.
- People sometimes feel I try and get too close and I scare them off.
- I can't cope on my own.
- I worry that my partner is going to abandon me during a difficult time.
- My parents had favourite children.

- I tend to assume the worst of people rather than the best.
- My emotions get in the way of achieving my goals and sometimes I find that I've damaged a valued relationship due to an emotional outburst.
- I find it very difficult to stay on an even keel if my partner is emotionally troubled. I want to be there for my partner, but I start to feel insecure myself and I find that hard to hide.

And they might say of their children:
- Sometimes I feel my baby is rejecting me, that he doesn't actually like me at all.
- I find it next to impossible to be consistent in my parenting.
- I never know if it's for real or if my children are just crying wolf.
- It's an emotional roller-coaster at our house.
- My children don't like me to go anywhere without them. (Please note that this is normal behaviour for children until about three to four years of age.)
- My child is my best friend.
- My child looks after me.
- My children don't explore, they stick right next to me.
- My children fight with each other a lot of the time.
- I have a favourite child, even though I know it's not a good thing, and everyone knows who it is.
- If my children are really upset it leaves me feeling completely swamped and unable to help them.
- On bad days I think my children would be better off without me.
- Sometimes one of my children reminds me so much of another family member I'm angry with, and it affects how I treat him.
- I believe you don't have to have the same rules for different children.
- My children are really hard to comfort.
- If I've been away from my children people tell me they only started playing up when I entered the room. They'll be good for everyone except me.
- My children tend to have wild emotional swings.

- I don't like my children to go far away from me because we live in a dangerous world.
- When my children seem to not need me I feel great hurt.

If these statements resonated with you, you would be said to be 'preoccupied' and your children 'ambivalent'.

Attachment is the focus of Part One. I do hope it helps you deal with some of the specific challenges you meet on this journey, because bringing up children is one of life's great journeys. Like every journey it is both an outward and an inward one. Books cannot replace the inner work that every parent needs to do to fully undertake that journey, but hopefully you will find some good support material in that first part of this book.

Appendix III

Troubleshooting active primitive reflexes

art Three was partly about the primitive reflexes. Briefly mentioned was the fact that they don't always 'disappear on cue' and that this can lead to problems in learning, attending and behaving. Seeing if a child has an active primitive reflex and strategies to integrate that reflex form the focus of this appendix.

Finding the information I've reproduced here was one of the great professional journeys Mum and I have taken over the last eight years. For many years we had just tested and treated children for two primitive reflexes. Then we came to the Murchison and discovered that more than these two reflexes could be kept past infancy. Once we'd worked this out, we began looking for information on how to treat children who'd kept a swag of primitive reflexes.

It was difficult to find because there was such a valuable market in selling reflex integration programs to parents. Practitioners can charge as much as $6000 per child for a program — and you, the parent, will still be doing the bulk of the work. We were amazed to discover that what should be the birthright of every human is subject to commercial confidentiality clauses. But not all practitioners refused to share. In this appendix you will find the knowledge developed by Australian occupational therapists, teachers and teacher's aides of the movements and strategies that will help your child.

You might be thinking, 'But surely the prescribing of movement sequences and carrying out a program will take a professional?' It definitely does help if you can see a professional to assist with working out what movements and games your child needs. But with waiting lists in excess of two years within the public system, and the high cost of private consultations, this is not something that is accessible to all parents. As for the carrying out of the program, the best results occur when parents work with their own child.

Parents are the better therapists for their own child because of the chemistry of attachment. Just as babies learn better from a secure attachment, so does a child. The 'feel good' from having a parent involved means a greater release of oxytocin, and so learning happens faster.

A retained reflex in action

David is a puzzle to his sporty parents. How can he be so different from them? Balancing their way around the outskirts of the oval on the low pine rail fence that surrounds it was a favourite game for them both as children. David, at seven, won't do it without a parent on either side, holding his hands. His posture is slightly stooped and his muscle tone and endurance are low. He gets carsick even on short journeys.

David's teacher has expressed concern that David's bank of sight words is not translating into smooth reading. Not only that, but he can't pick out words that he should know in a sentence: David has told her that 'the words keep shifting'. She has noted that his 'cooped up' posture seems to be interfering with his ability to do jigsaw puzzles or colour-in. If the pieces or pencils aren't right in front of him he doesn't pick them up. She says she has to remind him to 'take a deep breath' to get his best performance out of him. That cooped-up posture is contributing to shallow breathing and less oxygen getting to his brain. Finally, his teacher has gently pointed out to his stunned parents that it almost certainly no coincidence that David's headaches always occur before his physical education class.

What is responsible for David's difficulties? He has retained the tonic labyrinthine reflex, which babies normally work through in the first months of life during 'tummy time'. He has kept this reflex because the rented house where he grew up had cold cement floors and rough carpet in the lounge room. As a baby he did not like being on the floor, and his mother, not surprisingly, did not like him being there either.

With the intention of ensuring that he was off the cold floor she kept him in his pram. Later, still wanting to keep him warm but also wanting him to be active, she purchased a walker and a jolly jumper. David spent a great deal of his 'awake time' in both pieces of equipment from four months onwards. He walked at 15 months and never crawled. The end result is that, rather than having *integrated* this reflex in infancy, David is suffering the typical consequences of a strongly *retained* tonic labyrinthine reflex.

Untreated, David's difficulties will increase in impact. The absence of the postural reflexes will mean that he doesn't have the grace of his peers. In fact, he has the kind of awkwardness that increases the likelihood that he will be targeted by bullies. As reading texts get harder and the print smaller, he will battle more and more with reading. All text work, especially mathematics written vertically, will be hard for David.

Looking down for David is accompanied by the sense that he's about to fall, due again to the action of the reflex, and this is translating into a fear of heights. No little boy wants this, so he has a deep and growing sense of disappointment in himself.

It is important to remember that the persistence of a reflex is not an all-or-nothing thing. At one end of the continuum you have the person with cerebral palsy, at the other the normal adult with a 'shadow' of a reflex that is barely detectable by a trained clinician. In fact, most of us have one or two primitive reflexes that persist in a shadow form. It is only the most physically coordinated among us, such as our ballet dancers and elite athletes, who have entirely integrated all their reflexes. But otherwise normal, healthy children can experience negative effects from the retention of a primitive reflex.

Why might a child keep a reflex, apart from having missed movement sequences in infancy? Some children just need to spend longer working towards integrating reflexes than others for genetic reasons. You might like to consider your own school days and see if you can relate to any of the markers listed below also.

In trying to help a child with a retained reflex, bear in mind that reflexes are normally integrated doing something meaningful: achieving a milestone. Movements to help with reflex integration need to be kept as meaningful as possible. There are some people who believe that the movements required need to be carried out 'exactly right'. Mum and I don't believe that, because babies aren't that precise in their movements. It is more important that the movements need to be kept meaningful. The best way to do this is to make them fun.

The ideas for activities are not just for parents, there are growing numbers of teachers who have replaced the Perceptual Motor Program with reflex integration programs in reflection of the fact that more children require 'earlier' skills to be addressed. The bad news is that, although children can integrate a retained primitive reflex later in life, it is much harder to do so. It's easiest for everyone, particularly children, if reflexes are integrated in infancy.

Could my child have an active primitive reflex?
You need to ask:
- Did my child spend a lot of time in the pram, walker or highchair?
- Did my child miss out on or have almost no tummy time, back time and time being carried by me?
- Did my child move through all the movement milestones or did she skip some steps?
- Was her early childhood a traumatic time in our family's life?

These are some of the general markers of primitive reflex activity in an older child. Ask yourself:
- Does my child have poor balance?
- Was she delayed with her motor milestones? (Not sitting until after 10 months, not crawling until after a year etc.)
- Does my child have low muscle tone? Does she fatigue quickly and have a soft, floppy body?
- Does my teenager get motion sick easily?
- Does my child battle to stay still?
- Does my child struggle to work out how to carry out a procedure, including mental procedures?
- Does my child struggle with organising herself in general, compared to other children her age?
- Does my child W-sit?
- Does my child find cutting-out difficult?

- Does my child sit either in a 'cooped up' or a 'spread right out' fashion? When her head is bent, does her whole body tuck up? Or when her head tips back, do her arms and legs straighten?
- Does my child have a 'hook grasp' in writing — their wrist hooked around so they can watch themselves write?
- Does my child have an ape-like walk?
- Does my child find it difficult to sit for long periods of time?
- Does my child find it hard to break up words into syllables?
- Is my child a messy eater?
- Is she often chewing or sucking on non-food items?
- Does she make noises constantly, such as little sucking sounds or lip smacking?
- Was she late developing hand dominance or had no clear dominance by 30 months of age?
- Does she have difficulty making her eyes track smoothly along a line of text after seven years of age?
- Does she struggle to concentrate in a busy environment?
- Does she find it hard to reach across her body to pick something up — to reach into the right side space with the left hand and the left side space with the right hand?
- Does she have a poor short-term memory?
- Could she cope okay with schoolwork at a primary level but not so well at high school?

If you agreed with points in this list, then please keep reading. If you have opened the book here (which is where my friend Cindy says she'd be starting), please consider reading the beginning of Part Three, which is all about how movement normally develops.

Starting with the gatekeepers

In 2003 education researchers at the University of Western Australia asked boys with ADHD to bring a friend without ADHD in to be tested for primitive reflexes. They found that the boys with ADHD had active primitive reflexes. Their friends did not. The researchers also found that if the primitive startle reflex was present, then that child would also have more reflexes. The startle reflex was a gatekeeper to higher development.[12] Throughout the book I've talked about the startle reflex but I did not mention another, even earlier reflex that may also act as a gatekeeper.

A stressful in-utero environment or birth trauma or some kind of in-utero accident is also considered to potentially lead to children who also keep the precursor to the startle reflex, which is called the fear paralysis reflex. This reflex is simply that 'freeze' that occurs in many of us in situations of great terror: although we want desperately to move, we cannot. For many people it is something they only experience in dreams. And, at a guess, it may be something that is 'retriggered' as part of panic attacks. It is barely mentioned in the wider research literature, although it is discussed on the internet, and as it is not something I have personally treated it is only getting the briefest of mentions here.

If you have a toddler who faints through holding her breath or seems to suffer occasional 'paralysis', you might like to investigate the fear paralysis reflex as a possible cause. (Adults very occasionally report these symptoms too, often coupled with hypersensitivity to sensation.) The fear paralysis reflex has also been suggested as a cause of sudden infant death, and the research reports suggesting this also strongly support recommendations to sleep babies on their backs.[13]

Sally Goddard, the Irish therapist who remains the most influential writer on the role of primitive reflex activity in learning, also links muteness (inability to speak) to the fear paralysis reflex. There is a treatment path available, so it is certainly something for parents of such children to consider.[14] Children who still have a fear paralysis reflex will not have been able to fully develop their primitive startle reflex, so they are one step further back on the journey.

We are going to focus more on the primitive startle reflex as it appears at this present time to be a far more common issue. You might be wondering why children from normal home environments might have a startle reflex retained. The answer to that is not at all clear, but the children that the UWA researchers were testing actually lived around the university, which is very much inhabited by middle-class families. Certainly with no generational poverty.

The strongest piece of connected research reinforces that there is no safe level of drinking in pregnancy. This shows that children whose mothers use alcohol, even at very low levels, both startle abnormally in the womb and for longer afterwards.[15] And supporting the idea that it is the startle reflex that contributes to some of the behaviours of disorganised attachment, mothers who drink are more likely to have children showing disorganised attachment.[16]

This is not to say that all children with ADHD had mothers who drank while pregnant. It has not been researched in humans, but clinicians and non-drinking parents have said to us that they suspect high doses of MSG in takeaway food at the wrong time during pregnancy might have been a factor. In rats similar effects from MSG have certainly been found, and, supporting clinicians' views that healing is possible, these effects are not necessarily permanent. The rat's development is very delayed, but not permanently damaged.[17]

If your child has a fear paralysis reflex she is likely to have difficulties with the startle and all other primitive reflexes. If your child has a startle reflex, then it is most likely she will also have retained most other primitive reflexes.

Identifying and integrating the primitive startle reflex in an older child

As you will see, this profile is very similar to a child with a lack of right brain development, met in the last appendix. Look for:

- a combination of primitive reflex signs, such as poor balance, motion sickness, poor coordination, poor auditory skills, delayed eye movements
- a semi-permanent upper respiratory tract infection
- difficulty coping with moving from one activity to another
- 'all or nothing' emotional responses
- photosensitivity; bright lights bother these children
- problems with reading and other visual-perceptual tasks
- hypervigilance: constantly scanning for a threat
- aggressive boys and withdrawn girls
- a 'fists up' movement pattern in response to a surprise (child jerks up clenched fists), or an absolute refusal to lie on her back and float in swimming
- stronger reactions to sensation than most children
- after a 'bad patch' at home, all gains in classroom skills will be lost.

Parents and teachers always need to consider this as an explanation when a child comes from a home with a history of domestic violence or has lived in a war zone or through a natural disaster.

How can parents and teachers help?

- If you feel that there are attachment and safety issues, the healing must start with you, the parent, and by changing the environment. (Some ideas on healing attachment are described in the previous appendix).
- Institute a routine so that the child always knows what is coming next.
- Movements that will assist are those that help in integrating the startle reflex in babies. Loving touch to the face and hands and feet, such as face painting, hand games ('Clap clap if you feel you want to', 'Round and Round the Garden'), feet games (being barefoot and playing 'This Little Piggy'). These are just suggestions, use your imagination!
- Strongly consider a massage program using essential oils like lavender to relieve stress.
- Balance games, specifically those that let the child move through the startle movements: rocking backwards on her bottom and throwing her arms and legs out wide and then drawing them back in. Making an office chair spin by thowing legs and arms out and then bringing them in again.
- Singing, particularly in a high voice as this stimulates the vestibular nerve.
- Eye movement exercises.

What will help this child cope in the school setting?

- For teachers these children can be very difficult to manage as the only thing that gets their attention in a normal classroom are big scary movements and loud angry voices, because they are scanning the room for threat and until a threat presents they don't attend. The only way through is a very quiet and controlled classroom, where students feel safe. Only when your students feel safe will they learn. Teachers who are imperturbably calm are the best for these students.

- We also strongly recommend the 'turtle technique'. This can be used across the school or the class. It is introduced by telling the story of a little turtle with anger management issues. He is always in trouble, so a wise, elderly turtle teaches him to pull back into his shell until he is able to come up with a response that won't get him into trouble. This position of pulling back into your shell is basically the foetal position. The class rule is any child in that position is left alone. It is the 'stopping and thinking' position.
- Position affected children away from each other. The Meekatharra District High School, in Western Australia, removed tables and chairs from one room and replaced them with tents. This has led to a much calmer, safer classroom, and one where children get much of the floor time they missed as babies.
- Deliberately burn off stress hormones in students before class. Exercise is one way. Fascinatingly, one school in the Murchison has a climbing wall, a high ropes course and a 'cage' that drops terrifyingly but safely to the ground. They have found that teenagers perform a great deal better in the classroom after adventure experiences and that the teenagers are happy to go again and again.
- The Massage-In-Schools program, which counters the stress hormones with oxytocin, is another recommended intervention.
- Finally, there are suggestions from research reports that an approach where children are given feedback on their heart rate variability will help them 'tune in' to their bodies and better manage their startle response.[18] (See Chapter 8 for more information on heart rate variability.)

The tonic labyrinthine reflex backwards retained

In the classroom there are always children who tip their chair backwards. Some children will be doing it to focus better — the feeling of falling backwards, with its echoes of the Moro, remains highly alerting throughout life. But if a child is always tipping back her chair, then losing control of herself and the chair, you should start suspecting not devilry but an active tonic labyrinthine reflex backwards. If the child has a lot in common with Jane in the following example, then it should be considered the most likely suspect:

> Four-year-old Jane is a very busy little girl. She bounces on tippy-toes and wriggles incessantly. She is charming, her verbal skills are excellent and she talks a great deal. The careful observer will note she employs these verbal skills to save her from actually having to 'do' very much. Her dad calls her his Muppet–Puppet and that is simply because, from early on, Jane has reminded him of a puppet. Her movements are jerky and her limbs are a little stiff. As she runs on her toes across the oval it looks for all the world as if someone is rapidly working strings above her. Despite her speed, Jane is not an athletic kid. If something catches her attention when she is running she will 'trip over her own feet' and she never seems to get her hands up to protect her face in time. Like David she gets carsick easily. She does not like looking at books or doing puzzles; her parents say that she is their 'free-range daughter'.

Jane has a retained tonic labyrinthine backwards. Her body is still dominated by the straightening and arching muscles on the back of her torso, so there is a profound imbalance between her front and back muscle compartments. As a baby, Jane learned to roll early to get where she wanted to go, and then began pulling herself into standing. She didn't sit at all. She was cruising (walking by holding onto furniture) very early and walking at ten months. Not having crawled she hasn't developed the near vision required for books and puzzles. Whenever she looks up her body extends a little more, her toes straighten and she trips.

Why is this little girl so busy? Our sense of self comes from feeling ourselves to be 'in our body' and knowing where we are in space. Jane is never quite sure; the constant 'tripping' of the reflex is interfering with her balance sense and there is a mismatch between the visual and balance information she has. Movement, though, provides information through touch receptors, about what is her body and what is not her body. This little girl races through a world that spins disorientatingly around her, constantly moving in an attempt to keep her sense of self intact in an unreliable world.

Does my child have a tonic labyrinthine reflex still in operation?

Remember that children may either have a TLR forwards, where the child has stronger 'curling up' than 'straightening out' muscles or a TLR backwards, where the reverse is the case. It's all about an imbalance between the two muscle groups.

Ask yourself:

- Was my baby a 'bum shuffler' (sitting up, she moved by pushing herself along with her legs instead of crawling)?
- Was my baby a 'bear walker' (she kept her legs straight in crawling)?
- Does my child have poor muscle tone? Does she lean on me, desks, walls and other children, fatigue rapidly and have a less expressive face? When you massage her back, does it feel 'jellyish' rather than muscular? TLR forwards — stronger curling up muscles.
- Does my child have jerky, puppet-like movements and walk on her toes? TLR backwards — stronger straightening out muscles.
- Does my child still get motion sick after puberty?
- Is my child always tripping over her own feet? Is she clumsy when putting things down? Make sure her vision is accurate, but also consider the TLR. For children who have an existing prescription, glasses being changed may 'set off' some TLR signs. Children with rapidly changing prescriptions are likely to have a number of these difficulties because this reflex is all about matching position to visual information, and if the visual information keeps changing it puts the system under stress.
- Does my child have terrible difficulty staying still; not fiddling, but moving her whole body continually? If she rocks on the chair and spins, consider an active TLR. Don't stop her if this occurs while she is concentrating as she is using it to help along brain growth. You must also 'exclude' for giftedness with this behaviour. If the child is also prone to lots of talking with rich idea development, strong response to sensory information or nervous 'tics' in movement when excited, giftedness is a potential diagnosis. Of course, there's nothing to stop a gifted

child also having an active TLR. It is a matter of looking at the whole child.

- Does my child have problems with space perception?
- Does my child struggle to work out how to do certain activities, such as knowing whether to push or pull? This also applies with problems mentally reversing procedures in maths or spatial problems. A lack of mental flexibility here can be directly related to the inflexibility created by a lack of fully developed mature reflexes, due to the presence of underlying primitive reflex activity.
- Does my child W-sit or sit with her legs wrapped around chair legs?
- Does my child have 'sight words' but great difficulty moving her eyes along a line of text? This may have to do with lack of eye dominance (see Chapter 19) also.
- Does my child have untidy handwriting? A retained TLR is one potential cause of this.
- Does my child have problems with maths problems when they are written vertically?
- Does my child have difficulties with organising space, such as keeping her desk and room tidy? If she has other TLR signs then strongly consider a TLR.

How can parents and teachers help? Remember that you are seeking to provide the movement sequences that the child missed or didn't have enough of as a baby:

- Get the child to spin around and around on her bottom to music.
- Ask the child to roll in as straight a line as possible. This is much harder than it sounds.
- Encourage her to rock on her back, moving from lying down to sitting in an uncurling, gentle and slow movement.
- Have your child climb into a barrel (you can purchase these from toy stores) and make it roll.
- Ask your child to lie on her tummy and throw her beanbags to catch.
- Make a scooter board for your child — a square of wood 300 mm x 300 mm covered with carpet with four castor

wheels on the bottom — and encourage her to scoot around
the house on it.

- Swimming is excellent for integrating the TLR — often
children show a massive improvement at school after their first
summer of swimming lessons. Particularly good exercises are
'duck' diving and kicking while holding a float.

How do I help a child with an active TLR cope with school?

- Awareness is important for teachers. When the teacher knows
that the child doesn't like physical education because the reflex
makes it impossible for her to succeed, or that the child will
struggle with maths presented in vertical sums, he can build a
stronger relationship with the student.
- Students of all ages should not be allowed to 'W-sit'. Teachers
need to look out for both this position and the child wrapping
her legs around chairs. This prevents the child integrating the
TLR in sitting as she uses her leg muscles instead of her trunk
muscles to achieve balance.

The asymmetrical tonic neck reflex retained

Donald is six. He is a dear little boy with a cooperative nature.
He wants to do well in school. He succeeds pretty well, except
for when he must put pencil to paper. He carefully holds the
pencil the way he has been taught, tightens his hold into a
'death grip' and bends his head over his paper. All sorts of ideas
are boiling in his head ready to be translated to paper! But
within short order, his hand stretches itself out straight. He lets
go of his pencil and looks at his outstretched hand and then his
attention switches to out the window where the school
principal can be seen, walking across the lawn with visitors.

Luckily, before the principal can notice him looking out
the window, Don's teacher (who understands the activity of the
asymmetrical tonic neck reflex) catches his attention and
reminds him to use his non-writing hand to hold his book. And
as soon as both arms are bent his attention returns to his writing.
Unfortunately, he is five minutes behind the other children yet
again.

There is a lot of controversy about when the asymmetrical tonic neck reflex should have been integrated by a child — some people saying at six months[14] and others in the school years.[19] While it may not sound very interesting, this argument underlies a far more controversial topic. By proving that an active ATNR is found in normal children, critics of movement programs seek to rebuff claims that such programs help children succeed in school, particularly with reading.[20] Equally, by showing primitive reflex activity in children who have problems in school, researchers hope to promote movement programs.[21]

Unfortunately, the research from both sides can be contaminated by the fact that these competing sets of researchers often have programs to sell to parents and teachers. I have seen movement programs contribute greatly to improvements in children's reading, however. I have also found a correlation between the children who are struggling with school and the presence of the ATNR in whole class screens. And there have been a number of studies that support this.[14]

So how could prescribing movement improve reading skills? I believe that better impulse control and attention (both are critical for the development of a good working memory) happens in part by the child becoming 'free' from the constraints of the primitive reflex movements. There is a lot of support for this theory. Research shows that both children with ADHD and those with reading difficulties (often called 'dyslexia') show particular movement difficulties.[22, 23, 24] For example, if a child still has an active ATNR it keeps both sides of her body doing opposing things. This makes bilateral movement very difficult, and bilateral movement builds the bridge between the right and left sides of the brain. This has huge implications for reading. The bridge between the two hemispheres is called the 'corpus callosum', and scientists have found that there are quite clear differences here between the brains of readers and non-readers.[24,25] The difference occurs in a part of the corpus callosum which they think connects up with the part of the brain responsible for eye tracking.[26]

If your child is struggling to read, I believe that, among the other issues (see Appendix V: Troubleshooting reading) you need to consider an active ATNR. Little boys are more likely to retain this reflex; something else for parents of boys to bear in mind.[27]

Does my child have a retained ATNR?

The way therapists check for an ATNR is to ask the child to go upon all fours, knees bent and fingers and thumbs pointing forward. If the hand is out to the side the child will be 'locking' her elbows. Then we explain to the child that we are about to turn her head to the side, and ask her consent to do this. If the elbow on the 'skull side' of her head bends, that is the ATNR in action. You might like to check this on your child. Also, ask yourself:

- Did my child miss the milestone of rolling as a baby?
- Does my child struggle to bring scissors and paper together when trying to cut?
- Does my child battle with keeping both arms bent when using a knife and fork. Does she prefer to use her fingers or just one implement?
- Does she hook her whole arm around her pencil when writing so she can watch herself form letters?
- Did my child develop a dominant hand later than three years of age?
- Does my child struggle to cross the midline of her body?
- Does my child find it difficult to converge both eyes on a single close object, like a word?
- Is my child is over eight years and reversing all the different types of symbols, including letters, words and numbers?
- Does my child seem to battle to write anything down because she is not able to hold paper and pencil simultaneously?
- Does my older child struggle to experience a free flow of ideas, even without being asked to write them down?
- Does my child have problems with attention, including difficulties with attending to the text she is reading?

How can parents and teachers help?
- Encourage rolling games.
- Make a scooter board for your child — a square of wood covered with carpet with four castor wheels on the bottom — and encourage her to twirl around and around.
- Sit down with her and do activities like jigsaws or building with construction toys and keep prompting her to keep both arms bent.

- Play games which actually 'move her' through the reflex position. Go back to pages 145–147 and read through all the ways in which babies work through the ATNR and see if you can play games that mimic this. For example, the child lies on her back with her eyes closed and brings her thumb down towards her nose and then opens her eyes to check how well she guessed where her thumb was compared to her nose. Another is to flip from side to side on her back. First of all, she is to follow the dictates of the reflex — the hand she is looking at is extended and the opposite arm bent. Then reverse this, so she keeps the hand behind her head extended and the hand she is looking at in close.
- Any games where both arms are bent or both arms straight are good, such as tug of war, paddling an imaginary canoe, cartwheels, wheelbarrows, pretend to drive.

How do I help a child with a retained ATNR cope with school?
- Teachers need to encourage this child to keep both arms bent. Otherwise, once an arm is extended, the child is likely to have difficulty keeping her attention on her flexed arm and her work. Her attention is drawn inexorably to her outstretched hand, and from there, out the window or to another child.
- Teachers need to particularly encourage this child to cross her midline, otherwise she draws on half the page, writes on half the page and reads half the page. So when she is colouring-in, ensure she is using sweeping, crossing-the-midline strokes and not tiny little movements. When reading, check that the finger traverses the whole line. Make sure she doesn't keep her work on the right or left of her body but in the middle, so that she must keep crossing her midline.

Children who are still sucking at school

So connected are the hands and mouth that we find that children who still have rooting and suck reflexes also have their involuntary grasp (Palmar) reflex as well. For this reason we have grouped the reflexes together here, because helping to integrate one will help in integrating the others.

Does my child still have a Palmar reflex and rooting/suck reflex?

Ask yourself:
- Does my child chew on pencils, erasers, hair, sleeves or collars?
- Is my teenager's voice more childlike than I would expect?
- Is my child hypersensitive around her lips and mouth?
- Does my child sometimes dribble while eating?
- Does my child have unclear speech?
- Does my child have poor fine motor skills?
- Does my child have an unusual pencil grip?
- Are her palms hypersensitive?
- If my child is talking, do her fingers twitch? And, when engaged in a challenging fine motor task, does she screw up and work her mouth?

How can parents and teachers help?
- Many teachers and parents stop the child sucking only to discover that her fine motor skills become worse still. The answer is to deliberately exploit the link between hands and mouth to improve her fine motor skills. Add the sucking back in, but in more socially acceptable ways. The 'Sip and Crunch' program, which encourages children to bring water bottles and carrot sticks to school, helps here as chewing and sucking during fine motor tasks assists children to integrate sucking and develop precision in fine motor activities.
- The Palmar reflex — involuntary closing of the hand to a touch on the palm — is integrated in infancy by touch to the palm. It is much harder to integrate later on, but the same principle applies — touching the palm in a way that motivates the child to keep it open is what you want. So pushing games, clapping games and games like 'Round and round the garden' where the parent is tracing a finger over the child's palm are still the best ones. Crawling games (playing 'What's the time, Mr Wolf?' where everyone has to crawl, for example) and chair push-ups are excellent for older children as both provide heavy pressure to the palms.
- The touching the face games used for a startle reflex are also helpful.

- These children also often show 'tactile' problems, so you might like to read through the list of markers in the following appendix and include those suggestions in your program.

The spinal galant retained

This reflex has only the briefest mention in Part Three, to say that baby needs time on her back to integrate this reflex. So what happens if your child has kept it?

> Lauren appears to have 'ants in her pants'. When she's sitting down, she's squirming about on her seat. When she's wearing shorts with a waistband that is a bit tight she also squirms. She drives her teacher mad with her inability to 'listen with her whole body'. The sitting very still that denotes attentive listening doesn't seem to be possible for Lauren.
>
> Her walk is a bit unusual, as though she is 'hitching up' one hip as she walks. And, although seemingly unconnected to her physical peculiarities, this little girl also has great difficulty remembering. Her memory is so poor that sight words that she knows on Friday have vanished by Monday, much to her distress. She loses maths facts overnight. The continued action of the spinal galant also makes it difficult to develop the mature reflexes required for fluency in movement. Now in Year Four, she's struggling to master the skills required for sport in upper primary. On top of everything else, she sometimes still wets the bed.

This is an extreme example, but as a clinician I have met two children like Lauren.

One of the interesting aspects of this reflex is the question posed about just why it has such an effect on short-term memory. Does it impact simply by decreasing attention span, which has a negative effect on working memory? Or is there something else going on as well? There is the barest hint in the research reports that the spinal galant may be used by babies in the womb to respond to and remember sounds.[14, 28]

Does my child have a retained spinal galant reflex?
Therapists ask children (or adults) to go onto hands and knees and then trace down one side of their lower spine with something soft like a feather or a brush. If they wriggle involuntarily to that side, then the reflex is still present. If the reflex hasn't been found after three 'strokes' then it isn't there.

Also, ask yourself:
- Does my child appear to have 'ants in the pants'?
- Does my child wet the bed?
- Does my child have a scoliosis or a limp?
- Does my child struggle with storing things in long term memory? Does she battle to recall maths facts, for example?
- Even though I can get my child to bring her attention to bear on something, does she struggle to keep on concentrating?

How can parents and teachers help?
- Just as in infancy, this reflex is integrated in an older child by having her lie on her back and kick. Due to the action of the reflex, this does make children very flatulent, so we've learned to always do these activities outside on the lawn!
- Such lying and moving around on her back games could include asking her to catch and throw beanbags with her feet, wriggling along on her back through a tunnel, asking her to pass balls to another child with all children lying on their backs, rolling games and teaching her forward rolls.
- Let her work on her tummy to learn new things: this way she can concentrate unhindered by involuntary squirming.
- Try to avoid her wearing something 'tickly' on her back if at all possible.
- The most commonly given suggestion is for children with a retained spinal galant to be given a soft cushion to sit on, as this makes their constant shifting less distracting for others.

The symmetrical tonic neck reflex retained
This was the reflex that gave baby a 'bend at the hips'. Of course, children who bum shuffle or bear crawl or only crawl very briefly haven't released this reflex. So how does this involuntary movement pattern affect older children?

If they are looking down, their arms bend and their knees straighten. If they are looking up, their arms straighten out and their knees bend. Imagine sitting at a desk. You look up in response to the teacher and your arms straighten, taking your hands from your work. When you look back down at your work, your arms bend but your legs and hips straighten, making sitting on a chair most uncomfortable. These children are consequently extraordinarily restless; being asked to sit and write unleashes an unconquerable urge to wander about the room.

With all the difficulties these children have in sitting and balancing, they often resort to the W-sitting we mentioned earlier. The position is bad for backs, knees and ankles: some long term W-sitters have needed surgery to loosen up ligaments in later life.

The STNR has been explicitly linked to ADHD by some researchers.[14] So will a program of movement designed to integrate primitive reflexes such as the STNR help every single child with ADHD? No. It will certainly help some, but only those for whom the primitive reflex is still active.

When Mum and I began working with children many years ago, she would only find about one child who had an active STNR every year or so. It was one of the more unusual findings. In the Murchison where we now work, it is more common than not. And, as children are spending less and less time crawling, it is an increasingly common finding around Australia.

Does my child have an active STNR?
Therapists test for an STNR by asking a child to go upon hands and knees and then bending her head gently up and down. If the child resists the movement or her hips, knees and elbow straighten or flex based on head position, the reflex is still active.

You might also like to ask yourself:
• Did my child miss crawling?
• Is my child very uncomfortable in sitting?
• Is my child over seven and without a dominant eye?
• Does my child W-sit?
• Does my child have an ape-like walk?
• Does she slump at the desk or table?
• Does she hate copying from the board?

- Does she have poor attention skills?
- Is she finding it hard to learn to swim?

How can parents and teachers help?

This reflex is still best integrated by the same movements used by infants on the way to crawling and by crawling itself.

- Play bunny-hops with your child.
- Make crawling games more fun by making tunnels and playing spotlight — your child creeps up on you in the dark, making sure to freeze when you switch on your torch. If you catch her moving, she must go back to the start point.
- Swimming is also important. Ask your child to swim with her face under water much of the time, blowing bubbles and using the flutter or kick board for support.
- For school, provide these children with tilted desks to help keep both arms bent even when their head is tilted back.

As each of these different reflexes fits into place — no longer active but lying tame in your child's brain — she will add the adult reflexes to her movement repertoires. Teachers and parents have found time and time again that these movement patterns really do help their children get ready for learning. (Circus, Brain Gym and the Alexander Technique also contain these same movement elements.)

But remember, just as she did when she was an infant, your child will require lots and lots of these movement experiences for the change to happen. Before starting I recommend you line up 21 consecutive days on which to put in the program. This will help doing the program to become a habit for you and your child. You might see changes in as little as six weeks but my experience is that it takes about 14 months on a program to see permanent change. And when your child has a growth spurt you may find you need to do the exercises again.

Troubleshooting perceptual sensitivity

In Chapter 17 (Growing perceptual sensitivity) I made a firm link between difficulties with perceptual sensitivity and insecure attachment; however, insecure attachment isn't the only reason for such difficulties. Some children who are securely attached still have difficulties with their senses. This was something originally identified by occupational therapist Dr Jean Ayres. She found there to be three groups of children whose sensory perceptions were faulty in quite different ways.

Best known are the children for whom the world is brighter, louder, busier, harder, sharper, steeper and smellier. It is hard to regulate yourself if that is your world. It is hard for parents to feel confident when handling or playing with such a baby. In fact, the biggest impact this kind of sensory difficulty may have is that the bond between parent and child is damaged. These children have a 'defensive' response to stimulation.

Often these defensive children grow into children other people describe as 'difficult' or as a 'Mummy's boy or girl' or 'with poor social skills'. Only their parents know a very different child because, at home, these children don't need to defend themselves against unexpected sensations. But away from their home, life can be very hard. I remember hearing of the behaviour of one poor little boy who had an over-the-top defensive reaction to sound at his end of year concert. As the rest of his class played their recorders he clapped his hands over his ears and screamed, 'No, no, no!' A family friend heard the story, suggested an occupational therapist and he is now finding life far more bearable.

The second group of children, and I don't think I know a child like this so this description is drawn purely from my research into the subject, have the signals from the world outside mixed in with some neurological 'white noise' of their own. It's hard to make sense ...ld like that, or to know if you can trust what your senses are telling you.

Finally, there is another group of children who register far less than most of us of the world around them. Touch is softer, sounds are less exciting. These are sometimes the 'easy' babies who show a slower developmental rate as there is simply not quite enough information flowing in to grow their brains at normal rates. These children are described as 'sensorily dormant'. These are children who are 'surprise' referrals to occupational therapy at the end of the school year. They are so very compliant in the classroom that it is only when the teacher does her end of year testing that she discovers how little they have learned. These children often have lower muscle tone and less expressive, 'softer' faces.

Before starting off exploring the world of the child for whom sensations have unpleasant intensity have some strong coffee. Put on some very warm, scratchy clothes that don't fit you comfortably. Play some music that you don't like and turn it up too loud. Make the room too bright. Spray some nasty smelling insect repellent around. Quickly throw some objects on the floor and muss any surfaces if you like things to be neat. Now try rocking forward on your toes and imagining yourself looking down to the floor and finding it a bit further away than you had thought. For these children the world is surreal, disorientating and exhausting; and touch, which usually brings such emotional comfort, is emotionally disruptive. This is the most involved case scenario, a child with most senses switched on to 'extreme' sensitivity. For some children just one sense may be affected, while for others it's a small cluster.

Now imagine a world with far less sensation. It is a dreamier place. Imagine a badly managed day spa with rather cloying scents, where the music is bland and too soft, and the masseur doesn't ever get to the really sore spots. It's much harder to feel really alert, really energised or engaged, satisfied and successful. And this is the world inhabited by the children who have only a poor registration of sensation.

The hardest world of all to imagine is the world where children have white noise from their own brain leaking into the sensation coming in from the outside world. I guess it would be like living with a waterfall or a freeway in your head. If you suspect this is the case for your child, I'd recommend seeking specialist attention.

In addition to the bombardment or 'underwhelmed' state of their senses, these children also experience great fluctuations in how their senses respond: good days, okay days, bad days. This makes an already difficult situation worse. If you are missing an eye you learn to compensate. But if you have an eye that works some of the time, to no particular pattern, it's much harder to develop a way of compensating.

So why do these fluctuations in sensory receptiveness occur? And how can parents help children for whom this is an issue? There won't be 'no reason at all', but it might take some figuring out. What we do know is that everyone 'spirals down' to a lower level of function under stress. Stress tends to show up first wherever we are already weakest. For these children this is in their brain's ability to understand sensation. And just about any kind of stress can be responsible. The wrong food, not enough sleep, a growth spurt, a distressing failure, a nasty additive, fighting off a tummy bug: many possibilities must be sifted through to find the reasons for bad days.

Perceptual sensitivity and difficulties with behaviour, attention and learning

Children with both a dormant and defensive response are going to have difficulties learning, attending and behaving. Take the following example of Andrew and Lila.

Four-year-old Andrew screams when he is pushed out of the way by three-year-old Lila. She is running around seeming not to notice the nasty gash on her knee. Observers are all too likely to conclude from watching that Andrew is a 'wuss' and that Lila is 'tough'. And it won't take long before Andrew and Lila apply those labels to themselves. Working out that sensations differ from person to person requires theory of mind that is beyond most young children, and it is something that some adults have difficulty accepting too.

In fact, what is happening with Andrew is that he can't make sense of the information coming in from his touch sense. It all feels angry and aggressive and meaningless to him. So he does everything he can to defend himself from experiencing even moderate amounts of tactile information. He's picky about his clothes: anything textured is experienced by him as rough and scratchy. He washes his hands and face between bites of his honey sandwich as he experiences stickiness as unpleasant and intrusive.

The extra sensory load that Andrew has to deal with means that he has been a poor sleeper since infancy. Even now, every single night, his exhausted parents are unwillingly reminded of the princess and the pea as Andrew finds blankets, sheets, pillow and even his pyjamas can keep him awake or, on bad nights, wake him up.

Generally, an area of discomfort slowly intrudes upon our attention. But Andrew is simply not able to organise touch information into what is important and what isn't important. He can't switch any of it off. And because he isn't able to do that, he has great difficulty learning from his touch sense. Learning to write is going to be very difficult for Andrew as he won't like to hold a pencil. His parents are dreading the start of school on his behalf as he spends all his time around other kids trying to avoid being touched by them.

Empathising with the sensorily disordered child

It is just so important to get inside your child's skin if he fits one of these profiles. Without this understanding it's all too easy to conclude that your child doesn't like you very much. Such a child might push away a loving hand, cry at the sound of your voice or fail to realise that he has hurt you as he pushes rapidly past. Once in his skin, you can see the vast gulf between the world he perceives and your own, and you can set out to help him normalise his perceptions.

Learning to write is going to be difficult for Lila too, but for the opposite reason. In marked contrast to Andrew, Lila was a good sleeper and pretty much an all-round easy baby. (The words 'easy baby' are sometimes a red flag.) She has always amused her parents by her complete obliviousness to temperature. In summer she likes to wear her bright pink gumboots. In winter she would run around naked if she was allowed to. Recently, however, her parents have noticed that she's rough with other children and animals. She has taken to throwing herself off the bed onto the floor. Even though Lila giggles when she lands, it looks painful to her mum and dad. What's happening? Lila is beginning to crave much more intense tactile stimulation: her brain is literally starving for sensation.

Her parents are already worrying about her fine motor skills. They have noticed that she has real difficulty doing puzzles that her little sister of two is able to easily complete. Why? Her hands aren't able to move precisely because she can't obtain precise sensation from them. She is turning into what therapists call a 'sensory seeker'. This is a good sign, actually, as Lila is seeking to normalise her dormant tactile system all by herself.

Andrew's dad is trying to normalise his response to touch by touching Andrew more and 'getting him used to it'. He wakes him up by tickling him. He lightly messes his hair. Andrew giggles, but also begs his dad to stop. His dad is away for a week, and when he returns his mum says that this has been a much better week for Andrew. He has slept better. He tolerated a smear of honey on his arm while eating a sandwich. He spent a whole hour with his train set by himself.[29]

The tickling games were triggering a defensive response early in the day, and in their absence, Andrew had a calmer base from which to explore. When Andrew's dad asks him what games he would like to play, Andrew announces that he would like to be squashed. And deep pressure does have the effect of normalising the tactile system: light touch is stimulating, heavy touch is soothing.

The older Lila's sister gets, the more Lila's mum realises something is not right with Lila. Her most recent discovery is that she doesn't notice odours. Her mother decided to try to get Lila to tell the difference between different smells. By dabbing different smells onto cotton wool she made up a smell box for Lila to try and pick out different smells. Lila couldn't smell anything on the cotton wool. Her mother then added different essential oils to the floor of the shower every night: eucalyptus, spearmint, orange. Within a week Lila was saying that the smell was, 'A bit strong'. Soon afterwards, she found Lila 'feeling' different textures with her face. Often the olfactory or smell sense has to come online before the other senses wake up.

The ways that Lila and Andrew behave, although likely to impress the observer as 'poorly parented' or 'naughty', are only to be expected in children with perceptual difficulties. For Andrew touch information is so overwhelming that it amounts to torture; for Lila, even quite strong sensation is barely registering. And the same child can have both experiences in different sensory domains.

Listed below are questions to help you identify if your child has difficulties organising or receiving sensory information. The questions begin at the infant or baby stage and move on to older children.

Vestibular (the sense of where you are in space) system
Defensiveness:
- Did my baby have colic starting at one to two weeks of age?[30]
- Did my baby get very distressed when I lay him down for nappy change, even vomiting in response to being laid flat?
- Did my baby 'startle' frequently to position changes after four months of age?
- Was my baby irritable after six months of age?
- Was my baby late to sit (after ten months) and late to crawl (after one year)?
- Does my child dislike balancing games, such as walking on garden walls, jumping off steps, being up high on Dad's shoulders?
- Does my child dislike climbing, possibly even on the furniture, but certainly on climbing frames?
- Does my child get carsick or sick from any other movement experiences?
- Is my child clingy? (This behaviour looks similar to the ambivalently attached child, but it occurs only in new, busy settings, or when the child is asked to climb, jump or balance. If your child is made anxious by new experiences rather than being 'anxious in general', suspect general sensory issues.)
- Does my child have poor organisational skills, battle with 'reversibility' in mathematics and get lost around the school grounds?

Dormancy:
- Was my child an easy baby?
- Was my baby slow to reach movement milestones such as sitting (after 10 months), crawling (after one year) and walking (after 18 months)?

- Do his movements now have a slow, blocky quality?
- Does he jump recklessly off high places and seem generally 'brave' but at the same time also have poor balance?
- Does he spin or twirl obsessively without ever getting dizzy or having his eyes show the classic nystagmus eye movement where the eyes keep moving after the spinning has stopped?
- Is he having difficulty moving his eyes along a line of text?

Visual system (the visual and vestibular systems co-develop to a great degree)

Defensiveness:
- Does my baby find it difficult to focus for even a minute on my face at 10 weeks?
- Does my baby prefer to look at my mouth rather than my eyes?
- Does my baby not show the sustained looking behaviour that normally appears before six months?[31]
- Does my baby get upset when there is a change in someone's appearance, such as when they change their hairstyle?
- Does getting too many new things upset my child? (Most babies and toddlers love new things.)
- Do too many bright lights, flashing signs and so on, upset my child?
- Does my toddler or child complain of headaches?
- Do words and pictures seem to 'jump' according to my child?
- Does my child complain of headaches after reading, watching television or using the computer?
- Do fast movements around my child seem to leave him feeling disoriented?
- Does my child avoid eye contact?

Dormancy:
- Did my baby not really pay attention to the world around him?
- Did my baby refuse to spend time on his tummy, preferring strongly to be on his back?
- Did my baby have poor tracking skills and not watch me walking around the room?
- Does my child find it difficult to remember what he has read?

- Does he 'resist' looking at something close up?
- Does he strongly prefer playing with 'big toys' like rockers and tricycles to playing in sandpits and with puzzles?
- Does my child trace letters in order to recognise them? (Don't stop him from doing this, he is scaffolding his visual sense with his proprioceptive sense. This might be a helpful pattern for you to copy.)
- Was your child late (after three years) to identify colours?

Olfactory (smell, and to some degree taste) system

Defensiveness:
- Did my baby's skin change colour or did he startle to unexpected and new smells?
- Does my child comment on smells as 'horrible' that seem quite mild to me?
- Does he refuse to eat some foods on the basis of their smell?

Dormancy:
- Does my child seem unaware of even quite strong smells?
- Would he even eat or drink something poisonous, having not felt warned by its 'chemical' smell?

Tactile (the touch sense) system

Research shows that parents often underestimate their child's degree of tactile defensiveness. If your child is old enough and you think this may be a concern, you might like to ask him how touch affects him.[32]

Defensiveness:
- Did my baby find transitions difficult: such as taking clothes off or putting them on, or getting in or out of the bath?
- Was my baby hard to get to sleep and hard to keep asleep, with irregular sleeping patterns?
- Did my baby resist cuddling, fuss, cry and seem generally 'colicky'?
- Did my baby have difficulty breastfeeding?
- Do I sometimes feel rejected by his moving away from my touch? And even now, cuddles have to be on his terms?

- Or is he now almost 'sticky' in his need for physical a[...]
  and contact? (This means he's beginning to normalise [...]
  touch system.)
- Is my child very aware of what is touching his skin: disliking
  lotions, labels, sock seams, high necklines and some materials
  and 'feeling' temperatures more than most children?
- Is my child very fussy about textures and the temperature of
  food?
- Does he hate haircuts and face washes?
- Does my child have a substantial personal space that he
  defends against siblings and classmates?
- Does my child prefer baths to showers?
- Does my child's teacher say that he can't concentrate in class
  (but you find this difficult to believe as he concentrates for
  long periods at home)?
- Does my child insist that stickiness (such as glue and honey)
  on his fingers has to be washed off straight away?
- Are his fine motor skills poor?
- Are my child's social experiences tainted by his need for
  personal space and 'moodiness', and is he perceived by others
  in consequence as aggressive?
- Is his self-esteem a concern for me?[32]
- Do people often ask me if my child has ADHD?

Dormancy:
- Was my baby placid even during immunisation injections?
- Does my toddler or child seem not to feel the temperature —
  hot or cold — or cuts and grazes?
- Is he an 'outside boy', preferring to play with big toys rather
  than toys that demand fine motor skills such as Lego and
  jigsaw puzzles?
- Does my child sometimes hurt other children accidentally but
  seem quite unaware that the contact would have caused them
  pain?
- Does he seem to need more sleep and generally have lower
  endurance than other children?
- Is his self-esteem a concern for me?[29]

Auditory (hearing) system

Defensiveness:
- Is my baby particularly distracted from face-to-face joy interactions by sounds, even slight ones from a fridge or clock?
- Is my baby or toddler frightened by and inclined to cry at noises that he should have become used to, like the vacuum cleaner?
- Do electronic toys that suddenly make noises upset him?
- Does my child talk a great deal, and especially when I want him to listen to me? In fact, does he seem to actually be talking so as to avoid having to listen to me?
- Does my child seem to be hypersensitive to very high pitch sounds and disharmonies and have a strong preference for mid-range sounds, like those made by the cello?
- Are special sounds or music required as part of the settling down to sleep routine?

Dormancy:
- Is my baby placid in the face of new and startling sounds?
- Did my baby not really have a 'babbling' stage?
- Is it hard to get my child to attend to what I say?
- Even if my child seems to have been listening, does he then forget most of what was said? (Children should only be expected to follow three-stage instructions at six years of age.)
- Was my child late in talking? Children should have a few single words at one, two-word phrases by two and be talking very much like an adult at three.
- Does my child not make noises to match his game — no 'brooming' for trucks or 'zooming' for aeroplanes?
- Does my child find it hard to retell familiar stories at six years of age?

Proprioceptive (the internal 'movement sense' — knowing where your body parts are in relation to each other without looking) system

Defensiveness:
- Does my baby feel a bit 'stiff' to cuddle, as though he is holding himself a little rigid?

- Did my baby not enjoy movement experiences like the 'kick kick' game, perhaps freezing when his body parts were moved by others?
- Did he not enjoy jolly jumpers or being bounced by me?
- Is my child bothered by other children bouncing and jumping around, tending to freeze and cling to me under such circumstances?
- Is my child ambidextrous, swapping hands halfway through a task?
- Does my child loathe going down slides and walking down stairs, or travelling in lifts and on escalators?
- Does my toddler panic when a shirt is put on over his head when dressing?
- Is my child a perpetual motion machine, seeming to feel a bit 'lost' when he's made to be still?

Dormancy:
- Does my baby feel a bit floppy to cuddle, as though his joints are a little looser than they should be?
- Does my toddler seem to struggle with moving from one position to the next?
- Is my child a crasher, seeming to enjoy walloping into walls, people and the floor?
- Is he a thumper who really enjoys banging things together?
- Does my child struggle to grade the amount of strength required for a task? Does he pat dogs too hard, hold his pencil too tightly, inadvertently hurt other children and animals in rough play or grind his teeth?
- Does my child find it hard to learn new movement skills, particularly ones requiring fine finger movements (doing up buttons, using a knife and fork)?
- Does my child have difficulty feeding himself, missing his mouth even with finger-feeding? (A child should be able to feed himself by 14 months.)
- Does my child get fatigued faster than other children?
- Does my child particularly like wearing tight, heavyweight clothes?
- Does he seek out heavy work activities?

- Is my child a 'bit flabby' even though he isn't overweight, or is he overweight with noticeably poor muscle tone? (Children with dormant proprioception are at greater risk for obesity because they find less meaning and pleasure in movement — it doesn't give them that 'rush' of oxytocin, and so they tend to move less.)

What you can do to help

Sensory systems can be normalised. Even when therapists are involved it is parents who do most of the work. In fact, the work of therapy sometimes builds a bridge between parent and child, and in such cases it is the repaired relationship that may make the biggest contribution to a child's better sensory perceptual skills. It certainly stands up to examination when you consider the mother's role in building her baby's perceptual skills in the first place.

Start by observing your child. What always gets his attention? Is it the ticking clock, the bird flying past, the smell of food? What kind of sensory information most destabilises him? This is likely to be his most 'hyperactive sense', and the one you need to be most wary of overloading. What kind of information is he most likely to miss: smells, tastes, sights or sounds? What information does he process most easily? Once this is identified you can work from this strength. The senses feed each other confirmatory information, so the strongest sense can be used to help organise any sense that might be dormant (under-active) or defensive (far too active).

Observe what your child does to calm himself down and which sense he uses to do it, particularly at the end of a school day. Does he move, does he sit and read a book, does he sing or talk to himself? Equally, observe what he does to 'ready himself for action', to focus better. Never intrude on such times as he is building self-regulation skills. Make a mental note so that you can 'scaffold' him by providing such time regularly in his day. Just as for babies, it's important for brain growth that your child spends most of his day 'well-regulated' rather than dysregulated (feeling 'out of kilter' both emotionally and physically).

With this information, deliberately set out to engage with your child as closely as you can. If you have a 'defensive' child and you are a spontaneous and exciting kind of parent, this may mean changing your way of relating to him. These children need predictability, slower movements, softer, slower voices. Shouting at an auditory defensive child, for example, is going to distress him rather than help him to comply. Most mothers with children like this actually use soft, almost whispery voices. In general, these children need just 'one channel of information' to be stimulated at a time, so try to avoid moving, touching him and talking all at once. Your overall goal is to 'dampen down' his need to defend himself against the world, to help him reduce his need to defend himself so he can open up enough to take in information and begin to organise it.

Some gifted children also present very similarly to the defensive child, and, of course, there is going to be some crossover. Children do not fit into neat categories. (There is an excellent free internet resource on giftedness. Type GERRIC into your search engine and then choose the DEEWR Professional Development Package for Teachers.)

The creative or gifted child who displays Dubrowski's 'over-excitabilities' — the hallmarks of giftedness involving talking at a great speed, jiggling madly with excitement, imagining whole forests of wild ideas — is equally likely to feel bombarded by sensory stimulation. This is not due to problems with sensory perception but from a heightened response to what they perceive. The environmental management ideas discussed below may be useful for helping gifted and creative children, but it is important to recognise that for these children this 'over-excitability' is part and parcel of their temperament. Help them find ways to order and use sensory information, but also accept that they will still whirl like a dervish when a new dinosaur is discovered.[33]

Defensive behaviours are also a feature of autism. If a child shows these defensive responses to sensations and also is not responding to his name or responding to your emotions and prefers objects to people then you need to suspect autism and get a professional opinion very quickly. (If you've read the description of the development of empathy and theory of mind in parts Two and Four, and thought, 'This isn't my child', again, I would recommend a visit to a paediatrician.) Early intervention with autistic children helps tremendously.[34]

If you have a child who fits the 'dormant' profile most of the time, and your own style is equally low key, you may need to develop a higher energy way of relating to wake him up to the world. You may find that he has one sensory channel that is more alerting, and you can use this to prompt him into really paying attention.

And from there you can begin playing the kind of games that help normalise sensory systems. The rules are simple: make sure it is fun and follow your child's lead. Never push; never force. When a parent pushes a child and they become overwhelmed by sensory information it is not just bad for the relationship, but for the child's growing brain. And to speed up learning, it has to be fun. Keep the oxytocin flowing with lots of laughter.

The ideas listed in the following pages are intended to be a general guide and a good starting point. Once you know what you are looking for you will find that together you and your child generate the most satisfying and therapeutic games.

Vestibular system

Start by checking whether your child has a physical problem such as an ear infection, because the vestibular nerve runs through the ear. Play games that build the vestibular system: rocking, rolling, twirling. The same games are used to 'normalise' sensation in dormancy and defensiveness.

- Play rolling games like 'There were four in the bed and the little one said, roll over, roll over'. Help your baby or child to roll, starting with quarter rolls and then back again.
- Encourage hanging upside down. When your baby has good head control, sit him on your lap, then lean back a little and bring him upright again. With an older child, encourage him to swing sitting up on a bar, and then slowly encourage him to hang upside down with his eyes closed. Two old tyres hung closely together on a rope will allow your child to lie inside them and twirl. This normalises the vestibular system as it mimics the time spent in that position in the womb. Your child *must* be in charge of the movement. If you force the twirling or spinning you will make him feel very ill and worsen the situation.[29]
- Holding your baby close, dance in a rocking motion to music with a steady beat. Rock an older child over a gym ball, with him in charge of the rocking.

- Sing to your baby, or sing with your toddler. Whatever stimulates the ear will also stimulate the vestibular nerve, so sing, sing, sing!
- Rockers, seesaws, gym balls, scooter boards, barrels and giant saucers are all excellent for this purpose. The static playground equipment is not recommended for children with vestibular difficulties as it doesn't re-create the early experience of being rocked by Mum as a baby.

How do you know it is working?

Initially there may be a brief regression to younger behaviour. You will know things are getting better when you see the flicker of nystagmus (eyes keep moving after the spinning has stopped) starting; and when the child takes over the therapy and spins, climbs, rocks and takes 'balance risks' of his own accord.

Visual system

- First of all, have your child's eyesight and eye health checked.
- Bear in mind that visual difficulties increase the likelihood that your child could be injured by a ball. Consider protective eyewear for sport.
- Make the environment as visually simple as you can. Think about keeping the number of toys out at any one time to a minimum: the one toy for each child rule is very useful here. For both defensive and dormant children you are aiming to increase visual attention: to 'tolerate' looking for longer periods and to sharpen focus.
- Find a noisy and intriguing toy that your baby loves, such as a flashing star on the end of a wand, or a rattle, and play 'Where's it gone? Here it is!' games.
- All games where your child gets the opportunity to track a moving object with his eyes are great. Encourage your baby to watch it move around the room. Roll balls and have your crawler chase them.
- Lie a child on his back and have him swipe at or try to catch a suspended object or even your hand. This game gets very giggly.
- Toys that operate by blowing and blowing bubbles are great for helping children focus close up.[35] For older children play

'puff ball' with straws and a ping pong ball — on a flat surface the children must blow the ball through the straw towards a goal. This is also a game you can play in teams — a team must defend their nominated sides of a table.

- Combine vestibular and visual stimulation by playing catch and throwing while a child is swinging, or grab playfully at baby's feet while someone else moves him.
- Books that have pop-out bits, books that make noises and books with different textures all encourage looking and touching and listening, which supports the development of visual attention.

How do you know it is working?

You will feel that your child is paying far more attention to you and that you are more strongly and deeply connected to him. You will also see an improvement in his length of attention.

Olfactory system

- The 'smell' part of sensory problems is a surprisingly important marker of dormancy or defensiveness. Barbara Knickerbocker, the occupational therapist who sorted children into 'dormant and defensive' felt that it was the first system that needed to be normalised for children who also had auditory and tactile issues.[29] While this might sound rather extraordinary, the value of smell to improving mood, attention, planning and alertness is now well researched.[36, 37] In addition, children with ADHD have been shown to have 'sharper noses' than their peers. The significance of this is unclear, but perhaps it is another example of where therapists have been significantly ahead of the research in simply doing 'what works'.[38]
- Create 'smell match' games. You could use essential oils such as lavender and eucalyptus to dab on your child's soft toys, but make sure the oil has dried before the child is given them to play with. Then challenge him to match his toys according to smell. You could also try scratch and sniff stickers or create 'smell jars' (small jars into which you have put herbs or spices or essential oil or dish detergent or perfume — anything that smells.)

- Ask your child to guess what's for dinner based on the smell, ask him to hunt out a smell in a room (hide a teddy that has been liberally doused in essential oil) and talk about smells with him.

How do you know it's working?

The dormant child will become aware of smells and the defensive child will not be so affronted by them. But you should also see improvements to his tactile and auditory sensory issues.

Tactile system

- Skin conditions like eczema can also cause defensive behaviours, so finding the right treatment for your child's eczema is important for learning and social experiences too.
- When interacting with a child with a touch disorder, always stay in front of him so he can see what you are doing.
- Light touch is the most uncomfortable for the defensive child and won't even impact on the dormant child. Heavy touch engages the other senses as well and so helps to normalise the touch system. Games that involve your child being squashed, squeezed and squished work extremely quickly, sometimes instantaneously. This is perhaps one of the most 'magic' experiences you can have with sensory therapy: a child who had been very uncomfortable in their skin becoming visibly more calm every second. It is hard to forget one boy with tactile dormancy who enjoyed having a gym ball rolled over him and asked for it to be made heavier and heavier until he finally begged both the therapist and his mother to sit on the ball together. 'Aaaah!' he said, as though relieved of a great weight rather than lying beneath one, because, finally, a touch sensation had registered.
- Start with finding the kind of touch your child enjoys and supplying it. Before bed is a good time, as sleeping difficulties come with the territory. It might be heavy touch (weighted blankets or pyjamas, heavy rolling with a gym ball, heavy compression down through the shoulders) or it might be hard touch (having their body and limbs brushed with a hard hairbrush or rubbed firmly with a rough towel). With the

dormant child, brushing is good place to start: for the defensive child, however, it could be torture.

- For the defensive child introduce the more challenging kinds of touch experience as 'fun' and pull back as soon as he requests. He will simply become more defensive if you do not. Finger painting with paint, foam or coloured glue is a good place to start, as is sand and water play, play dough and textured play dough.
- Trying to reduce defensiveness to touch around the mouth usually needs to wait until last. Games that involve blowing (like blowing bubbles and straw paintings), sucking (trying to suck up different kinds of drink) and chewing are all helpful because they all encourage increasingly precise movements to build better sensation.

How do you know it is working?

As the touch system normalises children 'stuff in' as many tactile experiences as they can, just in the same way the eight month old does. It's catch-up time! You may also notice changes to the way the child relates to others. For example, it can be a time of upheaval in class pecking orders (and even within families) as the child is more able to claim 'equal rights' with other children.

Auditory system

- Start by ensuring that his ears are healthy, as ear infections and hearing loss can lead to these same behaviours.
- Use a soft and calm voice to speak, and keep the environment mostly quiet. For the defensive child this will reduce the chance of a defensive response and for the dormant child it will assist him to pick out and focus on the sounds you want him to hear.
- Put him in charge of the noise. Let him bang away on the pots and pans, make scraping sounds with a shovel, sing songs with him where he gets to 'turn the music up or down', and hammer or jump on bubble wrap.
- Use books with 'sound buttons' to stimulate listening and remembering.
- Put music or sounds (like white noise or wave music) into his going to sleep routine.

- Talk about sounds with him as they happen, like birdsong and vehicle noises. Play games where you try and pinpoint just where the noise has come from, and then see if you can work out together what made the noise. Finally, play games to do with the sequence in which noises happen. (This is the normal developmental sequence — where is it, what is it, what's the order in which it happened.) Some of the sound remembering games could include:
  — singing nursery rhymes with one line missing and asking your child to spot what was missing. (Further refinements here including missing just one word or eventually just a sound.)
  — making 'mistakes' when reading well-known books. Start by missing out words at the end of rhyming sentences, as they are the easiest to spot
  — playing tapping games where you copy your child's rhythm and he copies yours
  — making up barrier games together, such as making up two sets of cards which can be put together to create different pictures: for example, an 'identikit photo' kit, or a garden or a beach scene. One person gives a set of instructions and the other person has to try and remember all the instructions to re-create the same picture
  — remembering and retelling jokes to build memory and rhythm, which build an awareness of movement through time and space.

How do you know it is working?

As your child improves his auditory skills, he will begin to use them in everyday life. He will refer to his favourite stories and music. In independent play he will begin to make more of the zooming and brooming noises and also 'voices' for his toys. He will be able to remember and act on more of what you say.

Proprioceptive system

- Again, the same activities work to help both the defensive and dormant child. The proprioceptive receptors are deep within the body, in our joints and muscles. They are activated by being stretched or squashed by movement, or by carrying heavy weight. So therapy to normalise children with problems in this area requires these elements.

- From my observations there appears to be more and more children with proprioceptive difficulties. It seems logical to link that increase to the decreasing amount of time children spend in heavy work or even heavy play. Toys are mostly made of lightweight plastic. Trampolines have been replaced with indoor play stations. Parents need to deliberately return these elements to children's lives.
- Rock your baby from side to side or compress his shoulder joints gently when he is rocking backwards and forwards preparatory to crawling.
- Encourage children to wear a weighted backpack or even a weighted vest.
- Wrap your child up tightly in a sheet or blanket and then play that he is a caterpillar hatching from a cocoon or a dragon hatching from an egg made of heavy pillows.
- Make objects your child likes to shift heavier — for example, tape phone books under chairs.
- Play wheelbarrows and wheel your child along.
- Encourage your child to push back against your hand with his feet or his hands.
- Play 'Angel in the Snow'. Just as it sounds, this game is one where your child lies on his back in the snow, and by moving his arms and legs makes a shape that looks a great deal like a winged and skirted angel. There is no snow in most of Australia, but this game can be played on any surface to build body awareness in children from about five upwards. Ask your child to lie on his back. Help him get absolutely symmetrical, his legs together, his arms down by his sides. Now ask him to move one leg, keeping it pressed to the ground and moving it out to the side. And then bring it in again. Now an arm, keeping it on the ground but sweeping it around all the way to above the head, and then back down again. When your child is able to do these movements easily and return to a symmetrical position, ask him to do two or three or four together. You can then start asking him to move his right leg and left arm. And then in different combinations. Finally, ask him to do various combinations with his eyes closed.

- Delay teaching handwriting to your child until his proprioceptive system has greatly improved.

How do you know if it is helping?

Your child will begin to seem a lot more comfortable in his skin and, as a result, in himself. Rather than missing many environmental cues, or being made timid by them, his movements will seem less at odds with the events around him.

Troubleshooting reading

This appendix can also make a good 'starting place' for the parent of the older child. All school skills are built on foundation skills so many strategy and activity suggestions refer to earlier chapters and appendices, but you may find it useful to pinpoint the 'skill gaps' that are preventing a child reading, writing, spelling or doing mathematics. Reading is a language-based skill so you might also like to reread chapters 9 and 15, which discuss language development.

In Chapter 19 is a list of the skills required for reading and the background of how they develop. Here they are again, but with strategies and activities to build each skill when it didn't happen 'the first time around'.

Reflex integration

Ask yourself, 'Has my child integrated her primitive reflexes, particularly her asymmetrical tonic neck reflex?' You need to work through Appendix III to answer this question and help your child if active primitive reflexes are still present.

Hand and eye skills

Ask yourself:
- Does my child have a dominant hand? If she doesn't then she will not have a dominant eye either.
- Does my child have a dominant eye?
- Can my child direct her eyes to track along a straight line without a 'jerk' in the middle?
- Do her eyes converge — that is, do both her eyes point at the same close object?

(Pages 216–218 in Chapter 19 tell you how to check for all these skills.)

Here are some suggestions to help develop eye dominance and convergence:

- Eye movement co-develops with the integration of primitive reflexes. Do go back and check through Appendix III if you feel that eye movement is a concern for your child. For example, if your child doesn't have eye dominance by around the age of six, suspect an active asymmetrical tonic neck reflex, tonic labyrinthine reflex and/or a symmetrical tonic neck reflex.
- A developmental optometrist (not just one that concerns himself with visual acuity but also visual perception) is the relevant professional here. However, the more reputable optometrists will not attempt to work with children who still have primitive reflexes in place. Primitive reflex integration is the bottom rung on the developmental hierarchy, which means it needs to be dealt with first.
- Encourage your child to play on equipment that moves, such as twirlers, rockers, barrels, seesaws, swings, gym balls, pillows, trampolines, hammocks, dangling tyres and so on. The point of the moving is that it re-creates early infancy, which is when these eye movements usually develop as the baby responds to an unexpected movement event.
- Slow movements are important here. It is during that gentle early rocking, where baby's eyes are fixed upon your face, that eyes become yoked together. Gently rock your child in a big rocker or on an inflatable ball, talking to her, so that she must move her eyes to keep them on your face.
- Encourage your child to twirl, roll and crawl to music.
- While she is jumping or swinging or rocking, encourage her to catch and throw a ball or beanbag with you.
- Playing with kaleidoscopes is great for pushing along eye dominance and convergence.
- Play the torch chasey game, where you and your child each have a torch. Cover the torches with different coloured cellophane paper, shine them on the ceiling and have the light beams chase each other.
- There are more ideas in Appendix IV for improving visual skills.

Here are some ideas for developing smooth visual tracking in your child:

- Crossing the midline is one of the frequent focuses of occupational therapists. Difficulty in doing this is a marker not just for difficulty in reading but also difficulty with fine motor skills. It is something babies normally learn in crawling, and playing crawling games with your older child will definitely help her.
- Play 'wheelbarrows'. Be aware that children frequently have a time period where they are suddenly unable to play wheelbarrows, and then the ability returns again. Children with an active asymmetrical tonic neck reflex must be careful when playing wheelbarrows not to suddenly lose power in one arm and land painfully on the side of the face. Add in 'crossing hands' to wheelbarrow walking once your child is a proficient 'little wheelbarrow'.
- Do puzzles with your child. First of all, ensure she is not W-sitting, then place the puzzle pieces on the non-dominant side of her body. She must reach across with her dominant hand to pick up the pieces. (When I was working with impulsive children who struggled with midline crossing, I would ask them to sit on their 'helper' hand.) Games like Chinese chequers or noughts and crosses can also be played in this way.
- If your child loves colouring-in, make sure she is not carefully colouring just a tiny piece of the picture at a time and then shifting the paper. This is classic midline-crossing avoidance. Insist on long strokes with the pencil.
- Blow bubbles with her and insist that she uses just her dominant hand to pop them.

Self-regulation skills

Ask yourself:

- Does my child have 'good enough' mood management skills to be able to keep trying in the face of the inevitable frustration that learning to read brings?
- Can my child shift her attention at will?
- Are her impulse control and attention sufficient so that she

doesn't impulsively respond to a 'c' and say 'cow' but stops and thinks for a minute?

If these skills are missing I would recommend working through appendices I, II and III and reading the main body of the book.

Auditory skills
Ask yourself:
- Can my child easily blend together 'c' (pause) 'a' (pause) 't' to make 'cat'?
- Can my child tell me what sound a word starts with? (For example, 'What is the first sound in zoo?')
- Can my child tell me what sound is in the middle and on the end of a word?
- Can she easily match letters with letter sounds?

If these skills are missing your child will struggle with reading. These activities (plus the blending games in chapter 17) will help these skills develop so she's ready to read:
- Sing with your child as much as you can. Both of you should hold your hands under your chins as you sing to help her hear the syllables.[39] Ballads and nursery rhymes with their greater melody and slower speeds should be your focus. You do not need to do this with the words in front of you initially as this is a 'hearing' activity not a reading one. Clear enunciation of sounds is required. Make sure you don't run the words together.
- Listen to music together. Teach your child the different sounds of the different instruments and ask her to tell you when she can hear the 'voice' of the bassoon or the viola. This is helping your child develop the ability to pick out one sound in a complex background. You can't go past 'Peter and the Wolf' for this exercise.
- Beat out rhythms with your child, not just with your hands but also with your feet and with your heads.
- In the car play 'I spy' or 'Spotto' (which is about things regularly appearing outside the car). 'I saw it again and it started with t!' Remember to use the sound the letter makes rather than its name.

- Write your child's stories out for her. Help her elaborate by asking questions, but remember to enjoy every word she utters. This is a more powerful contributor to your child's ability to link sounds with letter shapes than reading.
- Make or purchase some sandpaper letters. Play 'Is this an "a"?', where your child must feel the shape with her eyes closed. You are matching visual, tactile and auditory information, and better phonemic awareness usually follows as a result. Along the same lines, also write letters on her back. You need to build up to this, though. Begin by drawing 'stories' on her back when she is little: 'And Revvy the little red truck screamed around the corner and suddenly there was a rabbit! He slammed on his brakes.' Accompany your story with matching movements. Then you can ask your child to say what animal movement you have drawn on her back, and what shape you have drawn. Eventually, when she is five or six, you will be able to start drawing letters.
- Card games such as Go Fish and Rummy build auditory memory.
- Make sure you speak more slowly. If you talk at breakneck speed it is much harder for anyone, let alone your child, to hear the component syllables. Habitually build some 'paused words' into your talking. 'If you go and get me a b (pause) oo (pause) k, I'll read it to you.' The motivation to decode and a clue is built right in.
- If this is a real area of concern for you — if you feel your child is strongly resisting listening — then consider finding a sound therapist. (Two of the big names in sound therapy are Samona and Tomatis.) Consider strongly that your child may have difficulties with other areas of sensory processing and return to Appendix IV. Choose some games that reduce 'auditory defensiveness' from those pages.

Visual perceptual skills
Ask yourself:
- Does my child have a good memory for what she has seen?
- Is she good at noticing subtle differences in pictures?

This is another very important set of skills for reading. Here are some suggestions:

- One classic game is Hunt The Thimble. Take any small object (a small plastic bear is a good one) and hide it in plain sight. You can give clues of 'hotter and colder' or 'higher and lower' while your child searches for it.
- The *Where's Wally?* and Usborne puzzle books (and all the other similar books) help your child practice finding just one object in a complex background.
- Sorting games are also very important, and sorting is something you need to directly teach children. A wonderful big box of assorted old buttons is an excellent teaching tool. Start with teaching size discrimination — big and little — and then move on to colour and finally examine shape. Don't expect your child to see the differences, you will have to teach her. In doing so you are sharpening her perception by adding language into the tool mix.
- Always start from large differences before progressing to smaller ones. Is it a pig or a cow? What is the difference between the two pigs on the page? Is one dog spotty and the other not? Is one face smiling and the other one sad? The first difference — between a pig and cow — is a lot more noticeable. The second difference — between two pink pigs — is going to be more challenging to detect. Being able to tell the difference between letters is obviously more challenging still.
- Barrier games are where you each have an identical set of cards to construct a room or a face or a scene to match the other person. Your child might say, 'My man has blue eyes, a pig's nose and a droopy moustache', and then you must build that. Then you both check to see if the two pictures match.
- Play 'find the' games in books — for example, Where is the horse? Where is the pig? — and all that is showing of each is the tail or an ear. These games can also be played while tidying up. 'Where is your elephant?' you ask, knowing that your child will only be able to see its trunk poking out from under a cushion.

- Jigsaws are excellent to build skills. Toy libraries and council libraries lend these out. We recommend doing just one at a time, and doing it with your child over and over. The first few times you are solving the puzzle using the different visual clues but eventually she learns to operate purely from the memory of how it goes together.
- It is really hard to go past playing cards. So useful are they that Mum helped a mother who belonged to a particularly strict religious order to gain dispensation to have a pack in her house to play card games with her daughter. Mind you, these were simple games like Old Maid, where the cards could not possibly be used for gambling. In the absence of card games Mum makes up games that involve remembering movement sequences. You do a hop, your child does a hop. You do a hop and clap and another hop and your child copies this. Then it is your child's turn to make up a movement sequence. Some of the really super card games to build visual memory include:
  — Clock Patience. You deal out a clock face, with another pile in the middle, making 13 piles of four cards each. You then pick up a card from the middle, and then put it in the right spot on the clock, and take a card from that pile. The game often 'comes out' and builds on number recognition and remembering position
  — Snap! The deck of cards is divided among the players and everyone has a turn putting a card down on the same central pile. You always have to hold in your mind the card at the top of the pile as well as the one that's just been put down. If there's a match, every participant tries to be the first to get their hand on the pile while screaming out 'Snap!'
- The board games that require visual memory as part of designing strategy are good, such as Chinese chequers, draughts and chess. It is not uncommon for little boys to be able to play chess in advance of being able to read.

Motivation
Finally, ask yourself:
- Does my child like books?
- Does she love stories?

- Has my child consistently said to me that she wants to learn to read?

If you are getting any 'no's' here then your child isn't motivated to learn. You need to think about how to create that motivation. The answer is both basic and drastic. Everyone (except most people with autism) loves stories. We are all hungry for the experience of living in the skins of those who are braver, bigger, stranger and grander than ourselves. Where is your child currently getting her story supply? From the TV set? From a regular diet of DVDs and videos? Or audio books? Cut off the non-storybook supply and explain to your child just why you are doing so.

Return to reading her stories, but choose those stories with a history of addicting readers. For the child who loves animals there are Gerald Durrell and James Herriot. For the little girl who loves acting and dancing there is Noel Streatfield. For the child with an appetite for the kooky and offbeat choose some of the non-fiction written by Herbie Brennan. Diana Wynne-Jones writes fantasy centred on children's relationships. Margaret Mahy's books show magic springing from the everyday. Try Justin D'Ath for adventure. Lie on the bed with your child, read aloud and point to the words as you read them. Stop in motivating places and leave the book by her bed.

Also, if you want your child to be a reader, never use 'No story time tonight!' as a punishment. Keep that time sacred until she is reading independently.

Troubleshooting maths, writing and spelling

In Chapter 20 there is an outline of the skills that underpin maths, writing and spelling. If your child is struggling with those parts of formal learning you might like to see if any of these skills have not yet developed.

Maths
Ask yourself:
- Is my child struggling with number concepts such as reversibility and orders of magnitude? If this is the case, I recommend you return to the age-old game of Stones described in Chapter 20 and play it for about half an hour a day.
- Is my child struggling with maths problems written vertically? If so, return to Appendix III and make sure that an active tonic labyrinthine reflex is excluded as the cause of the difficulty.
- Does my child struggle with the visual-spatial maths tasks like rotating an image in his mind? Again, the problem here may well be connected to a lack of fully developed adult reflexes.
- Is my child easily distracted and a bit 'scatty'? I suggest that his body awareness, his sense of being housed deeply and strongly in his body, might be poor. This is called 'position in space'. The game Angel in the Snow, which is described on page 320 in Appendix IV will be helpful.
- Does my child struggle to recall maths facts? This is often a sign of a poor auditory memory. The exercises in appendices III and IV for auditory skills are recommended. Consider also

that your child may have an active spinal galant reflex (see Appendix III to check for this and to find ideas to help).

The vexed question of reversals

So often people say, 'Oh, reversing letters still, he must be dyslexic!' When children are reversing letters and numbers in reading there can be a number of causes. To begin with, reversals are actually normal until age eight, particularly with boys.

For a child who reverses letters, numbers and small words in both reading and writing, you need to work more on his visual skills. Also, go back and spend some time on the most frequently reversed letters and numbers to make sure he can actually hear the differences. Make sure that he understands the differences between 13 and 30 by showing him each number made out of real objects: 13 buttons compared to 30 buttons. Reversals can also indicate that a child has an active asymmetrical tonic neck reflex, so go back and read Appendix III.

However, if a child is only reversing letters you can be sure that he has a problem with auditory skills and/or a problem with position in space. Angel in the Snow (see page 320) is an excellent game to build this sense. You might also like to ask him to shut his eyes while you massage different parts of his body and ask him to tell you what you are touching. And check how well your child understands the 'position' words such as 'up' and 'down', 'diagonal', 'sideways'. Learning visual differences is all about talking about them.

Check too for problems with auditory discrimination. Can he hear those differences or not? If he cannot, it is time to bring in some of the tools that can improve children's perception: mirrors, touching your face as you talk and feeling his own face as he produces sounds. A speech pathologist is the relevant professional to see here. When he can see and feel a difference he will find it easier to hear it too. Saying the sound over and over again, feeling the difference over and over again — it's all about practice.

Spelling

Ask yourself:

- Does my child learn a word and then forget it quite quickly? If so, the problem is one of poor visual skills. The visual perceptual games that help with reading (see Appendix V) will also help here.
- Does my child struggle to 'spell aloud' and do far better when asked to write the word? Does he seem to become particularly confused when asked to spell aloud using the letter names? If so, give up on the letter names straightaway. This is a sign of a lack of connection between the sound and the shape of letters, so get this solid first. Make sure your child can actually hear all the sounds, and then begin on the process of matching them to the letters. Letter names are optional for some time to come.[40]
- Does my child have difficulty remembering and knowing when to apply spelling rules? As with recalling maths facts, this is a memory issue. Consider the spinal galant reflex as a potential culprit. You might also like to consider these games to improve his memory:
  — ask your child to make something from a construction kit. Take a quick photo, then disassemble it and ask him to remake it from memory
  — go around the house hiding a number of objects with your child next to you, then ask him to remember where each one is
  — Kim's game is the classic memory game. Collect a group of items (just a small number to begin with) and place them in a group. Ask your child to memorise them and then accurately tell you what has been removed. Once your child has become a gun at this level you can rotate objects rather than removing them, or change their position relative to each other
  — play Memory with a deck of playing cards, where your child and you turn over the cards trying to find matching pairs
  — memorise a poem or song with your child.

Spelling is difficult! Reread Chapter 20.

Writing

Ask yourself:

- Does my child watch his pencil forming the letters? This is an indication that his proprioceptive sense is poor. In exploiting the proprioceptive sense to help your child learn letter shapes, the focus is on touch and movement rather than on vision. Ask him to write with his eyes closed. Take his hand and draw the letters gently on the sand or on the carpet (little fingertips are sensitive, so don't push hard). Make sure that you insist on clearly defined 'starting points' for letters and numbers.

- Does my child struggle with 'getting everything written tidily'? Some children with untidy handwriting are those who fatigue quickly. They usually have 'soft', less expressive faces and generally lower muscle tone. If this is the case, you must suspect an active tonic labyrinthine reflex (Appendix III) and do the activities suggested. One useful activity for increasing muscle strength to support grasp is to ask children to paint above shoulder height. You can just use water and a decorator's paint brush on a wall if you are short on paper and paint.

- Does my child battle to hold onto the pencil and paper at the same time? Does my child twist his paper or his body so that the paper is rotated 90 degrees away from him? Does he avoid crossing the midline of his body when he is writing (see Chapter 29)? All of these are markers for an active asymmetric tonic neck reflex. You will need to remedy that and also teach him to cross the midline of his body (see page 322 in Appendix V).

- Does my child forget how to write letter shapes all the time? This is often a marker for visual-perceptual issues and eye movement problems. Eye movement problems, of course, are strongly connected to primitive reflex retention. See Appendix III.

- Does my child struggle to get his ideas down on the page? This is considered to be a sign of a poorly developed corpus callosum or 'bridge' between the left and right sides of the brain. Consider that an active asymmetrical tonic neck reflex could be 'holding' your child in one hemisphere at a time when a free-flowing exchange between the hemispheres is required.[12] See Appendix III.

Endnotes

Introduction

1. Centre for Community Child Health and Telethon Institute for Child Health Research, A Snapshot of Early Childhood Development in Australia — AEDI National Report 2009. Canberra: Australian Government, 2009.
2. Kochanska G, Knaack A. Effortful control as a personality characteristic of young children: antecendents, correlates and consequences. Journal of Personality 2003; 71(3).

Part 1

1. Shonkoff J P. From neurons to neighbourhoods. In: The neuroscience of nurturing neurons, Children of the Code, 2004. Available from: ttp://www.childrenofthecode.org/interviews/shonkoff.htm.
2. Williams M, Nicholson W (illust.). The Velveteen Rabbit. New York: Doubleday & Company Inc., 1922.
3. Veríssimo M, Salvaterra F. Maternal secure-base scripts and children's attachment security in an adopted sample. Attachment and Human Development 2003; 8(3): 261–273.
4. van IJzendoorn M H. Adult attachment representations, parental responsiveness, and infant attachment: a meta-analysis on the predictive validity of the adult attachment interview. Psychological Bulletin 1995; 117(3): 387–403.
5. Fonagy P. Transgenerational consistencies of attachment; a new theory. Paper presented to the Developmental and Psychoanalytic Discussion Group, American Psychoanalytic Association Meeting 1999.
6. Slade A G, Grienenberger J, Bernbach E, Levy D, Locker A. Maternal reflective functioning, attachment, and the transmission gap: a preliminary study. Attachment & Human Development 2005; 7(3): 283–298(16).
7. Macfie J, Fitzpatrick K L, Rivas E M, Cox M J. Independent influences on mother-toddler role reversal:

infant–mother attachment disorganization and role reversal in mother's childhood. Attachment & Human Development 2008; 10(1): 29–39.

8. Sable P. Accentuating the positive in adult attachments. Attachment and Human Development 2007; 9(4): 361–374.

9. Fortuna K, Roisman G I. Insecurity, stress, and symptoms of psychopathology: contrasting results from self-reports versus interviews of adult attachment. Attachment & Human Development 2008; 10(1): 11–28.

10. Fonagy P, Target M. Bridging the transmission gap: an end to an important mystery of attachment research?. Attachment & Human Development 2005; 7(3): 333–343.

11. DeOliviera CA, Moran G, Pederson D P. Understanding the link between maternal adult attachment classifications and thoughts and feelings about emotions. Attachment & Human Development 2005; 7(2): 153–170.

12. van IJzendoorn M H. Adult attachment representations, parental responsiveness, and infant attachment: a meta-analysis on the predictive validity of the adult attachment interview. Psychological Bulletin 1995; 117(3): 387–403.

13. Adam E K, Gunnar M R, Tanaka A. Adult attachment, parent emotion, and observed parenting behaviour: mediator and moderator models. Child Development 2004; 75(1): 110–122.

14. Jansson T., Comet in Moominland, London: Penguin, 1946.

15. Lyons-Ruth K, Bronfman E, Parsons E. Maternal frightened, frightening, or atypical behavior and disorganised infant attachment patterns. Monographs of the Society for Reseach in Child Development 1999; 64(3): 67–96.

16. Berlin L J, Yair Z, Amaya-Jackson L, Greenberg M T, eds. Enhancing early attachments: theory, research, intervention and policy. Duk Series in Child Development and Public Policy, New York: The Guildford Press, 2007.

17. Crittenden P M. Danger and development: the organization of self-protective strategies. Monographs for the Society of Research in Child Development 1999; 64(3): 145–171.

18. van IJzendoorn M H. Disorganized attachment in early childhood: meta-analysis of precursors, concomitants, and sequelae. Development and Psychopathology 1999; 11: 225–249.

19. Hennighausen K, Lyons-Ruth K. Disorganization of attachment strategies in infancy and childhood. Rev. ed. In: Tremblay R E, Barr R G, Peters R de V, Boivin M, eds. Encyclopedia on Early Childhood Development [online]. Montreal: Centre of Excellence for Early Childhood development; 2010: 1–7.

20. Cicchetti D, Cohen D J. Developmental psychopathology: Theory and method. New York: John Wiley and Sons, 2006, p. 1104.

21. Fox M, Lofts P (illust.) Koala Lou. Australia: Penguin Books, 1988.

22. Rholes W S, Simpson J A. Adult attachment: theory, research, and clinical implications. New York: Guilford Press, 2006, p. 482.

23. Vaughn B E. Discovering pattern in developing lives: reflections on the Minnesota study of risk and adaptation from birth to adulthood. Attachment & Human Development 2005; 7(4): 369–380.

24. Maier M A, Bernier A, Reinhard P, Zimmermann P, Strasser K, Grossmann K E. Attachment state of mind and perceptual processing of emotional stimuli. Attachment & Human Development 2005; 7(1): 67–81.

25. Weinberg M K, Tronick E Z. Infant affective reactions to the resumption of maternal interaction after the still-face. Child Development 1996; 67(3): 905–914.

26. Schore A N. The effects of early relational trauma on right brain development, affect regulation and infant mental health. Infant Mental Health Journal 2001; 22: 201–269.

27. Schore A N. Dysregulation of the right brain: a fundamental mechanism of traumatic attachment and the psychopathogenesis of posttraumatic stress disorder. Australian and New Zealand Journal of Psychiatry 2002; 36: 9–30.

28. Holmes J. Disorganized attachment and borderline personality disorder: a clinical perspective. Attachment & Human Development 2004; 6(2): 181–190.

29. Cooper G. Circle of security. J J King, ed. 2009: Perth. Two Day Circle of Security Workshop.

30. Mahy M. Dangerous Spaces. Great Britain: Hamish Hamilton, 1991.

31. Kinsley C H, Lambert K G. The maternal brain: Pregnancy and motherhood change the structure of the female mammal's brain, making mothers attentive to their young and better at caring for them. Scientific American, January, 2006.

32. Pawluski J L, Walker S K, Galea L A M. Reproductive experience differentially affects spatial reference and working memory performance in the mother. Hormones and Behavior 2006; 49(2): 143–149.

33. Kinsley C H, Madonia L, Gifford G W et al. Motherhood improves learning and memory: Neural activity in rats is enhanced by pregnancy and the demands of rearing offspring. Nature, 1999, 402, 137–138.

34. Kinsley C H, Madonia L, Gifford G W et al. Motherhood improves learning and memory. Nature, 1999; 401(6758): 137–138.

35. Lemaire V, Millard J M, Dutar P et al. Motherhood-induced memory improvement persists across lifespan in rats but is abolished by a gestational stress. European Journal of Neuroscience, 2006; 23(12): 3368–3374.

36. Marmot M, Wilkinson R G, eds. The social determinants of health. 2nd ed. Oxford: Oxford University Press, 2006, p. 366.

37. McKie R. Want to boost your brain power? Just have a baby!. The Observer [newspaper on the internet]; January 15 2006 [cited February 18 2010]. Available from: www.guardian.co.uk/science/.

38. Noonan E. Giving birth to a better brain: Do babies sharpen parents' minds? The Boston Globe [newspaper on the internet]; October 31 2005 [cited February 18 2010]. Available from : www.boston.com/news/globe/health/.

39.   Palmer L F. Bonding matters ... the chemistry of attachment. Attachment Parenting International News [serial on the internet] 2002; 5(2) [cited February 18 2010]. Available from: www.attachmentparenting.org/support/articles/.

40.   Schore A N. The effects of a secure attachment relationship on right brain development, affect regulation, and infant mental health. Infant Mental Health Journal, 2001; 22(12): 7–66.

41.   Ginott H. Teacher and child. New York: The Macmillan Company, 1972.

42.   Ginott H. Between parent and child. New York: The Macmillan Company, 1965.

43.   Chang L, Schwartz D, Dodge K A, McBride-Chang C. Harsh parenting in relation to child emotion regulation and aggression. Journal of Family Psychology, 2003; 17(4): 598–606.

44.   Woodward L J, Fergusson D M. Parent, child, and contextual predictors of childhood physical punishment. Infant and Child Development, 2002; 11(3): 213–235.

45.   van Duijvenvoorde A C K, Zanolie K, Rombouts S A R B, Raijmakers M E J, Crone E A. Evaluating the negative or valuing the positive? Neural mechanisms supporting feedback-based learning across development. The Journal of Neuroscience, 2008; 28(38): 9495–9503.

46.   Davies D. Child development: a practitioner's guide. New York: Guilford Press, 2004.

47.   Klein R, Shrout P, Brotman L M, Gouley K K, O'Neal C, Huang K Y, Rosenfelt A. Preventive intervention for preschoolers at high risk for antisocial behavior: long-term effects on child physical aggression and parenting practices. Journal of Clinical Child & Adolescent Psychology, 2008; 37(2): 386–396.

48.   Petrosino A, Turpin-Petrosino C, Buehler J. 'Scared straight' and other juvenile awareness programs for preventing juvenile delinquency. The Annals of the American Academy of Political and Social Science, 2003; 589(1): 41–62.

49.   Henderlong J, Lepper M R. The effects of praise on

children's intrinsic motivation: a review and synthesis. Psychological Bulletin, 2002; 128(5): 774–795.

50.   Mueller C M, Dweck C S. Praise for intelligence can undermine children's motivation and performance. Journal of Personality and Social Psychology, 1998; 75(1): 33–52.

51.   Dweck C S. Mindset: the new psychology of success. New York: Random House, 2006.

52.   Kipling, Rudyard, Animal Stories. London: Macmillan & Co. Limited, 1956.

53.   Huston A C, Rosenkrantz A S. Mothers' time with infant and time in employment as predictors of mother–child relationships and children's early development. Child Development, 2005; 76(2): 467–482.

54.   Belsky J, Vandell D L, Burchinal M et al. Are there long-term effects of early child care? Child Development, 2007; 78(2): 681–701.

55.   Love J M, Harrison L, Sagi-Schwartz A et al. Child care quality matters: how conclusions may vary with context. Child Development, 2003; 74(4): 1021–1033.

56.   Harrison L J. Does child care quality matter? Associations between social-emotional development and non-parental child care in a representative sample of Australian children. Family Matters, 2008; 79: 14–25.

57.   Harrison L J, Ungerer J A. Children and child care: a longitudinal study of the relationships between developmental outcomes and use of nonparental care from birth to six. Panel Data and Policy Conference. Canberra: Department of Family and Community Services, 2000.

58.   Belsky J, Bakermans-Kranenburg M J, van IJzendoorn M H. For better and for worse: Differential susceptibility to environmental influences. Current Directions in Psychological Science, 2007. 16(6): 300–304(5).

59.   Wachs T D, Kohnstamm G A, eds. Temperament in context. Mahwah, New Jersey: Lawrence Erlbaum, 2001.

60.   Crockenberg S C. Rescuing the baby from the bathwater: how gender and temperament (may) influence how child care affects child development. Child Development, 2003; 74(4): 1034–1038.

61 McMahon C A, Barnett B, Kowalenko N M, Tennant C
    C. Maternal attachment state of mind moderates the
    impact of postnatal depression on infant attachment.
    Journal of Child Psychology and Psychiatry, 2006; 47(7):
    660–669.

62. Fisher J R, Feekery C J, Rowe-Murray H J. Nature, severity
    and correlates of psychological distress in women admitted
    to a private mother-baby unit. Journal of Paediatrics and
    Child Health, 2002; 38(2): 140–145.

63. Dennis C L, Ross L. Women's perceptions of partner
    support and conflict in the development of postpartum
    depressive symptoms. Journal of Advanced Nursing, 2006;
    56(6): 588–599.

64. Dennis C L, Ross L. Relationships among infant sleep
    patterns, maternal fatigue, and development of depressive
    symptomatology. Birth, 2005; 32(3): 187–193.

65. Slattery D A, Neumann I D. No stress please! Mechanisms
    of stress hyporesponsiveness of the maternal brain. Journal
    of Physiology, 2008; 586 (2): 377–385.

66. Mayes L C, Swain J E, Leckman J F. Parental attachment
    systems: neural circuits, genes, and experiential
    contributions to parental engagement. Clinical
    Neuroscience Research, 2005; 4(5–6): 301–313.

67. Gray M, Qu L, Weston R. Research paper no. 41: Fertility
    and family policy in Australia, Australian Institute of Family
    Studies, February 2008.

68. Lockhart K, Reilly N, Thiele W. Perinatal mental health
    consortium perinatal mental health national action plan
    2008–2010. Australia: beyondblue: the national depression
    initiative, 2008. Available from: http://www.gpsa.org.au/
    media/docs/mentalhealth/perinatal_national_action_plan.pdf

69. Joseph S, ed. Encyclopedia of women & Islamic cultures.
    Leiden-Boston: BRILL, 2003.

70. Crawley R A, Dennison K, Carter C. Cognition in
    pregnancy and the first year post-partum. Psychology and
    Psychotherapy, 2003; 76(1): 69–84.

71. des Rivières-Pigeon C, Saurel-Cubizolles M-J, Romito P.
    Division of domestic work and psychological distress 1 year

after childbirth: a comparison Between France, Quebec and Italy. Journal of Community & Applied Social Psychology 2002; 12(6): 397–409.

Part 2

1. Schore A, Carrol R. An interview with Allan Schore — 'the American Bowlby'. The Psychotherapist; Autumn 2001.
2. cited in Shaffer C R, Anundsen K. Creating Community Anywhere: Finding Support and Connection in Fragmented World. New York: G. P. Putnam's Sons, 1993, p. 6.
3. Fox M, Argent K (illust.). Wombat Divine. Sydney: Omnibus Books: 1995.
4. May C P, Hasher L. Synchrony effects in inhibitory control over thought and action. Human Perception and Performance, 1988; 24(3): 363–379.
5. Sung J H, Dice J, Hsu H-C. Developmental links of infant temperament to attachment security and behavioral adjustment assessed in toddlerhood. XVth Biennial International Conference on Infant Studies, 2006: Kyoto, Japan.
6. Kaye K L, Bower T G R. Learning and intermodal transfer of information in newborns. Psychological Science, 1994; 5 (5): 286–288.
7. Goddard S. Reflexes, learning and behaviour: a window into the child's mind. Eugene, Oregon: Fern Ridge Press, 2002.
8. Marmot M, Wilkinson R G, eds. The social determinants of health. 2nd ed.: Oxford: Oxford University Press, 2006, p. 366.
9. Schore A N. The effects of early relational trauma on right brain development, affect regulation and infant mental health. Infant Mental Health Journal, 2001; 22: 201–269.
10. Cooper G. Circle of security workshop. Perth, Western Australia: 2009.
11. Schore, A N. The effects of a secure attachment relationship on right brain development, affect regulation, and infant mental health. Infant Mental Health Journal, 2001; 22: 7–66.

12.   Zeifman D M. An ethological analysis of human infant
        crying: answering Tinbergen's four questions.
        Developmental Psychobiology, 2001; 39: 265–285.
13.   Savino F, Castagno E, Bretto R, Brondello C, Palumeri E,
        Oggero R. A prospective 10-year study on children who
        had severe infantile colic. Acta Paediatrica, 2005; 94(449):
        129–132.
14.   Canivet C, Ostergren P O, Jakobsson I, Hagander B. Higher
        risk of colic in infants of nonmanual employee mothers
        with a demanding work situation in pregnancy.
        International Journal of Behavioral Medicine, 2004; 11(1):
        37–47.
15.   Akman I, Kuşçu K, Özdemir N et al. Mothers' postpartum
        psychological adjustment and infantile colic. Çevre Sok,
        2006; 54(6): 06680.
16.   Wachs T D, Pollitt E, Cueto S, Jacoby E, Creed-Kanashiro
        H. Relation of neonatal iron status to individual variability
        in neonatal temperament. Developmental Psychobiology,
        2005; 46(2): 141–153.
17.   Savino F. Focus on infantile colic. Acta Pædiatrica, 2007;
        96(9): 1259–1264.
18.   Kagan J. Temperament. In: Enclopaedia of Early Childhood
        Development. Tremblay R E, Peters R DeV, eds., Montreal,
        Quebec Centre for Excellence in Early Childhood
        Development, 2005.
19.   Schmidt L A, Fox N A. Fear-potentiated startle responses in
        temperamentally different human infants. Developmental
        Psychobiology, 1998; 32: 113–20.
20.   Aron E N. The clinical implications of Jung's concept of
        sensitiveness. Journal of Jungian Theory and Practice, 2006;
        8(2): 12–43.
21.   van Zeijl J, Mesman J, Stolk M N et al. Differential
        susceptibility to discipline: The moderating effect of child
        temperament on the association between maternal
        discipline and early childhood externalizing problems.
        Journal of Family Psychology, 2007; 21(4): 626–636.
22.   Belsky J, Makermans-Kranenburg M J; van IJzendoorn M H.
        For better and for worse: differential susceptibility to

environmental influences. Current Directions in Psychological Science, 2007; 16(6): 300–304.

23.   Sears W. Keys to Calming the fussy baby. New York: Barron, 1991.

24.   Elizabeth Goudge, *The Heart of the Family*, London: Hodder and Staughton, 1953

25.   Simons R C. Boo! Culture, experience and the startle reflex. New York and Oxford: Oxford University Press, 1996.

26.   Richards J E. Development of multimodal attention in young infants: modification of the startle reflex by attention. Psychophysiology, 2000; 37: 65-75.

27.   Sabatinelli D, Bradley M M. Startle reflex modulation: perception, attention and emotion. In Experimental Methods in Neuropsychology. Hughdahl K, ed. Norwell Massachusetts: Kluwer Academic Publishers, 2003, p. 65–87.

28.   Kaitz M, Maytal H. Interactions between anxious mothers and their infants: An integration of theory and research findings. Infant Mental Health Journal, 2005; 26(6): 570–597.

29.   Evans L G, Oehler-Stinnett J. Structure and prevalence of PTSD symptomology in children who have experienced a severe tornado. Psychology in the Schools, 2006; 43(3): 283–295.

30.   Perry B D, Blakley T L, Baker W L, Vigilante D. Childhood trauma, the neurobiology of adaptation & use-dependent development of the brain: how states become traits. Infant Mental Health Journal, 2006; 16(4): 271–291.

31.   Dixon Jr W E D, Smith P H. Who's controlling whom? Infant contributions to maternal play behaviour. Infant and Child Development, 2003; 12(2): 177–195.

32.   Putnam S P, Rotherbart M K, Gartstein M A. Homotypic and heterotypic continuity of fine-grained temperament during infancy, toddlerhood, and early childhood. Infant and Child Development, 2008; 17: 387–405.

33.   Adolphs R, Damasio H, Tranel D, Cooper G, Damasio A R. A role for somatosensory cortices in the visual recognition of emotion as revealed by three-dimensional lesion mapping. Journal of Neuroscience, 2000; 20(7): 2683–90.

34. Zeedyk M S. From intersubjectivity to subjectivity: the transformative roles of emotional intimacy and imitation. Infant and Child Development, 2006; 15: 321–344.

35. Hobson P. The Cradle of Thought: Exploring the origins of thinking. London: Pan Macmillan, 2004.

36. Feldman R. Parent-infant synchrony and the construction of shared timing; physiological precursors, developmental outcomes, and risk conditions. Journal of Child Psychology and Psychiatry, 2007; 48(3–4): 329–354.

37. Sarkadi A, Kristiansson R, Oberklaid F, Bremberg S. Fathers' involvement and children's developmental outcomes: a systematic review of longitudinal studies. Acta Paediatrica, 2008; 97(2): 153–158.

38. Williams M, Nicholson W (illust.). The Velveteen Rabbit. New York: Doubleday & Company Inc., 1922.

39. Young, C. The science of mother love: is science catching up to mother's wisdom? Mothering Magazine, 2002.

40. Hobson J A, Hobson P R. Identification: the missing link between joint attention and imitation? Development and Psychopathology, 2007; 19(2): 411–431.

41. Thayer J F, Friedman B H, Ruiz-Padial E. Neurovisceral integration, emotions and health: An update. International Congress Series, 2006; 1287: 122–127.

42. Thayer J F, Lane R D. Claude Bernard and the heart-brain connection: Further elaboration of a model of neurovisceral integration. Neuroscience & Biobehavioral Reviews, 2009; 33(2): 81–88.

43. Guarneri D M. The Heart Speaks: A Cardiologist Reveals the Secret Language of Healing. London: Fusion Press, 2006.

44. Beauchaine T. Vagal tone, development, and Gray's motivational theory: Toward an integrated model of autonomic nervous system functioning in psychopathology. Development and Psychopathology, 2001; 13: 183–214.

45. Marsh P, Beauchaine T, Williams B. Dissociation of sad facial expressions and autonomic nervous system responding in boys with disruptive behavior disorders. Psychophysiology, 2008; 45: 100–110.

46. Schore A N. Dysregulation of the right brain: a fundamental mechanism of traumatic attachment and the psychopathogenesis of posttraumatic stress disorder. Australian and New Zealand Journal of Psychiatry, 2002; 36: 9–30.

47. Feldman R, Weller A, Eidelman A I, Sirota L. Testing a family intervention hypothesis: The contribution of mother-infant skin-to-skin contact (kangaroo care) to family interaction and touch. Journal of Family Psychology, 2003; 17(1): 94–107.

48. Fonagy, P. Transgenerational consistencies of attachment: a new theory. In: Paper to the Developmental and Psychoanalytic Discussion Group, American Psychoanalytic Association Meeting. 1999: Washington DC.

49. Fonagy P, Gergely G, Target M. The parent-infant dyad and the construction of the subjective self. Journal of Child Psychology and Psychiatry, 2007; 48(3–4): 288–328.

50. Uvnäs-Moberg K. Antistress pattern induced by oxytocins. News in Physiological Sciences, 1998; 13(1): 22–25.

51. Porges S W. Cardiac vagal tone: a physiological index of stress. Neuroscience & Biobehavioral Reviews, 1995; 19(2): 225–233.

52. Jensen-Urstad M, Jensen-Urstad K, Ericson M, Johansson J. Heart rate variability is related to leucocyte count in men and to blood lipoproteins in women in a healthy population of 35-year-old subjects. Journal of Internal Medicine, 1998; 243(1): 33–40.

53. Stern D N. The First Relationship: Infant and Mother. Cambridge, Massachusetts: Harvard University Press, 2002.

54. Milne A A, Shephard E H (illust.). The House at Pooh Corner. London: Methuen and Co., 1928.

55. Heal C, Cooper C. Other implications of disposable nappies. Archives of Diseases in Childhood, 2001; 85(3): 268.

56. Belsky J, Fearon R M. Early attachment security, subsequent maternal sensitivity, and later child development: Does continuity in development depend upon continuity of caregiving? Attachment & Human Development, 2002; 4(3): 361–387.

57.   Soderstrom M. Beyond babytalk: Re-evaluating the nature and content of speech input to preverbal infants. Developmental Review, 2007; 27(4): 501–532.

58.   van IJzendoorn M H, Dijkstra J, Bus A G. Attachment, intelligence, and language: a meta-analysis. Social Development, 2006; 4(2): 115–128.

59.   Tamis-LeMonda C S, Bornstein M H, Baumwell L. Maternal responsiveness and children's achievement of language milestones. Child Development, 2001; 72(3): 748–767.

60.   Magorian M. Goodnight Mister Tom. Great Britain: Puffin Books, 1981.

61.   Oddy W, Kendall G E, Li J et al. The long-term effects of breastfeeding on child and adolescent mental health: A pregnancy cohort study followed for 14 years. The Journal of Pediatrics, corrected proof published online December 2009.

62.   Winberg J. Mother and newborn baby: Mutual regulation of physiology and behavior — A selective review. Developmental Psychobiology, 2005: 47(3), 217–229.

63.   Blyth R, Creedy D K, Dennis C-L, Moyle W, Pratt J, De Vries S M. Effect of maternal confidence on breastfeeding duration: an application of breastfeeding self-efficacy theory. Birth, 2002; 29(4): 278–284.

64.   Doan T, Gardiner A, Gay CL, Lee KA. Breast-feeding increases sleep duration of new parents. Journal of Perinatal and Neonatal Nursing, 2007; 21(3): 200–206.

65.   Osborn D A, Sinn J K. The Cochrane Library and dietary prevention of allergic disease and food hypersensitivity in children: an umbrella review. Evidence-Based Child Health: A Cochrane Review Journal, 2007; 2(2): 541–552.

66.   Dörner G, Rodekamp E, Plagemann A. Maternal deprivation and overnutrition in early postnatal life and their primary prevention: historical reminiscence of an 'ecologic experiment' in Germany. Human Ontogenetics, 2008; 2(2): 51–59.

67.   Lauredhel. Flimsy. Wimpy. Weak. The Parliamentary Breastfeeding Inquiry Report. Hoyden About Town. Date Accessed: 16 November 2008. Available from:

hoydenabouttown.com/20070809.824/flimsy-wimpy-weak-the-parliamentary-breastfeeding-inquiry-report/.

68.   Gribble K D. Long-term breastfeeding: changing attitudes and overcoming challenges. Breastfeeding Review, 2008; 16(1): 5–15.

69.   Goodwin B, How The Leopard Changed Its Spots: The Evolution of Complexity. London: Weidenfeld & Nicholson, 1994.

70.   Marín-García J, Goldenthal M J, Moe G W. Aging and the Heart: A Post-Genomic View. New York: Springer, 2007, p. 574.

71.   Feinberg A P, Ohlsson R, Henikoff S. The epigenetic progenitor origin of human cancer. Nature Reviews Genetics, 2006; 7(1): 21–33.

72.   Oakes C C, La Salle S, Smiraglia D J, Robaire B, Trasler J M. A unique configuration of genome-wide DNA methylation patterns in the testis. Proceedings of the National Academy of Sciences of the United States of America, 2007; 104(1): 228–233.

73.   Danese A, Pariante, C M, Caspi A, Taylor A, Poulton R. Childhood maltreatment predicts adult inflammation in a life-course study. Proceedings of the National Academy of Sciences of the United States of America, 2007; 104: 1319–1324.

74.   Ridker P M. C-reactive protein and the prediction of cardiovascular events among those at intermediate risk: moving an inflammatory hypothesis toward consensus. Journal of the American College of Cardiology, 2007; 49: 2129–2138.

75.   Miller A H, Raison C L. Immune system contributions to the pathophysiology of depression. Focus, 2008; 6: 36–45.

76.   Pradhan A D, Manson J E, Rifai N, Buring J E, Ridker P M. Reactive protein, interleukin 6, and risk of developing type 2 diabetes mellitus. Journal of the American Medical Association, 2001; 286(3): 327–334.

77.   Gluckman P D, Hanson M A, Beedle A S. Early life events and their consequences for later disease: a life history and evolutionary perspective. American Journal of Human Biology, 2007; 19(1): 1–19.

78. Weaver I C G, Cervoni M, Champagne F A et al. Epigenetic programming by maternal behavior . Nature Neuroscience, 2004; 7(8): 847–854.

79. McGowan P O, Sasaki A, D'Alessio A C et al. Epigenetic regulation of the glucocorticoid receptor in human brain associates with childhood abuse. Nature Neuroscience, 2009; 12(3): 342–348.

80. Marcus G. Making the mind. The Boston Review, 2003/2004; 28(6): 32–35.

81. Perry B D. Incubated in terror: neurodevelopmental factors in the 'cycle of violence'. In: Children, Youth and Violence: The Search for Solutions, Osofsky J, ed. New York: Guilford Press, 1997, pp. 124–148.

82. Sly P, Hanna E, Giles-Corti B, Immig J, McMichael T. Environmental threats to the health of children in Australia: the need for a national research agenda. Australian Research Alliance for Children and Youth, 2008.

83. Stanley F. The greatest injustice: why we have failed to improve the health of Aboriginal people. 2008 Annual Hawke Lecture, Adelaide Town Hall: The Bob Hawke Prime Ministerial Centre.

Part 3

1. Goddard S. The Well-Balanced Child. Stroud: Hawthorn Press, 2003.

2. Goudge E. The Heart of the Family. London: Hodder and Stoughton, 1953.

3. Ilg F L, Ames L D. The Gessell Institute's Child Behavior. New York: Dell, 1961.

4. Milne A A. When We Were Very Young. Suffolk, Great Britain: The Chaucer Press, 1924.

5. Taylor M, Houghton S, Chapman E. Primitive reflexes and attention–deficit/hyperactivity disorder: developmental origins of classroom dysfunction. International Journal of Special Education, 2004; 19(1): 23–37.

6. McPhillips M, Jordan-Black L A. The effect of social disadvantage on motor development in young children: a

comparative study. Journal of Child Psychology and Psychiatry and Allied Disciplines, 2007; 48(12): 1214–1222.

7. Thompson P. 'Down will come baby': prenatal stress, primitive defences and gestational dysregulation. Journal of Trauma & Dissociation, 2007; 8(3): 85–114.

8. Goddard S. Reflexes, Learning and Behaviour: A Window Into The Child's Mind. Eugene, Oregon: Fern Ridge Press, 2002.

9. Froebel F. Mother Play, The International Education Series, Volume XXXI. New York and London: D. Appleton and Company, 1912.

10. Garlick D. The Lost Sixth Sense: A Medical Scientist Looks at the Alexander Technique. Kensington, NSW: Laboratory for Musculoskeletal and Postural Research, School of Physiology and Pharmacology, the University of New South Wales, 1990.

11. Teitelbaum P, Teitelbaum O, Nye J, Fryman J, Maurer R G. Movement analysis in infancy may be useful for early diagnosis of autism Proceedings of the National Academy of Sciences of the United States of America, 1998; 95(23): 13982–13987.

12. Fagard J, Monzalvo-Lopez K, Mamassian P. Relationship between eye preference and binocular rivalry, and between eye-hand preference and reading ability in children. Developmental Psychobiology, 2008; 50(8): 789–798.

13. Winberg J. Mother and newborn baby: Mutual regulation of physiology and behavior — a selective review. Developmental Psychobiology, 2005; 47(3): 217–229.

14. Thelen E, Fisher D M, Ridley-Johnson R, Griffin N J. Effects of body build and arousal on newborn infant stepping. Developmental Psychobiology, 1982: 15(5), 447–453.

15. Dietz V. Spinal cord pattern generators for locomotion. Clinical Neurophysiology, 2003; 114: 1379–1389.

Part 4

1. Axline V M. Dibs, In Search Of Self. London: Penguin Books, 1964.

2.	DeJong M, Sendak M (illust.). The Wheel on the School. Great Britain: Puffin Books, 1961.

3.	Ananthaswamy A. Language may be key to theory of mind, *The New Scientists*, 23 June 2009.

4.	Hobson P. The Cradle of Thought: Exploring the origins of thinking. London: Pan Macmillan, 2004.

5.	Zimmerman F, Christakis D, Meltzoff A. Associations between media viewing and language development in children under age 2 years. The Journal of Pediatrics, 2007; 151(4): 364–368.

6.	Moore C, Mealiea J, Garon N, Povinelli D J. The development of body self-awareness. Infancy, 2006; 11(2): 157–174.

7.	Focquaert F, Braeckman J, Platek S M. An evolutionary cognitive neuroscience perspective on human self-awareness and theory of mind. Philosophical Psychology, 2008; 21(1): 47–68.

8.	Cooper P M. Literacy learning and pedagogical purpose in Vivian Paley's 'storytelling curriculum'. Journal of Early Childhood Literacy, 2005; 5(3): 229–251.

9.	Paley V G. The Boy Who Would Be a Helicopter: Uses of Storytelling in the Classroom. Harvard: Harvard University Press, 1991.

10.	Fletcher K L. Picture book reading with young children: A conceptual framework. Developmental Review, 2005; 25(1): 64–103.

11.	McGuiness D. Growing A Reader From Birth. New York: W. W. Norton & Company, 2004.

12.	Ramus F, White S, Frith U. Reply to peer commentary: weighing the evidence between competing theories of dyslexia. Developmental Science, 2006; 9(3): 265–269.

13.	Nicolson R I, Fawcett A J. Do cerebellar deficits underlie phonological problems in dyslexia? Developmental Science, 2006; 9(3): 259–262.

14.	Reynolds D, Nicolson R I. Follow-up of an exercise-based treatment for children with reading difficulties. Dyslexia, 2007; 13(2): 78–96.

15.	Covey S R. The 7 Habits of Highly Effective People. New York: Simon and Schuster, 1989.

16. Pliszka S R, Liotti M, Woldorff M G. Inhibitory control in children with attention-deficit/hyperactivity disorder: event-related potentials identify the processing component and timing of an impaired right-frontal response-inhibition mechanism. Biological Psychiatry, 2000; 48(3): 238–246.

17. Sung J H, Dice J, Hsu, H-C. Developmental links of infant temperament to attachment security and behavioral adjustment assessed in toddlerhood. Paper presented at XVth Biennial International Conference on Infant Studies, 2006: Westin Miyako, Kyoto, Japan.

18. Dixon W E, Hull Smith P. Who's controlling whom? Infant contributions to maternal play behaviour. Infant and Child Development, 2003; 12: 177–195.

19. Wachs T D, McCare R R, Kohnstamm G A, eds. Temperament in Context. Mahwah, New Jersey: Lawrence Erlbaum, 2001.

20. Wachs T D. Nature of relations between the physical and social microenvironment of the two-year-old child. Early Development and Parenting, 2006; 2(2): 81–87.

21. Schmidt M E, Pempek T A, Kirkorian H L, Lund A F, Anderson D R. The effects of background television on the toy play behavior of very young children. Child Development, 2008; 79(4): 1137–1151.

22. Brocki K C, Randall K D, Bohlin G, Kerns K A. Working memory in school-aged children with attention-deficit/hyperactivity disorder combined type: Are deficits modality specific and are they independent of impaired inhibitory control? Journal of Clinical and Experimental Neuropsychology, 2008; 30(7): 749–759.

23. Juster N. The Phantom Tollbooth. London: Collins, 1974.

24. Goddard S. Reflexes, Learning and Behaviour: A Window Into The Child's Mind. Eugene, Oregon: Fern Ridge Press, 2002.

25. Frick S M, Hacker C. Listening With The Whole Body. Madison: Vital Links, 2002.

26. Yeh S S, Connnel D B. Effects of rhyming, vocabulary and phonemic awareness instruction on phoneme awareness. Journal of Research in Reading, 2008; 31(2): 243–256.

27.   Smith S L, Scott K A, Roberts J, Locke J L. Disabled readers'
        performance on tasks of phonological processing, rapid
        naming, and letter knowledge before and after kindergarten.
        Learning Disabilities Research & Practice, 2008; 23(3):
        113–124.

28.   Rigg D. Workshop Promoting Literacy Development.
        Geraldton, Western Australia, April 2007.

29.   Winberg J. Mother and newborn baby: Mutual regulation
        of physiology and behavior — A selective review.
        Developmental Psychobiology, 2005: 47(3), 217–229.

30.   Marlier L, Gaugler C, Messer J. Olfactory stimulation
        prevents apnea in premature newborns. Pediatrics, 2005;
        115(1): 83–88.

31.   Sullivan T E, Schefft B K, Warm J S, Dember W N, O'Dell
        M W, Peterson S J. Recent advances in the neuropsychology
        of human olfaction and anosmia. Brain Injury, 1995; 9(6):
        641–646.

32.   Park R, Young N (illust.). The Muddle-headed Wombat at
        School. Sydney: Angus and Robertson, 1966.

33.   Putnam S P, Stifter C A. Reactivity and regulation: The
        impact of Mary Rothbart on the study of temperament.
        Infant and Child Development, 2008; 17: 311–320.

34.   Rothbart M K, Ahadi S A, Hershey K L, Fisher P.
        Investigations of temperament at three to seven years: the
        children's behavior questionnaire. Child Development,
        2001; 72(5): 1394–1408.

35.   Pesonen A-K, Raikkonen K, Heinonen K et al. Transactional
        development of parent personality and child temperament.
        European Journal of Personality, 2008; 22(6): 553–573.

36.   Ilg F L, Ames L D. The Gessell Institute's Child Behavior.
        New York: Dell, 1961.

Part 5

1.   Cited in 'School Readiness', Australian Research Alliance
        for Children and Youth, 2007. Prepared by Dr Estelle Farrar,
        Dr Sharon Goldfied and Dr Tim Moore.

2.   Frances Lillian Ilg and Louise Bates Ames, The Gessell
        Institute's *Child Behavior*, 1961.

3.   Talcott J B, Witton C, Hebb G S et al. On the relationship between dynamic visual and auditory processing and literacy skills; results from a large primary-school study. Dyslexia, 2002; 8: 204–225.

4.   Office for Standards in Education. The education of six year olds in England, Denmark and Finland: an international comparative study. Education, 2003.

5.   Organisation for Economic Co-operation and Development. First results from PISA 2003: executive summary. In PISA 2003 Reports. Paris: OECD, 2003.

6.   Knickerbocker B M. A Holistic Approach to the Treatment of Learning Disorders. Thorofare, New Jersey: Slack Incorporated, 1980.

7.   Bristow P. The new era of singing training. In: Why breakthrough methods can dramatically improve your voice — faster than you ever knew possible, 2008. Available at www.perbristow.com

8.   Fagard J, Monzalvo-Lopez K, Mamassian P. Relationship between eye preference and binocular rivalry, and between eye-hand preference and reading ability in children. Developmental Psychobiology, 2008; 50(8): 789–798.

9.   Camarata S, Woodcock R. Sex differences in processing speed: developmental effects in males and females. Intelligence, 2006; 34(3): 231–252.

10.   Durand M, Hulme C, Larkin R, Snowling M. The cognitive foundations of reading and arithmetic skills in 7- to 10-year-olds. Journal of Experimental Child Psychology, 2005; 91: 113–136.

11.   Volker M A, Lopata C, Cook-Cottone C. Assessment of children with intellectual giftedness and reading disabilities. Psychology in the Schools, 2006; 43(8): 855–870.

12.   Vuontela V, Steenari M-R, Carlson S. Audiospatial and visuospatial working memory in 6 to 13 year old school children. Learning & Memory, 2003; 10: 74–81.

13.   Richardson U, Thomson J M, Scott S K, Goswami U. Auditory processing skills and phonological representation in dyslexic children. Dyslexia, 2003; 10(3): 215–233.

14. Kephart N C. The slow learner in the classroom. Columbus, Ohio: Charles E. Merrill Books, 1971.

15. Meyler A, Breznitz Z. Visual, auditory and cross-modal processing of linguistic and nonlinguistic temporal patterns among adult dyslexic readers. Dyslexia, 2005; 11(2): 93–115.

16. Rubia K, Halari R, Christakou A, Taylor E. Impulsiveness as a timing disturbance: neurocognitive abnormalities in attention-deficit hyperactivity disorder during temporal processes and normalization with methylphenidate Philosphical Transactions of the Royal Society of Biological Sciences, 2009; 364(1525): 1919–1931.

17. Overy K, Nicolson R I, Fawcett A J, Clarke E F. Dyslexia and music: measuring musical timing skills. Dyslexia, 2003; 9(1): 18–36.

18. Kipling R. Just So Stories for Little Children. London: Macmillan and Co., 1950.

19. Rigg D. Workshop Promoting Literacy Development. Carnarvon, Western Australia. February 2010.

20. Butterworth B, Reeve R, Reynolds F, Lloyd D. Numerical thought with and without words: Evidence from indigenous Australian children. Proceedings of the National Academy of Sciences of the United States of America, 2008; 105(35): 13179–13184.

21. Ehri L C. Learning to read and learning to spell: two sides of a coin. Topics in Language Disorders, 2000; 20(3): 19–36.

22. Cooke A. Learning to spell difficult words: why look, cover, write and check is not enough. Dyslexia, 1997; 3: 240–243.

23. Evans M A, Shaw D. Home grown for reading: parental contributions to young children's emergent literacy and word recognition. Canadian Psychology, 2008; 49(2): 89–95.

24. Duff J. Dealing with the reluctant writer. Workshop: Geraldton, Western Australia, 2008.

25. Mahy M, Horse H (illust.). A Villain's Night Out. London: Puffin Books, 1999.

26. Gumpel T P. Are social competence difficulties caused by performance or acquisition deficits? The importance of self-regulatory mechanisms. Psychology in the Schools, 2007; 44(4): 351–372.

27. Warnes E D, Sheridan S M, Geske J, Warnes W A. A contextual approach to the assessment of social skills: Identifying meaningful behaviors for social competence. Psychology in the Schools, 2005; 42(2): 173–187.

28. Hane A A, Cheah C, Rubin K H, Fox N A. The role of maternal behavior in the relation between shyness and social reticence in early childhood and social withdrawal in middle childhood. Social Development, 2008; 17(4): 795–811.

29. Lucas-Thompson R, Clarke-Stewart K. Forecasting friendship: How marital quality, maternal mood, and attachment security are linked to children's peer relationships. Journal of Applied Developmental Psychology, 2007; 28(5/6): 499–514.

30. Zunshine L. *Why We Read Fiction: Theory of Mind and the Novel.* Columbus Ohio: Ohio State University Press, 2006.

31. Rigby K, Slee P T. Australia. In: The nature of school bullying, Catalano R, Junger-Tas J, Morita Y, eds. London: Routledge, 1999, 324–329.

32. Berger K S. Update on bullying at school: Science forgotten? Developmental Review, 2007; 27(1): 90–126.

33. Finkelhor D, Turner H, Ormrod R. Kid's stuff: The nature and impact of peer and sibling violence on younger and older children. Child Abuse & Neglect, 2006; 30(12): 1401–1421.

34. Thompson M, O'Neill-Grace C, Cohen L J. Best Friends, Worst Enemies: Understanding the Social Lives of Children. New York: Ballantine Books, 2001.

35. Woods S, White E. The association between bullying behaviour, arousal levels and behaviour problems. Journal of Adolescence, 2005; 28(3): 381–395.

36. Monks C P, Smith P K, Swettenham J. Psychological correlates of peer victimisation in preschool: social cognitive skills, executive function and attachment profiles. Aggressive Behavior, 2005; 31(6): 571–588.

37. Modry-Mandell K L, Gamble W C, Taylor A R. Family emotional climate and sibling relationship quality: influences on behavioral problems and adaptation in preschool-aged children. Journal of Child and Family Studies, 2007; 16(1): 61–73.

38.   Idsoe T, Solli E, Cosmovici E M. More evidence on their relative etiological significance for bullying behavior. Aggressive Behavior, 2008; 34: 460–474.

39.   Rohde P A, Atzwanger K, Butovskaya M et al. Perceived parental favoritism, closeness to kin, and the rebel of the family: the effects of birth order and sex. Evolution and Human Behavior, 2003; 24(4): 261–276.

40.   Lamarche V, Brendgen M. Boivin M, Vitaro F, Pérusse D, Dionne G. Do friendships and sibling relationships provide protection against peer victimization in a similar way? Social Development, 2006; 15(3): 373–393.

41.   Wolke D, Samara M M. Bullied by siblings: association with peer victimisation and behaviour problems in Israeli lower grades. Journal of Child Psychology and Psychiatry, 2004; 45(5): 1015–1029.

42.   Rhode P. Perceived parental favoritism, closeness to kin, and the rebel of the family: the effects of birth order and sex. Evolution and human behaviour, 2003; 24(4): 261–276.

43.   Froebel F. Mother Play, The International Education Series, Volume XXXI. New York and London: D. Appleton and Company, 1912.

44.   van Duijvenvoorde A C K, Zanolie K, Rombouts S A R B, Raijmakers M E J, Crone E. Evaluating the negative or valuing the positive? Neural mechanisms supporting feedback-based learning across development. The Journal of Neuroscience, 2008; 28(38): 9495–9503.

45.   Csikszentmihalyi M, Csikszentmihalyi I S. Optimal Experience: Psychological Studies of Flow in Consciousness. Cambridge, England: Cambridge University Press, 1988.

46.   Laible D J, Thompson R A. Mother–child discourse, attachment security, shared positive affect, and early conscience development. Child Development, 2000; 71(5): 1424–1440.

47.   Oppenheim D, Koren-Kari N, Sagi-Schwartz A. Emotion dialogues between mothers and children at 4.5 and 7.5 years: relations with children's attachment at 1 year. Child Development, 2007; 78(1): 38–52.

48. Fiese B H, Hooker K A, Kotary L, Schwagler J and Rimmer M. Family stories in the early stages of parenthood. Journal of Marriage and the Family, 1995; 57(3): 763–770.

49. de Rosnay M, Harris P L. Individual differences in children's understanding of emotion: the roles of attachment and language. Attachment and Human Development, 2002; 4: 39–54.

50. Garner P W, Dunsmore, J C, Southam-Gerrow M. Mother–child conversations about emotions: linkages to child aggression and prosocial behaviour. Social Development, 2008; 17(2): 259–277.

51. Goleman D. Working With Emotional Intelligence. New York: Bantam Books, 1998.

52. Bernard M E, Stephanou A, Urbach D. ASG student social and emotional health report. Australian Council for Educational Research. Australian Scholarships Group 2007.

53. Ilg F L, Ames L D. *The Gessell Institute's Child Behavior.* New York: Dell, 1961.

Appendices

1. Blunden S L, Chervin R D. Sleep problems are associated with poor outcomes in remedial teaching programmes: A preliminary study. Journal of Paediatrics and Child Health, 2007; 44(5): 237–242.

2. Gau S S F, Kessler R C, Tseng W L et al. Association between sleep problems and symptoms of attention-deficit/hyperactivity disorder in young adults. Sleep, 2007; 30(2): 195–201.

3. Barclay L, Murata P. Sleep duration in 7-year-old children varies among individuals. Sleep, 2008; 31(1): 71–78.

4. Touchette E, Petit D, Tremblay R et al. Associations between sleep duration patterns and overweight/obesity at age 6. Sleep, 2008; 31(11): 1507–1514.

5. Eggermont S, Van den Bulck J. Nodding off or switching off? The use of popular media as a sleep aid in secondary-school children. Journal of Paediatrics and Child Health, 2006; 42(7–8): 428–433.

6. Pheloung B. School floors. Sydney: Iceform Pty Ltd, 2006.

7.   Hart K, Bishop J, Truby H. Changing children's diets: developing methods and messages. Journal of Human Nutrition and Dietitics, 2003; 16: 365–370.

8.   Wake M J, Nicholson J M et al. Preschooler obesity and parenting styles of mothers and fathers: Australian national population study. Pediatrics, 2007; 120(60): e1520–1527.

9.   Allen, J, Director of the Geraldton Regional Community Education Centre. Resilience Workshop, Geraldton, Western Australia: April 2009.

10.   Simons R C. Boo! Culture, experience and the startle reflex. New York and Oxford: Oxford University Press, 1996.

11.   Whittle S, Yap M B, Yücel M et al. Prefrontal and amygdala volumes are related to adolescents' affective behaviors during parent–adolescent interactions. Proceedings of the National Academy of Sciences, 2008; 105(9): 3652–3657.

12.   Taylor M, Houghton S, Chapman E. Primitive reflexes and attention-deficit/hyperactivity disorder: developmental origins of classroom dysfunction. International Journal of Special Education, 2004; 19(1): 23–37.

13.   Kaada B. Why is there an increased risk for sudden infant death in prone sleeping? Fear paralysis and atrial stretch reflexes implicated? Acta Pædiatrica, 2000; 83(5): 548–557.

14.   Goddard S. Reflexes, Learning and Behaviour: A Window Into The Child's Mind. Eugene, Oregon: Fern Ridge Press, 2002.

15.   Hepper P, Dornan J, Little J. Maternal alcohol consumption during pregnancy may delay the development of spontaneous fetal startle behaviour. Physiology & behaviour, 2005; 83(5): 711–714.

16.   O'Connor M J, Sigman M, Brill N. Disorganization of attachment in relation to maternal alcohol consumption. Journal of Consulting and Clinical Psychology, 1987; 55(6): 831–836.

17.   Kiss P, Tamas A, Lubics M et al. Development of neurological reflexes and motor coordination in rats neonatally treated with monosodium glutamate. Neurotoxicity Research, 2005; 8(3–4): 235–244.

18.   Thayer J F, Friedman B H, Ruiz-Padial E. Neurovisceral

integration, emotions and health: An update. International Congress Series, 2006; 1287: 122–127.

19.   Parmenter C L. The Asymmetric Tonic Neck Reflex in normal first and third grade children. American Journal of Occupational Therapy, 1975; 29(8): 463–468.

20.   White S, Milne E, Rosen S et al. The role of sensorimotor impairments in dyslexia: a multiple case study of dyslexic children. Developmental Science, 2006; 9(3): 237–242.

21.   McPhillips M, Jordan-Back J A. Primary reflex persistence in children with reading difficulties (dyslexia): a cross-sectional study. Neuropsychologia, 2007; 45(4): 748–754.

22.   Cruddace S A, Riddell P M. Attention processes in children with movement difficulties, reading difficulties or both. Journal of Abnormal Child Psychology, 2006; 34(5): 672–680.

23.   Kooistra L, Crawford S, Dewey D, Cantell M, Kaplan B J. Motor correlates of ADHD: contribution of reading disability and oppositional defiant disorder. Journal of Learning Disabilities, 2005; 38(3): 195–206.

24.   Willcutt E G, Olson R K, Chhabildas N, Hulslander J. Neuropsychological analyses of comorbidity between reading disability and attention deficit hyperactivity disorder: in search of the common deficit. Developmental Neuropsychology, 2005; 27(1): 35–78.

25.   Deutsch G K, Dougherty R F, Bammer R, Siok W T, Gabrieli J D, Wandell B. Children's reading performance is correlated with white matter structure measured by diffusion tensor imaging. Cortex, 2005; 41(3): 354–363.

26.   Ben-Shachar D R, Wandell B A, White matter pathways in reading. Current Opinion in Neurobiology, 2007; 17: 258–270.

27.   Jordan-Black J A. The effects of the Primary Movement programme on the academic performance of children attending ordinary primary school. Journal of Research in Special Educational Needs, 2005; 5(3): 101–111.

28.   Sallenbach W B. Claira: A case study in prenatal learning. Journal of Pre- & Perinatal Psychology and Health, 1998; 12(3–4): 175–196.

29. Knickerbocker B M. A Holistic Approach to the Treatment of Learning Disorders. Thorofare, New Jersey: Slack Incorporated, 1980.

30. Desantis A, Coster W, Bigsby R, Lester B. Colic and fussing in infancy, and sensory processing at 3 to 8 years of age. Infant Mental Health Journal, 2004; 25(6): 522–539.

31. Posner M, ed. Cognitive Neuroscience of Attention. New York, The Guilford Press: 2004.

32. Stephens C L, Royeen C B. Investigation of tactile defensiveness and self-esteem in typically developing children. Occupational Therapy International, 1988; 5(4): 273–280.

33. Ackerman C M. Identifying gifted adolescents using personality characteristics: Dabrowski's overexcitabilities. Roeper Review 1997; 19(4): 229–236.

34. Muratori F. Early indicators of autism spectrum disorders. Zero To Three, 2008; March: 18–23.

35. Frick S M, Hacker C. Listening With The Whole Body. Madison: Vital Links, 2002.

36. Marlier L, Gaugler C, Messer J. Olfactory stimulation prevents apnea in premature newborns. Pediatrics, 2005; 115(1): 83–88.

37. Sullivan T E, Schefft B K, Warm J S, Dember W N, O'Dell M W, Peterson S J. Recent advances in the neuropsychology of human olfaction and anosmia. Brain Injury, 1995; 9(6): 641–646.

38. Romanos M, Renner T J, Schecklmann M et al. Improved odor sensitivity in attention-deficit/hyperactivity disorder. Biological Psychiatry, 2008; 64(11): 938–940.

39. McGuiness D. Growing A Reader From Birth. New York: W. W. Norton & Company, 2004.

40. Swallow G. Teach Your Child To Spell. Burwood: Dellasta, 1998.

Acknowledgements

This book wouldn't have happened at all without other people.

Without being asked to write such a book by Jo Mackay I wouldn't have thought to try.

Without my mother – a very experienced occupational therapist who can usually answer the curliest questions from parents – I'd never have had the nerve to take up the opportunity.

Without the encouragement of Associate Professor Ivan Lin at the Combined Universities Centre for Rural Health I'd not have had the confidence to undertake the research required.

Without my husband, Martin, my mum and dad and my three sons helping with such things as meals, housework and running the schoolroom, and their willingness to discuss child development at length and their faith that this book will be helpful to other people – I'd have given it away half a dozen times.

This book is a synthesis not just of the research but of other people's experience. I've talked to many people over the years about multiple generations in their families; to many clinicians, teachers and parents about children and, of course, to children themselves. The following people have challenged and shaped my ideas and, while I'm sure they don't all entirely agree with me, I'd like to thank them very much.

The parents, grandparents and child development aficionados: Stephanie and Bradley Degens, Megan Jackson and Adrian Cutler, Sally Mather, Kathryn Bryson, Lisa Crake, Bevan and Noelene Turner (who made me wonder about the real story of the human heart), Jenny and Greg Watters, David and Ann Anderson, Chandra Ridley, David and Tracy Bent (for giving me a practical perspective on childcare), Bernard and Di Bent (specially for her insights into boys), Greg and Cindy Payne, Caroline and Simon Thomas, Mark and Carolyn Halleen, Rebecca Handcock and Michael O'Brien, Fe Waters and Shay Telfer, Quentin and Shelly Fowler, Emma and Rossco Foulkes-Taylor, Sue Wilding, Jo Johnson, Rob and Ros Gillam, Daniel

Oi, Bridget Cameron, Emma Hawkes, Kate and Bill Moses, Elaine Sharplin, Robin and Alec Edgar, Kathy and David Lovelock, Christine and Christopher Gillam, Philippa and John Bostock, Mia Bostock, Darren Longbottom and Frances Brigg, Anna Hepburn and Art Diggle, Minnie and Nick Sabatino, David Chandler and Lara Hopkins, Christina Orow, Elizabeth Bowyer, Stuart Hill, Tanya Brown, Penny Johns, Rosie O'Connor, Maria and Geoff Pocock, Tracie Blair, Annette Prendergast, Sharon and Glen Grey, Sheryl Major, Ernie Stringer and Rosalie Dwyer, Penny and David Giorgi, Katie and Peter Jeffries, Lian and Patrick Walsh, Nita Human, Des and Phyllis Thompson, Tanya Lupton, Gina Goddard and Terry Chilvers, Merete Osborne and Paul Talbot, Kerry and George Hamilton, Jenny and Andrew Bailey, Sarah Xu, Margaret Watts, Sandra Norman and Deborah Costello, Sue Hamilton, Gladys King, Dave Cake and Karen McKenna, Elizabeth Jackson and Lynette Gillam.

The colleagues: Glenda Pitman, Helen Webb, Brendin Flanigan, Amanda Jackson, Margaret Oakley, Alma Dender (for helping me place sensory-motor theory within an attachment framework), Cathie Gillzan, Tania Wiley, Gary Davies, Meg Roche, Steph Bateman-Graham, Debbie Dowden, Sharyn May, Florence Robinson, Rebekka Sinclair, Karren Wood, John McCloy, Jim Peletier, Mike Henderson, Annette Evans, Ann Larson, Ariane Van Der Peyl, Marg Dines, Sue Van Uden, Phillip Gardiner, Karen Morissey, June Doyle, Mary Ash, Lyndy Richmond, Judy Young, Clive Reardon, Mandy Mitchell, Melinda Croke, Rebecca Smythe, Libby Lodge, Davina Fraser, Dorothy Stephens, Winsome Richards and Marissa Don.

The Combined University Centre for Rural Health, the Health Department of WA Library and the Education Department of Western Australia between them gave me access to books and journals from around the world. The In-Home Care Scheme has meant that the family business could afford for me to write this book: thank you Frontier Services, Ranitha Rachindar and Lesley de Grussa-Macaulay.

Thank you too to all my editors and readers for their detailed critiques, patience and intuitively-timed encouragement – Jo Mackay most of all, but also Ali Lavau, Megan Jackson, Tom Jackson, Glenda Downing, Jessica Dettmann and Catherine Page. Jessica, Catherine and indexer Susie Easton are all pregnant as I write – very serendipitous as knowing your own baby is coming makes child development fascinating – and they have brought an extraordinary degree of care and attention to getting this book right. The wonderful cover and book design are by Jane Waterhouse.

Finally, the practical wisdom of this book is due mostly to my mother Barbara – any mistakes are mine.

Index

WHO code of practice for
formulas, 109
Brain
effect of parenthood on, 33–6
engaging right brain, 271
epigenetics and right brain,
116-17
left brain, 123, 168
movement and right brain, 123
right brain, 35–6
right brain dysfunction, 269
right brain growth, 36–7, 52, 59,
96, 123
use dependent organ, 79
Breastfeeding, 104–11
attaching correctly, 105–6
benefits of, 104, 111, 133, 142
confidence, 108
cracked nipples, 106
decrease among Australian
women, 105, 109
decreasing milk supply, 107, 110
disinformation about, 107–8
empathy and, 104
feeding baby to sleep, 108
harassment in public, 108
help with, 106, 107, 111
information about, 111
mastitis, 106
paid maternity leave and, 109
problems with, 107, 110
pumping to boost supply, 110
reading to toddler while, 178
return to work and, 109
sleep and, 108
thrush, 106
Bullying, 242–8
aggression and, 243–4
awkwardness and, 282
behavioural, 243
dealing with the school, 248
insecure attachment and, 27, 32,
244
low self-esteem and, 14, 243

physical, 243
poor impulse control and, 64
'pure' bully, 244
relational/verbal, 243
reporting, 248
siblings, 244–8
'Bunny roll', 140–1

Catecholamines, 6, 66
Child becoming caregiver, 17, 29–31
Childcare, 51–5
attachment of carers, 54
centre-based, 54
effect on attachment, 51–2
impact on children, 52–5
mentors for parents, 52
moving between different
settings, 55
quality in Australia, 54
temperamentally vulnerable
children, 55
Childhood experiences of parent,
7–10, 28, 38
ghosts of the past, 38–40
preoccupied parenting, 28–31,
277–8
Child's perspective, 5, 21, 22
Chores see Household chores
Circle of Security parenting
approach, 39, 40
Clingy children, 28, 31–2
Colicky babies, 68–73
back time, 145
heart calming technique for
mother, 90
highly susceptible children, 70–2
'parenting to sleep', 73
parents' belief about colic, 71–3
temperament and, 70–1
tips for sensitive parenting, 73
treatment, 69–70
Communication see also Language
skills
development, 177–84

self-regulation skills impaired, 19
thinking skills impaired, 169
Dominant eye, 218, 219, 299, 322
Dominant hand, 151–3, 218, 220,
    322
Duff, Judith, 232
Dummy, 143
Dyslexia, 217, 223, 293
    asymmetrical tonic neck reflex
        and, 293
    impaired timing skills, 223
    movement difficulties and, 293
    processing speed, 217

Eating *see* Food
Eight year olds, 260
Emotional connection, 5
Emotional signature, 114
Emotions, 6
    baby learning about, 100
    child amplifying, 28, 29
    child hiding, 24
    embryo feeling, 113–14
    learning difficulties and, 14
    movement skills impacted by, 13
    parent not responding, 24–8
    parent responding
        inappropriately, 29
    parent showing understanding,
        41–4
    'states become traits', 6
Empathy, xv, 87–96
    babies learning, 5, 87–96, 100
    breastfeeding and, 104
    childcare and, 54
    chores helping grow, 253
    dismissive parent not showing, 27
    friendship skills, 233
    heart, starting with, 88–91
    impulse control and, 87
    insecure attachment and lack of,
        27
    integrated body and mind, 123
    perceptual sensitivity and, 195

play improving, 175
showing understanding to child,
    41–3
Enforcing rules, 17, 18
Environment, 264–8
Epigenetics, 112–20
    abuse in childhood, effect, 115
    changes during pregnancy,
        113–14
    DNA sequence, 112
    emotional signature, 114
    environment where baby
        conceived, effect, 114–15
    epigenetic marks, 112, 113, 115
    inflammatory markers, 114
    relationships and, 115–16
    relevance to parents, 113
    reversibility of epigenetic marks,
        115
    societal pressures on parents,
        117–20
Eye movements, 219
    convergence, 323
    developing skills, 322–4
    dominant eye, 219, 299, 322
    reading and, 219, 322
    visual perception and, 220

Fair play, teaching, 237–9
Fatigue
    new mothers, 56–9
Fear, 15–17, 78
    parents' behaviour causing, 16–
        17
Fear paralysis reflex, 285–6
Financial problems
    harsh parenting and, 46
Five to six year olds
    attention and concentration, 192
    stage of development, 210
'Flow' experiences, 254–5
Focus on behaviour, not child, 42,
    44
Food, 264–6

Formula *see* Bottle feeding
Four to five year olds
    attention and concentration, 192
    stage of development, 209
Friendship, 233–9
    exclusivity, 238–9
    line between 'funny' and
        'hurtful', 239
    shy children, 234–5
    teaching good skills, 233–7
Frightened parents, 16
Frightening parents, 15, 45, 47
Fussiness, 127

Games *see* Play
Gazing at baby, 91–6
    baby's sense of self and, 91–6
    premature baby, 92–3
Gesell Institute's behavioural stages,
    125
    birth to one year, 125–6
    one to two years, 126–7
    two to three years, 127–8
    three to four, 208–9
    four to five years, 209–10
    five to six years, 210
    six to seven years, 210
    eight years, 260
    nine years, 260
    ten years, 260
Ghosts of the past, 38–40, 226
Gifted children, 254, 313
Ginott, Haim, 11, 40–50, 183, 256,
    272
Goddard, Sally, 285
Grasping, 141–7

Hand and eye skills, 218, 322–4
Hand dominance, 151–3, 218, 220,
    322
Harrison, Dr Linda, 54
Harsh parenting, 44–7, 186
    impulse control, difficulty with, 47
    marital/financial trouble and, 46

negative opinion of child and, 46
warning against, 44
Hearing, sense of, 203–4
    defensiveness, 310, 318
    dormancy, 310, 318
    helping child develop, 318–19
Heart
    baby and mother's heart beat,
        88, 89, 94
    biofeedback, 90
    calming technique, 90
    disease, 114, 116
    empathy starting with, 88–91
    epigenetics and, 116–17
    highly variable, 88
    inflammatory markers and heart
        disease, 114
    stress affecting, 89–90
Highly reactive children, 70, 71
Highly sensitive children, 70, 71
Highly stressed children, 114
Highly susceptible children, 70–2,
    81
Hormones
    cortisol (stress), 6, 65, 66
    oxytocin (love), 6, 34, 94, 95,
        134, 266
Household chores
    fairness, teaching, 238
    impulse control, 162
    organised attachment, 17, 256
    reward for effort, 255
    self-regulation skills, growing,
        253
    walking practice, 162–3
    work, teaching child to, 253
Hyperactivity, 269

Impulse control, xiv, 63–73,
    185–93
    attention and concentration,
        188–93
    babies, 67–70
    bullying and, 64

Moro reflex *see* Startle reflex
Motherhood
    anxiety and fatigue, 56–9
    effect on brain, 33–6
    mothering new mothers, 59
    postnatal depression, 55–9
Motivation
    reading, 328–9
    toilet training, 250–1
Movement skills
    attachment and, 124
    baby equipment affecting,
        137
    back time, 145–7
    balance and vision, linking,
        143–4, 158
    behaviour shaped by, 125
    birth to one year, 125–6
    concentration span and, 124
    controlling head, 128
    crawling, 130, 153–60
    disorganised attachment,
        impacted by, 13, 124
    four to five years, 209
    grasping, 141–7
    hand–eye coordination, 145
    hands, eyes and ears, linking,
        144–5
    importance of, 123–34
    impulse control and, 124
    insecure attachment, impacted
        by, 124
    integrated body and mind, 123
    inward journey, 123
    neck muscle receptor sensitivity,
        138–9
    one to two years, 126–7
    perceptual sensitivity and, 124
    reflexes *see* Reflexes
    resisting gravity, 136
    right brain growth, 123
    rolling, 135–41
    secure, organised attachment
        and, 124

    sitting, 148–53
    social disadvantage and poor
        skills, 129
    startle reflex and, 128–30, 132–4
    straightening out, 135–6
    three to four years, 209
    tummy time, 139
    two to three years, 127–8
    walking, 160–3
MSG during pregnancy, 286
Music
    reading and, 222–4
    singing to baby, 80, 82–3, 99,
        103, 156, 204

Nature and nurture, 116
Neck muscle receptor sensitivity,
    138–9
Negative feedback, 45
    children under 11 not learning
        from, 45, 252
    toilet training, 252
Negative opinion of child, 46
Nine year olds, 260
Non-maternal care, 52–5
Number concepts, 227–9

Obesity, 265
Oculo-headrighting reflex, 138,
    140
Olfactory system, 202–3, 308
    defensiveness, 308, 316
    dormancy, 305, 308, 316
    helping child develop, 316–17
One to two year olds
    attention and concentration,
        191–2
    stage of development, 126–7
Organised attachment, 11, 12
    childcare workers, 54
    enforcing rules, 17, 18
    household chores, 17, 256
    impulse control and, 186
    movement skills and, 124

teaching children to amuse
themselves, 188
tummy time, 139
Positive feedback, 45
Postnatal depression, 55–9
anxiety and fatigue, 56–8
feeling alone, 58–9
insecure attachment, 55
support of partner, 55–6, 118
whole family affected, 58
Praise, 48–50, 256
appreciative, 48
child becoming hooked on, 49
child's evaluation of, 49
effect on child, 48
evaluative, 48
'growth mind-set', encouraging,
50
insincere, 49
negative inferences from, 48
reward for effort, 256
toilet training, 252
Pregnancy
alcohol use during, 285–6
effect on brain, 33–4
epigenetic changes, 113–14
MSG consumption during, 286
Premature baby, 92–3
Preoccupied parents, 28–31, 98, 169,
277–9
Prop-feeding, 142–3
Prophesising, 43
Proprioceptive sense, 197, 310
defensiveness, 310–12, 319
dormancy, 311, 319
helping child develop, 319–21

Reading
alphabet books, 202
asymmetrical tonic neck reflex
and, 293
auditory skills, 325–6
best way of learning, 225–7
bibliotherapy, 237

book selection, 225
comparing school systems,
214–16
difference between boys and
girls, 217
difficulties, 293
dyslexia, 217, 223, 293
eye movements, 219, 220, 322
good children's books, 178–9,
182, 202, 220, 237, 329
hand and eye skills, 218, 322–4
home readers, 226–7
motivation, 328–9
movement difficulties and, 293
music and, 223–4
pre-reading games, 204
processing speed, 217
puzzle books, 220
reflex integration, 322
rhyme books, 202
self-regulation skills, 324–5
skills required before, 216–24
theory of mind learnt from
books, 236–7
time perception, 222–3
to children, 80, 178–9, 182, 202
troubleshooting, 322–9
understanding what is heard,
221–2
understanding what is seen,
220–1
visual perception skills, 326–8
wanting to read, 219
Reflexes
ADHD and primitive reflexes, 284
amphibian reflex, 131, 155
asymmetrical tonic neck reflex
see Asymmetrical tonic neck
reflex
crawling and, 130, 154
fear paralysis reflex, 285–6
integrating, 131, 132–4, 322
integration programs, 280
movement milestones and, 132

breastfeeding parents getting
more, 108
deep sleep and SIDS, 108
problems, 263–4
Smacking, 44
Smell, sense of, 202–3
defensiveness, 308, 316
dormancy, 305, 308, 316
helping child develop, 316–17
Social skills
childcare and, 54
coping with being different,
240–2
fair play, 237–9
friendship, 233–7
line between 'funny' and
'hurtful', 239
play improving, 175
school, 233–48
shy children, 234–5
theory of mind, 235, 236–7, 240
Societal pressures on parents, 117–
20
Sound remembering games, 204
Speech see Language skills
Speech pathologist, 179–82
Spelling, 229–30, 332
Spinal galant reflex, 146–7
helping to integrate, 298
identifying in older child, 298
retained, 297–8
Startle reflex, 75–9, 128–9
after four months, 79, 129
babies, 75–6, 128
emotional triggers, 78
hand-foot-mouth link, 133, 142
hand-neck feedback loop, 132–3
helping to integrate, 132–4, 287–
8
identifying in older child, 286
integrating, 132–4, 286–8
movement skills and, 128–30
older children, in, 77–9, 129,
286–8

retained, 77–9, 129, 284–8
school setting, 287–8
Stepping reflex, 160, 161
Stimulation, 5
Stress
embryo feeling mother's, 113
environment where baby
conceived, 114
epigenetic marks, 114, 115
harsh parenting and, 46
heart beat affected by, 89
highly stressed children, 114
hormones, 6, 65, 66, 89, 98
inflammatory markers, 114
Sucking, 142
breastfeeding benefits, 133, 142
dummy, 143
fine motor skills and, 133, 143,
296
school children still, 295–7
Sucking reflex, 105, 142, 295
helping to integrate, 296
identifying in older child, 296
newborn baby, 105
school children retaining, 295–7
Surprise games, 82–3, 99
Symmetrical tonic neck reflex, 150,
298
ADHD and, 299
crawling, 154, 155–6
helping to integrate, 300
identifying in older child, 299
retained, 298–300
Sympathy and understanding, 41–3

Tactile system, 203
defensiveness, 304, 308, 317
dormancy, 305, 309, 317
helping child develop, 317–18
Talking see Language skills
Television, 80, 175, 176, 179, 190,
204, 270
Telling off child, 44
Temper tantrums, 18, 126, 127